MW01199255

Vahagn Dilbaryan

100BUSINESS SECRETS

TOP 100 SECRETS
HOW TO CHANGE YOUR LIFE

Book 1 (1-25)

Edited by:
  Nazeli Karapetyan
  Jim Teepen

Cover design by:
  Arabo Sargsyan

Dear reader,

There was a time I thought hard about why some people change their lives and achieve great success while most others do not. And I thought about how to join this small group of people. These reflections led me to consider the path of my life. I know that many of you want to have your business or a good career, but you face the most difficult problem – what to do?

I faced the same problem a few years ago and started to think about how to change my life, how to achieve success, and what successful people do that others do not. And I found out that everything starts with a goal: When you have a clear goal, you start thinking of ways to reach it. And, indeed, when I had a clear goal, I started to think about methods to achieve the goal. What are these methods? One of the most effective ways, of course, is to study the lives of successful people, and I decided to explore the lives of hundreds of successful people from different fields, from business to politics.

I started reading: I read a lot. I was immersed in another world, a world of winners, a world of business and marketing, a world in which competition allows only the fastest, smartest, strongest, and most flexible to win - a world, finally, where I wanted to be.

I studied the lives of many successful entrepreneurs - their business strategies, the right and wrong decisions they made, their thoughts, applied techniques, and innovations, in a nutshell, everything - and, as a result, I "was armed" with a lot of options to apply in different situations. This knowledge gave me more self-confidence. It generated new ideas in me that changed my life and became the basis of my success.

I enjoy accumulating knowledge and then sharing it. *100 Business Secrets* presents the insights and advice I have gathered over the years, along with my own thoughts and experiences, since I'm also involved in sales and marketing. I have introduced the most interesting and crucial stages of the lives of many successful people, as well as a part of my success story, to demonstrate how to achieve success in a short period of time.

The book comprises 4 parts, each of which includes 25 business secrets that introduce influential businessmen, marketing techniques, and motivational stories. It took me almost three years to write this book, during which time I read more than 250 books. That is, I read 7 books a month. This was not so much the result of hard work as a goal that became one of the most important investments of my life. Each person presented in the book has been a mentor for me, a person who gave me something most valuable – knowledge.

All this was rather time-consuming, but you are given the chance to save both your money and time by reading and getting to know 100 practical ways, methods, tools, strategies, and secrets that can change your life and build your success. Do you want to reach your goal? If yes, *100 Business Secrets* will give you the practical tools to help you on your journey.

And now it's in front of you.

Enjoy the book.

From the third to the twenty-fifth secrets the texts in italics are pieces of advice from the author.

Contents

Book 1
Secret 1. The Secret of Achieving Success
Secret 2. The Secret of Achieving Success
Secret 3. Tracinda (Kirk Kerkorian)
Secret 4. Google (Sergey Brin, Larry Page)
Secret 5. Google (Laszlo Bock)
Secret 6. Inditex Group (Amancio Ortega)
Secret 7. Wal-Mart (Sam Walton)
Secret 8. Virgin Group (Richard Branson)
Secret 9. Virgin Group (Richard Branson)
Secret 10. JP Morgan and Chase (John Pierpont Morgan)
Secret 11. Examples of Motivating the Employees
Secret 12. Keith Ferrazzi (Ferrazzi Greenlight)
Secret 13. Keith Ferrazzi (Ferrazzi Greenlight)
Secret 14. 11 Interesting Stories
Secret 15. Berkshire Hathaway (Warren Buffett)
Secret 16. Sewell (Carl Sewell)
Secret 17. Ford (Henry Ford)
Secret 18. Tinkoff Credit Systems (Oleg Tinkov)
Secret 19. How to Influence the Purchase Decisions
Secret 20. How to Influence the Purchase Decisions
Secret 21. How to Influence the Purchase Decisions
Secret 22. How to Influence the Purchase Decisions
Secret 23. How to Influence the Purchase Decisions
Secret 24. Calouste Gulbenkian
Secret 25. IKEA (Ingvar Kamprad)

Book 2
Secret 26. Panasonic (Kōnosuke Matsushita)
Secret 27.
Secret 28.
Secret 29.
Secret 30.
Secret 31.
Secret 32.
Secret 33. Tesla, SpaceX, SolarCity (Elon Musk)
Secret 34.
Secret 35.
Secret 36.
Secret 37.
Secret 38.
Secret 39.
Secret 40. Apple (Steve Jobs)
Secret 41.
Secret 42.
Secret 43.
Secret 44.
Secret 45.
Secret 46.
Secret 47. Alibaba (Jack Ma)
Secret 48.
Secret 49. Never Give Up
Secret 50.

Book 3
Secret 51.
Secret 52.
Secret 53. Loyal Customers
Secret 54.
Secret 55.
Secret 56.
Secret 57.
Secret 58. Yum Brands (David Novak)
Secret 59.
Secret 60.
Secret 61.
Secret 62.
Secret 63. Auchan (The Mulliez family)
Secret 64.
Secret 65.
Secret 66. Fedex (Fred Smith)
Secret 67.
Secret 68.
Secret 69.
Secret 70. Tesco (Jack Cohen)
Secret 71.
Secret 72.
Secret 73.
Secret 74.
Secret 75.

Book 4
Secret 76.
Secret 77. Guerrilla Marketing
Secret 78.
Secret 79.
Secret 80.
Secret 81.
Secret 82.
Secret 83.
Secret 84.
Secret 85.
Secret 86.
Secret 87.
Secret 88. Pepsi vs Coca-Cola
Secret 89.
Secret 90.
Secret 91.
Secret 92. Singapore (Lee Kuan Yew)
Secret 93. Ritz-Carlton (César Ritz)
Secret 94.
Secret 95.
Secret 96.
Secret 97.
Secret 98. How to Reach Your Goal
Secret 99.
Secret 100.

Secret 1

To achieve your goals in life, I realized that it matters less how smart you are, how much innate talent you're born with, or even, most eye-opening to me, where you came from and how much you started out with. Sure, all these are important, but they mean little if you don't understand one thing: You can't get there alone. In fact, you can't get very far at all.

Keith Ferrazzi

The Secret of Achieving Success

From the author – In our days, many ask themselves one specific question: How can I achieve success? There is no precise formula as such. It is specific for each person, but there are certain factors that bring you closer to success once you practice them. Yes, you may have read and heard a lot and even seen examples of success, but you have always wondered - ok, and how do I become successful? Sometimes you are not told how; only examples, perseverance, and ambition are mentioned. Many would argue that success requires hard work. Yes, I agree, it does require hard work, but if you work harder on the same thing, you get just a slightly better result. There are many approaches, but in the first and second secrets, I'll try to show you what I think are the two most important keys to success. You might not agree with me, but I'm going to demonstrate my conviction through many examples. Many times we hear that if we want something very much, it will happen.

Indeed? Then you're misled, just as I used to be. I should note that wanting is not enough, we must act. We all think that if we keep working hard, reading much, learning, being better than others, and persistently striving, success will come to us. But many people who read and work and are even sometimes better than others are not successful. So up to when should we train, try hard, and work? There's no answer. No, this is delusion – nobody achieves long-term success alone.

Luck, knowledge, skills, work, connections, education, experience – these are all parts of success. Initially you get everything because of your personal qualities – diligence, courage, willpower, initiative - but as Alexander Kravtsov says: "We gain the main skills and knowledge between the ages of 20-30, after which every successful person faces the problem of the transition to the next level and doing more. As a rule, this level should already be achieved with other people, uniting their abilities, say, with your abilities." Connections are always needed because they give you the opportunity to find people who can make a difference in your life by giving advice, money, a word, a call, a phone number, an opinion, or aid.

I have yet to see a serious athlete who has no coach. There needs to be someone who will support you, at least by giving his advice, opinion, help, or cooperation. Forget the idea that by working relentlessly you can succeed all by yourself. Yes, you need to work, persevere, and have a strong will. You must exercise and not give up. But can you do this alone? Maybe in order to climb Everest we need endurance, strong muscles, will, good equipment, and experience. But can we do it alone? Hardly. In any case, you'll need a team or an escort. Let me show this by examples from different fields.

What would Napoleon have achieved had he not been saved by Murat, Ney and Desaix? Hard to say, but he could probably not have defeated his enemies alone. Bonaparte relied on the skills, courage and flexibility of these people. It was in the Battle of Marengo that Napoleon was in trouble when Desaix's legions could be seen approaching.

Desaix, that skillful and courageous general, died in that battle, but the victory was given to Napoleon, though it was another person who changed the outcome of the battle. Had Crixus, the bravest slave among Spartacus's friends, not agreed, Spartacus would probably not have incited a slave rebellion and climbed up the peak of Mount Vesuvius, where he was joined by Gannicus' slave units. Without General Sabotai, Batu Khan would have faced big problems in the times of Mongol invasions, particularly in Rus.

Or don't you think that World War II could have taken a different direction had Hitler's most skillful general, Friedrich Paulus, not been taken prisoner in the Battle of Stalingrad, as right after that battle the Soviet troops attacked? We all know that the teacher of Alexander the Great was Aristotle, who had taught everything to the capable child. If it were not for this man, could Alexander have achieved such a result? And also Aristotle's teacher was Plato, and Plato's teacher was Socrates.

There always needs to be a person who can truly see, help you identify your skills, and give you a boost to conquer heights, in other words, someone who will help you discover your potential. We come across this phenomenon in every step of our lives; if a teacher at school does not encourage you to participate in Olympiads, you probably won't. Or if your employer is smart enough, he notices your potential at once, and you're hired.

After graduating from college in 1978, Jeff Immelt worked for Procter & Gamble, but some time later he graduated from Harvard with his MBA. During his studies he had a job interview with GE where he was noticed by Dennis Dammerman. Dammerman personally handed Immelt's CV to the HR department, and in 1982 Immelt started working in GE's marketing department. Immelt learned Jack Welch's strategy - either become the best or appear in the street - through his own experience.

When Immelt didn't accomplish his monthly sales plan, the boss warned that he would be fired if it was repeated. Immelt worked very hard. Once, when a client had not received his order on time, Jeff spent the whole weekend packing the product to fix the problem. Of course, it wasn't his duty, but his diligence was soon noticed. He had appeared in the list of 150 prospective managers, and Jack Welch himself followed their growth. Subsequently, he was chosen to be the CEO of General Electric and succeeded Welch. You must be noticed and be taken care of: Nobody achieves success alone.

Ruben Vardanyan says: "We live in a period of transition, when many processes are still not built, despite the fact that more than twenty years have passed since the beginning of the changes in our country. The level of mistrust between different groups of society, between business and investors is still very high. My competitive edge is in the fact that I know many and many know me as a banker and trust me on both a professional and human level."

Results are not achieved alone. You must be known, and you must have some value for the contacts to increase. It is crucial for many people to know you, and it is even more important for these people to be ready to take action for you.

The grandmother of the US Vice President Dan Quayle would tell him that he could do anything he wanted if he just set his mind to it and went to work. I agree. He worked hard. But what if Bush had not chosen him? None of us knows what would have happened, but Bush chose him as Vice President. Putin received the offer through Yeltsin, and Medvedev through Putin. My point is that success depends not only on you, but on the people you've chosen to be in your environment: They, to a great extent, change your life.

It is known that Bill Clinton has carried a black notebook with him since his student years. When he met other students, he would ask them questions about what they did, why they were at Oxford, and who they knew. Then he wrote down the answers in his notebook. When asked why he did this, Clinton answered that he wanted to become the governor of Arkansas. He was taking the contact information of people he thought could be of help in the future. Coming home in the evening, he would sit at his desk and put together all the contact information. Clinton, at 32, became the youngest governor in US history. He was re-elected more than 4 times and later became the 42th president of the United States. Many would just switch on the television and watch American football, while Clinton was collecting other people's contacts. Relationships with other people are vital in your life, and believe me, in many cases they are decisive.

There was a time when an employer could notice who worked hard and well and appreciated them. But today many work well and invest all of their potential. Yet, competition gets more intense in the workplace. Then a question arises: What to do? The answer to this question is – get to know your boss and let him get to know you. It's known at General Electric: "If Jack Welch doesn't know you personally, you're not going to go anywhere at GE, even if you've worked there for 20 years."

As a college president said to his students: "Be nice to your A students because they'll come back and be your colleagues, but be especially nice to your B students and C students because they will come back and give us a new auditorium and a new science building." Peter McColough, the former CEO and Chairman of the Board of the Xerox Corporation, made the following observation about his fellow students, graduates of Harvard Business School, class of 1949: "The record of accomplishment corresponds negatively with the standing of the class," McColough reported. "The top people did not do that well. The middle third did. The guys who got the highest marks tended to be in the middle in accomplishment."

If you believe that good grades are the key to success, you should attend your twenty-fifth high school reunion. Success in studies and success in the boardroom have little in common. There is a reason why success is not directly derived from the intellect. The more intelligent a person is, the more he relies on himself. After all, he knows everything. He relies on himself in achieving his life goals as well.

Less intelligent people know that they are not that smart. Consequently, they are more prone to look for others who can help them climb the stairs. There is nothing wrong with being smart. In no way do I imply that average education is advisable. Of course it is not. We should learn well and be educated, but no matter how smart you are, try using connections instead of walking alone. Have a team, connections, or someone who will contribute to your success. Long-term success is not achieved alone.

Studying 268 Harvard alumni over sixty years (1940-2000), psychiatrist George Vaillant came to the conclusion that success in relationships with people determined how high they rose and how happy they eventually were. There is nothing strange here.

Connections can be used for solving any problems. You even use the help of your acquaintances to get some minor information such as where the best restaurant or café is, etc. For example, Peter Thiel and Max Levchin did not make an announcement when recruiting a team for Paypal. They just sat, took a piece of paper, and wrote the names of 30 people they went to college with. They hired 24 people from that very list. Yes, it's not possible to achieve results alone.

How can you make someone else recognize your talents? If you are an artist, you need a gallery to let people know about you. If you are a writer, you need a publisher. If you are a musician, you have to find a record company. In a nutshell, you need the recognition of a person who will help you succeed. Or if you are a singer, unless someone notices and speaks about you, can you have an army of fans? Of course, not! Let's consider The Beatles. Paul McCartney failed an audition for the Cathedral choir in his hometown, Liverpool. He would he probably not have reached great heights without Brian Epstein. John Lennon, the most influential music creator of his generation, had a silver plaque made on which his aunt's words were inscribed, words that she often told him: "The guitar's all right John, but you'll never make a living out of it." Without Brian Epstein, Lennon indeed would not be able to earn a living with his guitar. Nobody achieves success alone.

Elvis Presley is a man who became one of the most successful musicians of our times. No one denies that he was a talent in his genre, but he also succeeded in his career in a most unusual way. The future King of Rock 'n' Roll recorded a couple of songs in the Sun Recording Studio as a gift to his mother. The studio's owner, Sam Phillips, spotted the talented guy, and later, when he was looking for a white man who had the sound and feel of a black man, decided to give Elvis a chance and recruited him into a music group. It was Phillips who boosted Elvis's professional music career. Was Presley alone?

At the same time, you need to have certain skills to be interesting for others. Usually, if you want to use other people's abilities, let them get to know you and trust you, because trust is most important in this world.

Yes, find those people or that person. Nothing gets done alone. Success starts after finding the right people.

Arnold Schwarzenegger was once so poor that the purchase of a refrigerator was a real   struggle for him. A person who was an athlete, an actor, and a politician – how was he able to achieve such a result? He simply made the right moves during his career: When he served in the army, he woke up very early, 1 hour earlier than everyone else to exercise with the barbells he kept in the tanks. His first success was achieved due to his personal qualities. Later, he left for the United States and became an actor, using his marvelous physique. But he could not conquer the third peak alone; his connections helped. Before entering politics, Schwarzenegger had long been prepared for it: He had trained senators, married Maria Shriver, who was a relative of President Kennedy, and accompanied George H. W. Bush at a campaign rally. President Bush subsequently appointed him chairman of the President's Council on Physical Fitness and Sports. As a result, he managed to create appropriate connections and get the votes of the electors. Do you want to achieve big results? Take Schwarzenegger as an example.

Here's another example that it's never possible to achieve anything alone. It was Bruce Lee who invited Chuck Norris to play a small part in one of his movies, and hence Norris's acting career began.

Don King is the man whose patronage helped many boxers succeed. There's no famous athlete who hasn't had a serious coach, someone who has been his source of inspiration and guidance. When Vince Lombardi became the head coach of the Green Bay Packers, the team was in a deplorable state, but in just a few years the Packers won the World Championship, and not only once. The team could not have achieved success if it were not for Lombardi.

As the co-founder and CEO of Likeable Media, Dave Kerpen, says: "The difference between success and failure is a great team." It has long been known in business that success is achieved by teams rather than by loners. As the greatest basketball player, Michael Jordan, would say: "Talent wins games, but teamwork and intelligence wins championships."

Famous Spanish singer José Mercé was Florentino Pérez's friend, and he had advised him to buy Sergio Ramos from Sevilla FC. José Mourinho was not a good football player, but he achieved success due to Sir Bobby Robson, who had come to Portugal to take the helm of Sporting. Mourinho was Robson's interpreter and helped him in everything. Hence, José Mourinho, who became Robson's right-hand man, became extremely successful as a coach.

Michael Schumacher's family was facing big financial problems because Schumacher initially needed money for a career in sports. Once one of their distant relatives, Jürgen Dilk, visited them and, learning about his achievements, decided to finance him. Yes, nobody achieves results alone.

Even the Pope is elected by the Cardinals. Attention: you have most probably heard about Vincent van Gogh. He painted numerous paintings, but only managed to sell one in his lifetime. If you want to be a painter like Vincent van Gogh and just paint but be poor, then you can seclude yourself in your studio and enjoy art. But if you want to achieve success in the sphere of art, get acquainted with Harvey Mackay's story.

Mackay was 54 years old when he wrote his first book, Swim with the Sharks, Without Being Eaten Alive. Before printing the book, he started collecting reviews of different famous people about his book. He turned to Robert Redford, Mario Cuomo, Gloria Steinem, Gerald Ford, presidents of companies such as United Airlines, 7-Eleven Stores, Porsche, Estee Lauder, Northwestern Bell, IDS, Dayton-Hudson, Carlson Companies, Cray Research, Farely Industries, Drescher, General Motors and Stanley Works, and the presidents of Kansas University and Sanford. And you know what? He sold more than 2.3 million copies, and for 40 weeks it headed The New York Times Best Sellers list. You just can't reach success alone.

Bill Gates: Was he alone? Of course, not! He would have hardly obtained such results without Paul Allen. Also consider the two Steves - Jobs and Vozniak; the founders of HP Company – Hewlett and Packard; the Yandex founders - Arkady Volozh and Ilya Segalovich, Niklas Zennström and Janus Friis; the founders of Skype - Chad Hurley, Jawed Karim and Steve Chen; the founders of Youtube - Sabeer Bhatia and Jack Smith; the founders of Hotmail - Albrecht, Johnson brothers, Walton, Mars and Hantz families. None of them was alone. After meeting with Jobs, Mike Markkula realized that this young man and his friend had great prospects and that he needed to support them instead of competing with them. This very Markkula became the springboard the two Steves made use of, as, through his connections, he took huge amounts of credit from the Bank of America. Donald Trump was sending his CV to numerous companies, but he got no response, and he succeeded through his father, after working in his company.

Aras Agalarov, the owner of Crocus International, held the "Miss Universe" beauty pageant in Moscow to seek common ground with Donald Trump, as the broadcast rights of the pageant belonged to Trump. Naturally, when Trump wanted to build a Trump Tower in Moscow, he was looking for partners, and the Crocus team was among the candidates.

William Procter, a British immigrant to the United States, and James Gamble, of Irish origin, started out together in Cincinnati. Procter had produced candles and Gamble had produced soap. Both had moved to the USA from Europe with an aim to start a new life, and they were both poor. You might wonder how they came to know each other. And I'll answer – they became related by marrying the Norris sisters and created the global giant, Procter & Gamble. The idea of doing business together belonged to the father of their wives, Alexander Norris, who insisted that his daughters' husbands should start a business together rather than compete with each other. Each invested 3596.47 dollars and established the Procter & Gamble.

After receiving a diploma, Gyulzhan Moldazhanova started working at Moscow State University. In order to improve her financial situation, she subsequently went to work for $200 a month in Oleg Deripaska's Rosaluminproduct Company. Then she became the assistant of the financial director, and after a year she was working in the department of foreign trade. In 2005 she headed the Basic Element Company, which comprised around 80 companies worth a total of $23 billion. This was one more example that shows that no result is achieved alone. You need a fulcrum in the form of aid, advice, or some other type of support.

Such examples are many, all of which come to prove that it's simply impossible to achieve success alone. Larry Page and Sergey Brin created Google. Pemberton invented Coca-Cola, and Caleb invented Pepsi, but they were alone and, interestingly, both sold their companies. Claude Hopkins – the advertising legend - was advised by his own boss to try advertising. David Ogilvy would have been a cook had he not followed his friend's advice. Ray Kroc achieved great success due to the McDonald brothers and bought the restaurant chain, and then he helped Fred Turner to rise. That's right. Morita was a very talented engineer, but it was only after uniting and exchanging ideas with Ibuka that Sony Corporation was created.

In 1981, after graduating from university, Sergei Sarkisov got his start at Ingosstrakh insurance company. In Soviet times it was a great job, and he would sometimes leave for Cuba to make payments for the insurance of various kinds of cargo. Through his work he established warm relationships with the president of Ingosstrakh, Vladimir Kruglyak, who later offered Sarkisov the job of heading the Russian-European Insurance Company. In fact, Kruglyak and Enric Bernat themselves were to start that business, and the idea, surprisingly, belonged to the founder of Chupa Chups lollipop company, Enric Bernat, who had come to Russia aiming to start an insurance business because he believed a boom in the insurance industry awaited Russia. As an investment, Bernat provided Sarkisov with a BMW 525, which he drove to meetings. This is how Sarkisov became the chairman of RESO and laid the foundation for its growth. Success is not achieved alone.

Giorgio Armani had medical background, but he worked for Nina Cerruti. At the age of 40, Giorgio made a decision to start a business with Sergio Galeotti. Was he alone? – Of course, not.

Armani sold his Volkswagen car and invested all the money in menswear business. The very first collection appeared in Time magazine and the rest is history.

Warren Buffett may not have been one whose actions are admired by all investors if his teacher Benjamin Graham had not revealed Buffett's abilities. Graham became the cornerstone of Buffett's success. If Jeff Bezos's parents had not helped him, I don't think we would have had this symbol, Amazon, of corporate USA.

No matter how mighty an engineer Gordon Moore was, he wasn't able to achieve success without Robert Noyce, but due to their union one more giant was born – Intel Corporation.

Yet for further development they needed one more catalyst. So Andrew Grove joined them, and there was no stopping Intel. Twitter, Youtube, Yahoo, Paypal and many similar websites were built by two or a few friends. Who was Henry Ford before getting married? And what an empire did he build after his marriage? Was he alone? No, he had his wife by his side. Yes, Ford's secret of success was his wife, and to the question, "Mr. Ford, would you like to be born again?" he answered, "Only if Clara would be my wife again."

Karl Benz said that his wife, Bertha Ringer, always gave him new energy, creative strength and a drive to succeed. What a picture of a strong woman!

When Robert Kiyosaki was literally crying because of debts, his wife, Kim, was by his side, and she also helped her husband to become one of the most successful people in the world. It's impossible to achieve success alone; having a true partner in life helps.

Let's observe Russian oligarchs. Most of them are students of the Metallurgy and Petroleum Engineering Departments. Berezovsky and Abramovich, Potanin and Prokhorov, Mikhail Fridman and Pyotr Aven are people who have supported one another. Many big problems lay ahead Chichvarkin, but he was noticed by Timur Artemyev, who became the source of his success as they founded Yevroset together. There's a wise Armenian folk saying: "One hand washes the other one, while two hands wash the face." Find that next hand: That's the key to success.

Ben Horowitz was one of the founders of Opsware, an enterprise software company, which he sold in 2007 to Hewlett-Packard for $1.6 billion in cash. This number is really amazing given that a few years before the shares of the company had sunk from $6 to $0.35 per share. No investor in the world would believe in the recovery of the company. NASDAQ even gave the company a deadline for the prices of the shares to rise to at least over $1. Opsware shares were 30 times lower than normal, so no one even wanted to hear about the company's plans.

Ben turned to an acquaintance of his, networking guru Ron Conway, who advised him to meet an influential investor, Herb Allen. Allen listened to Horowitz and said he would see what he could do. Within a few months Allen's investment company bought Opsware shares. Some of Allen's colleagues did the same. This step could not remain invisible to the eyes of other investors, and the prices Ben Horowitz's shares began to rise. Opsware resisted the pressure, experienced a crisis and, as a result, became a billion-dollar business. All this wouldn't have happened had Horowitz not met Ron Corway. And when Horowitz met Allen, the latter told him that Ron's recommendation meant a lot for him.[1] No one achieves long-term success alone.

Whatever your location or nationality, look around. The reality is that many people have seized the moment, regardless of their education. In

1 Kravtsov A. – The Next Level. A Book for Those Who've Reached Their Ceiling, 2016

his youth, Alfred Krupp left school and spent all day in a factory. He was interested in nothing but getting weapon orders. In 1843, after many efforts, Krupp created a type of steel used to make the best cannons in all of Europe. He emphasized the quality of the cannons, which were precise, were lighter, and shot farther than those of the rivals. Alfred Krupp went around Europe with his cannon, but in vain. Nobody bought it until Emperor Wilhelm 1 noticed him at one of the exhibitions. From that time on, business relations started between the emperor and future businessman. Wilhelm ordered around 300 cannons. The interesting thing is that these cannons were more expensive than the English ones, but Wilhelm pointed out that the national production was preferable to that of the enemy.

The expression "Krupp steel armor" spread throughout Europe due to Wilhelm, which came to be the brand of the Krupp family. Poor Wilhelm. He didn't even imagine that right after his first order Alfred would start selling the cannons to the enemy – the French. In the Franco-Prussian war both sides were using Krupp cannons, while Krupp was growing rich.

Success does not depend on one person. Find someone who will give you a boost, notice you, advise you, or believe in you, and you will achieve success together. Archimedes said, "Give me but one firm spot on which to stand, and I will move the earth."

Yes, find that firm spot. That is the key to success. It can be your boss, friend, business partner, supplier, or customer. It might be an acquaintance, someone you've just briefly met, your wife, a child, a teacher, or a coach. This list can be very long. Be attentive. Such moments are missed at great cost. Perhaps a person's word, advice, offer, phone number, or opinion can become the beginning of your success.

Secret 1. Success is not achieved alone.

Secret 2

Success depends on how you react to unexpected opportunities.

Ross Perot

The Secret of Achieving Success

From the author - There are many factors for success, but in this case I have distinguished two of them. Why these two in particular? Because all of us encounter at least one of these factors in our lives. I already spoke about the first factor and will further elaborate on it through the example of Kate Ferrazzi in Secret 12, and this secret relates to the second factor. Yes, a person can be smart, hard-working, talented, and persistent - but still not successful. If the first factor was about not being alone, the second one is about seizing the moment. Why do I say so?

How many times have you been in situations when you regretted not doing something? Every such thought prevents you from achieving possible success. Every phenomenon contains certainty and uncertainty. If you don't take steps, uncertainty follows, and if you take steps, regardless of whether you succeed or not, you have certainty. So it's better to try, to use that moment. Sometimes that favorable moment happens only once. If you don't seize the moment, you fall into uncertainty, which oppresses you for years. Am I right? Therefore, it is better to take action without fear, seize that moment. If you succeed, you'll move forward. If not, you'll try again, but this time with a different plan.

The founder of Mary Kay Cosmetics, Mary Kay Ash, would say, "For every failure, there's an alternative course of action. You just have to find it. When you come to a roadblock, take a detour." And now I'm going to illustrate my conviction by examples.

James Lafferty was a fitness instructor and worked for Procter & Gamble, training the top-managers of the company. He carefully listened to the managers and sometimes even told them about his dream – he wanted to try himself in business. He befriended many, and one of them offered Lafferty the position of Brand Assistant. Ultimately, James Lafferty headed the Procter & Gamble division in Philippines and the Coca-Cola division in Africa. He became the CEO of the British American Tobacco. He was offered the position, wasn't he? Seize the moment!

When Lee Iacocca became the CEO of Chrysler Corporation, he announced that there wasn't a new class of cars in the market. He had taken his minivan plans with him to Chrysler after Ford nixed the concept. Having been fired by Mr. Ford, everyone predicted that he would fail at Chrysler, but he decided to create minivans at the most favorable moment and became a legend. Iacocca took advantage of the appropriate moment – people needed a family car. The minivan was created.

When the McDonald brothers opened their restaurant, it occurred to no visitor that it was an excellent business. Ray Kroc, on the other hand, was stunned seeing how people were buying hamburgers and whispered to himself that the future belonged to that business. Kroc also took advantage of the chance that was given to him.

When Levi Strauss arrived in San Francisco during the Gold Rush, he learned that there was no special clothing for the miners, as it quickly got worn out. Being well aware of the famous fabric in Genoa used for making tents, he made clothing for the miners out of this fabric, which later came to be known as jeans. Strauss also took advantage of the right moment.

Across the Atlantic, Gustave Leven became as famous in France as Levi was in the United States. In early 1946, Leven's father, the head of a family brokerage firm, asked him to find a buyer for a small spring, which the owner wanted to sell, in the south of France. Junior Leven contacted an old friend of the family, Samuel Bronfman, heir to the Seagram Corporation, and asked him if he wanted to add a spring to his empire of soft drinks. Bronfman asked his friend to wait until the fall when he would come to France and see the spring.

Leven did not wait long. He came to Vergèze town where the spring was. The springs of this town had been known since the Roman times. Leven decided to buy the spring and the bottling production, despite the fact that they were obsolete. He watched the workers filling small green bottles with water by plunging them into the spring by hand. Sometimes, the workers even filled the bottles with their feet. The bottles were Perrier, of course, and they made Leven one of the richest people in France. He owns almost 20% of Source Perrier SA Company, which sells $4 billion in bottles in 125 countries. Be flexible and use the moment.

Alan Dabbiere, AirWatch, 800 jobs, www.air-watch.com – "When I watched Steve Jobs reveal the iPhone at Macworld, I knew that device would dramatically change the way people interact and the way businesses operate. We immediately recalibrated our operations to manage smartphones for the business market. Since then, AirWatch has grown to support more than 4,000 customers and manage millions of smartphones and tablets in 47 countries." Simon Khalaf, Flurry, 100 jobs, www.flurry.com – "I saw the iPhone App Store in July 2008 and thought, 'This is the next trillion dollar opportunity.' After that, we placed Flurry on the path to be the platform for app measurement and advertising. Today, we employ more than 100 people, have a sizeable revenue stream and are cash-flow positive.[1]"

These examples remind us of how people have been able to take advantage of the opportunities that are given to all of us at least once. Take advantage of the opportunity given to you, and I'll proceed with sharing examples. In 1998, Max Levchin appeared in Silicon Valley, still unsure what he was going to do with his life. One day, Levchin attended a small lecture by Peter Thiel at Stanford University. Only six persons were present at the lecture, but it did not bother him. Levchin had heard about Peter but did not know him personally. They had a chat after the lecture and ended up meeting at a breakfast a few days later.

Levchin recalls, "I had two different ideas that I was considering starting companies around, and I pitched him on both evenly. Peter was running a hedge fund at the time. For a few weeks we kept talking and eventually he

1 http://www.forbes.com/sites/alanhall/2012/10/15/100-founders-share-their-top-aha-moments-guess-how-many-jobs-theyve-created-so-far/3/#6c0d66742e6c

said, 'Take this idea, because this one is better, and you go start a company around it, and then I can have a hedge fund invest a little bit of money in it.'-like a couple hundred thousand dollars. I had just moved from Champaign; most of my contacts and friends were in Chicago. One of them I was trying to convince to be the CEO. He wasn't really available, so I wound up being without a CEO. I called Peter and said, 'This investment is a great thing, but I have no one to run the company. I'm just going to write the code and recruit the coders.' And he said, 'Maybe I could be your CEO.' So I said 'That's a really good idea.'"

"The thing that kept us going in the early days was the fact that Peter and I always knew that both of us would not be in a funk together. When I was like, 'This fraud thing is going to kill us,' Peter said, 'No, I've seen the numbers. You are doing fine. Just keep at it. You'll get it.' On the flip side, when Peter would be annoyed by some investors or board dynamics or whatever, I was usually there trying to support him. That sort of sounds touchy-feely, but I think you have to really have good people. If you have a good team, you are halfway there." This is how the basis of Paypal's creation was laid, in which Levchin used the opportunity that came his way. They helped each other for a common purpose, and needless to say, it's difficult to achieve long-term success alone.

When the two Steves brought their Apple computer to their bosses at Atari and Hewlett-Packard and proposed that the companies take up the product, they were both rejected. Wozniak tried to get to his supervisor several times at Hewlett-Packard. But this man said that Wozniak had no college degree and no diploma in computer design. Today both Atari and Hewlett-Packard produce personal computers, but they are far behind Apple. And what if they had taken advantage of the moment?

Michael Dell was a first-year student at the University of Texas in 1983. It was a time when the IBM personal computer was hot stuff. Dell made a key observation as to how the system worked, "A dealer could order 10 and actually receive just 1. Or sometimes he'd order 100 and only receive 10. So sometimes, even if they only wanted 100, they'd order 1000 – and, lo and behold, 1000 would be delivered." So dealers would sell him the extra computers at or below cost, just to keep their cash flowing. He invested one thousand dollars from his savings to make his first deal.

Once Dell received computers, he modernized them, adding new parts, and then sold them to his fellow students at bargain prices. April of 1984 was the last month he did business from his dorm-room, with sales reaching $80,000. The next month he incorporated and moved into an office. Dell's next step was to buy hardware parts wholesale and assemble them into clones of IBM computers. But he did not try to sell them through major computer stores. Instead, he found a channel none of the computer companies used - the channel of direct marketing. Dell placed ads in computer magazines, and customers placed orders by dialing a toll-free number. As a result, his computers became a top brand name in the direct mail market. Dell dared to be different and used the right moment.

In 1947, George Soros left for London on his father's advice. In 1949, he became a student at the London School of Economics. After graduating, Soros found it difficult to find a job; he sent letters to all the managing directors of banks, an unusual act for those days. Someone called Walter Solomon appointed a meeting with Soros just to point out that the latter had misspelled his name. During one of these interviews Soros was told the following, "Here in the City we practice what we call intelligent nepotism. That means that each managing director has a number of nephews, one of whom is intelligent, and he is going to be the next managing director. If you come from the same college as he did, you would have a chance to get a job in the firm. If you came from the same university, you may still be all right. But you're not even from the same country." He advised Soros to stay away from the City. After this interview, he got a job at Singer & Friedlander, where the managing director was a Hungarian. I should mention that Soros was also born in Hungary. Connections worked, and Soros was hired. While at the bank, one of Soros's colleagues offered him the position of an arbitrage trader at his father's brokerage house. "Why not me?" Soros thought. It was an opportunity he used to change his life and moved to the United States in 1956. Seize the moment.

And why do people not take advantage of the moment in many cases? In the majority of cases, they are either afraid or find that it's not the right time yet; a better chance might be en route. Perhaps many of you doubt whether it's the right moment. Or what if you try but fail? The fear of failing prevents you from trying. Yes, the fear. You will probably be interested to know that around 7 billion people live in the world, and they all have fears. Look around. Everyone fears something. Some fear death; some fear disease; others fear the loss of close people, poverty, or snakes. Some fear bandits; bandits themselves fear the police; the police fear that the authorities can leave them without rewards or fire them. The authorities fear their authorities, and, of course, their wives. And the wives have fears too. Everyone fears something. The people you fear are even more afraid of you!

Like everything else in our lives, we create our own fears – in our heads. Fear was given to us to save our lives in dangerous times. There was a time when losing one's life was easier than losing a wallet today. But we use our fear wrongly. Most people use it to spoil their and others' lives. A few use fear to achieve success, and they become great heroes: Julius Caesar, Theodore Roosevelt, and many other leaders who feared to live an empty and colorless life. It's not enough just to dream and do nothing because you fear failure. Try. Use your moment, your chance.

The main cause of our fears is that we focus of our attention and thoughts on whatever bad and terrible may happen if we perform a certain act, if we start to move towards the realization of our dreams. A person imagines all kinds of scary options and does not understand that they are all an illusion, a fantasy. This type of fear is paralyzing and does not let us move forward. And what if to try to ask yourself a question differently? For example, "What bad thing will happen if I do not do this?" (And scare yourself with consequences of inaction.) "What good thing will happen if I do this?" Why not use this very moment? Dear reader, grab the opportunity as soon as it pops out. Choose success! Choose happiness, choose and seize the moment and do not wait for someone to give it to you on a platter. Come and take it. Let's go on with our examples – Adobe Systems.

While at Xerox PARC, Charles Geschke and John Warnock developed a language called Interpress that allowed any computer to talk to any printer. But the two friends soon had problems with Xerox and decided to quit their jobs and start their own company. Geschke recalls, "My mother and father thought I had lost my mind, because I had this great job at Xerox, a nice big office overlooking the whole Bay Area. They said, 'What are you doing?'" He answered, "You know, my ego may get bruised if this doesn't work, but I'll always have a job. If you have a PhD in computer science, you're not going to be looking for work very long. This is something to give a try and branch out on my own."

"Both John and I were in our early 40s. Maybe my kids were nervous that I wouldn't be able to put them through college, but no, I really wasn't nervous because I knew I could get another great job, partly from the experience at PARC and from watching people in the venture world. I knew one founder who seemed to get more money every time one of his companies failed than the last time! You fail and people figure that you won't make the same set of mistakes the next time. So I never really felt scared. The only thing that would have been hard to deal with would be the stigma of failing. But I thought we had a reasonable chance of succeeding."

"John Warnock's thesis advisor at the University of Utah was a man by the name of Dave Evans, and Dave sat on the board of Hambrecht & Quist, a venture capital company up in San Francisco. He introduced us to Bill Hambrecht, and we went up and met with him. The idea that we talked about was to build laser printers and typesetting equipment that could produce not only text, but also images – imagesetters they're called today – combine that with all the software and market it to the Fortune 500 as internal publishing systems that they could use to have more control and more rapid response in their printing needs."

"Bill liked the idea - partly because he was always frustrated with the financial printers to get his prospectuses out – and so he said that he would support it. 'But neither one of you guys have ever run a business before, right?' And we said, 'That's correct.' He said, 'Well, I've checked around and you have a lot of respect in the technical community, but I'm going to hire a guy to be a consultant for you who is a marketing person. He'll help you write a business plan because I need to have business plan to talk to the investors.'" Without missing the opportunity, I should mention again – success is not achieved alone.

"We said, 'Fine.' So we wrote our business plan. John and I had managed enough projects that we knew what the costs would be to bring out a first product. We put that together in a plan, gave it to Bill, and he said, 'Fine, you can quit your jobs.' We said, 'We don't exactly have the money yet.' He said, 'You'll have to trust me.' So John and I quit. Bill loaned us $50,000 just as a personal note so that we could go out and start leasing a Vax computer to do our work on. We eventually found the name Adobe Systems and we were in business."

"Before long I got a phone call from one of my professors at Carnegie Mellon, Gordon Bell, who had since left Carnegie and gone back to Digital Equipment and was running research and development for the company. He said, 'I hear you started a business and I want to come out and talk to you about what you're doing.' So he came out and we showed him. We explained our business plan about building the computers and the printers and putting it all together in a package and he said, 'That all sounds great, but I don't need computers. I'm Digital Equipment. I already have a deal with Ricoh for laser printers, so I don't need the printers. My problem is that I've got several development teams trying to build the software to interface between the two of them and they're getting nowhere. That's very frustrating to me. Why don't you just sell me the software?' – which we had already shown him. The precursor of what became PostScript – 'That's what I need.'"

"We said, 'Well, Gordon, we raised $2,5 million and this is our business plan and that's what we're going to do.' He said, 'I'm disappointed, but if you change your mind, give me a call.'"

"About 2 months later we got a call from a fellow by the name of Bob Belleville, who had been at Xerox and then had moved on to Apple and was responsible for the overall engineering management for the Macintosh. He said, 'I want to bring Steve Jobs over and see what you guys are doing.' So they came over, we went through the same spiel, and Steve said, 'I've got this computer coming out called the Macintosh,' which he showed us, and he said, 'so I don't need a computer. And I have a deal with Canon on the laser printer. But the development team trying to interface between the computer and printer is just failing miserably. Why don't you sell me your company?' We said, 'Steve, we're not for sale, we're really out to build a business on our own.' He said, 'All right, why don't you just sell me the software?' We said, 'We have this business plan, we raised $2,5 million, and this is what we said we are going to do.' He said, 'I think you guys are crazy. Think about it a little bit and I'll call you back.'"

"So John and I went to talk to the fellow that Bill Hambrecht had asked to chair our board, named Q. T. Wiles. He'd been in business for a long time and, when we described what had happened with both of these episodes, he said, 'You guys are nuts. Throw out your business plan. Your customers – or potential customers – are telling you what your business should be. The business plan was only used to get you the money. Why don't you have a business plan that is focused just on providing what your customers want?'" As a result, Charles and John took advantage of the appropriate moment.

Let's consider Paul Allen and Bill Gates. Allen worked in Honeywell and Gates was a student at Harvard. Once while walking in Harvard Square, Allen read an announcement in the January 1975 issue of Popular Electronics "World's First Minicomputer Kit to Rival Commercial Models... ALTAIR 8800." Allen hurried to Gates to tell him that their dream could come true. They knew that those computers needed software. In other words, they could write computer programs and sell them. The two friends got very little sleep at night. In a few weeks, Allen went to ALTAIR 8800 makers and introduced the software. For the beginning, success was ensured, and Microsoft started rising and expanding. Of course, take advantage of the opportunity.

In 1978 Steve Jobs went to Xerox and said, "Look, I will let you invest a million dollars in Apple, if you sort of open the kimono at Xerox PARC."

The Palo Alto Research Center was the ultimate high-tech laboratory in Silicon Valley.

Xerox allowed Jobs to visit the place where Jobs first saw the computer mouse and picked up the idea. Of course, Jobs used the moment: Soon Apple's Macintosh revolutionized the PC market with the mouse-centered interface.

Edwin Land was walking along a street in New Mexico with his three-year-old daughter. The girl asked her father, "Dad, why can't I see at once the picture you took of me?" Land didn't know what to answer, as he was unable to produce a photo immediately with his camera. But he undertook the task of solving the puzzle she had set him. In 5 years, after an enormous research program and hard work, Land publicly demonstrated an instant camera, called the Polaroid Land Camera, which made it possible for a picture to be taken and developed in 60 seconds or fewer.

When Phil Knight met coach Bill Bowerman, the latter told him that American athletic shoes were too heavy and not fit for running; no serious athlete would buy and train in such footwear. Knight didn't forget this moment. He left for Japan to observe how sneakers were produced there. Knight bought 300 pairs of Tiger athletic shoes, which were in great demand in the United States, from Onitsuka company . And why not produce his own? As a result Nike, Inc. came into being.

Sponges didn't sell well in Wal-Mart. Sam Walton was angry. One of his employees was constantly thinking of selling sponges. And one day Walton learned that sponges sold incredibly well in one of his supermarkets. He caught a plane, visited the supermarket, and was astounded to see a Ford pickup truck inside the store, the back of which was filled with sponges. People would pick up sponges when passing by it, and the sales were secured. Walton granted that employee shares in the company's stock as a reward. Seize the moment.

Let's think about the next example: Tim Brady was the first Yahoo! employee. Yahoo! started as a collection of links to research papers maintained by two Stanford graduate students, Jerry Yang and David Filo. They gradually added links to new types of information, and this led to a rapid increase in popularity of the site. Jerry and David would add new sites to their list for eight hours a day (sometimes even more) for eight months. At the end of 1994, Yang and Filo decided to turn the site into a startup and asked Tim Brady to write a business plan for it. I must note that they were not alone either. They had a team. Tim Brady had been Jerry Yang's college roommate and at the time was getting his MBA at Harvard Business School. He was planning to finish the semester, but as the popularity of Yahoo! was growing rapidly, he could not wait and joined. Brady turned in the business plan of the new company as his final assignment in the courses and left for the West Coast to become Yahoo's first employee.

Brady explains, "This was fortunate because, as it turns out, by February of '95, they were saying, 'We need you now; we don't need you in June when you graduate.' My reply was, 'I'm in school, and my dad paid for it. Are you suggesting that I tell my dad that I'm not going to come away with a degree?' And Jerry was like, 'I'm not telling you to do anything, but we need you now.' So I talked to some of my professors, and you can fail a certain number of classes at HBS throughout your tenure – it's a pass/fail grading system. I hadn't failed any yet, so I could fail three classes and technically graduate. I was taking five classes, so I tuned in my business plan as a final paper for two out of five, and passed with those." And I should note – take advantage of the moment.

Jessica Livingston founded Y Combinator in 2005 with Paul Graham, Robert Morris, and Trevor Blackwell. Y Combinator developed a new approach to venture funding: to fund startups in batches, giving them just enough money to get started, working closely with them to refine their ideas, and then introducing them to later-stage investors for further funding. In three years they have funded more than 100 startups.

Jessica Livingston says, "There had been one group, two guys from UVA, who were still seniors and were graduating that spring—Alexis Ohanian and Steve Huffman. They came to us with an idea that we just thought was wrong for two young guys with no connections in the fast food industry. Their idea was ordering fast food through your cell phone. And we didn't fund them. We told them, 'Sorry, we really liked you guys, but we just think your idea would be a bit too challenging.' But that morning when I was at work, Paul called them and said, 'We like you guys. Would you be willing to work on another idea?' They were on an Amtrak train heading back to Virginia. I remember Paul emailed me and the subject line was 'muffins saved.' I had nicknamed them 'the muffins,' because I just loved them. It was just sort of an affectionate name." This idea was later used in the Reddit project.

"I remember thinking, 'This is so exciting.' [Seizing the moment] They had gotten off the train in Hartford or something and headed back to Boston to go meet with Paul to brainstorm new ideas. I thought, 'These are the kind of people I want to fund – people who would get off the train and go back and make it happen.' So we wound up funding eight companies that summer." Reddit is a social news website founded by Steve Huffman and Alexis Ohanian in 2005. Users registered in it can submit content, such as text posts or direct links to any information they liked on the Internet.

As CEO of IBM, one of the oldest, most powerful companies in the world, Ginni Rometty is no stranger to public speaking. She gave a commencement speech at her alma mater, Northwestern University, in June, 2015. In her speeches she hardly ever mentions her husband of 35 years, Mark Rometty, who prefers to stay out of the spotlight. Apparently, he noticed. So Rometty included him in one of the funniest portions of her speech, telling this great anecdote about how he set her on her career path, "I had worked for a senior executive, and he decided to go to a new job. He came in to me one day and he said, 'Wonderful, you are the candidate to replace me.' So, I was called in the office and with great excitement told I'd be offered this job."

"Well, I can remember my reaction: it wasn't the same great excitement. I looked at him and I said, tsk, it's too early. I'm not ready. Just give me a few more years and I'd be ready for this. I need to go home and I need to go sleep on that. Well, that evening, my husband, now up there [she pointed upward, which made it look like she was pointing at heaven] ...well, he's up in the stands, I don't mean too far up. My husband of 35 years. Oh, boy. He says I never mention him, and then I do and I mess it up, you know. He sat and listened patiently to my story, like he always does. And then he looked at me and he said one thing. He said, 'Do you think a man would have answered the question that way?' He said, 'I know you. In six months you'll be ready for something else.' And you know what? He was right. And I went in the next day and I took that job."

"And that takes me to my second lesson to leave you with: growth and comfort never co-exist. I want you to close your eyes ... and ask yourself, when have you learned the most? I guarantee it's when you felt at risk[2]." Of course, the moment must not be missed.

Let me introduce my example, too. I was getting numerous letters from people asking me advice on what books to read. Then, as I recommended books, they would ask me if there were the Armenian versions of them. Interesting idea. I thought why not combine the results of all my research and what I've learned from prominent businessmen in one book? And so the idea was born.

2 http://www.businessinsider.com/ibm-ceo-ginni-rometty-tells-inspiring-story-about-her-husband-2015-6

The examples are too many, so I'll wind up at this point. This is why I insist that success depends on not being alone and seizing the moment.

In our further topics you will see that all our heroes had either used the moment to their advantage or had someone else with them, followed that person's advice, or reached substantial results due to someone else's help.

Secret 2. Remember, the moment has to be seized.

Secret 3

If economists were good at business, they would be rich men, instead of advisers to rich men.

Kirk Kerkorian

Tracinda (Kirk Kerkorian)

This quiet and shy man gave very few interviews He didn't have a credit card or an e-mail address. He didn't give speeches in public. He did his job and considered that his activities defined him. His greatness was in that he, an eighth-grade dropout, was a self-made man, ranking 41st on the Forbes list of the world's richest people with a net worth of $16 billion in 2008. Kerkorian was the youngest of four children in his family. Born June 6, 1917, in the city of Fresno, he was the son of Armenian immigrants who had moved to the United States to escape the Armenian Genocide. His father had managed to achieve some success, but in the years of Great Depression the family lost all its property - hence necessity forced every family member to work and bring in money.

The 9-year-old Kirk had to lie about his age to employers so he could get a job. He did everything he could to make money; he was a paperboy, golf caddie, steam cleaner, car refurbisher, street cleaner, porter, furnace installer, etc. When still in junior high school, Kirk was drawn to boxing, as his elder brother was involved in it. Soon Kirk became amateur welterweight champion. That was the reason he decided to go into professional boxing. But meeting Ted O'Flaherty became pivotal in his life.

In 1939, the 22-year-old Kirk was earning 45 cents an hour helping O'Flaherty install furnaces. O'Flaherty tried to convince Kirk to go on a ride in a single-engine airplane, but he consistently refused, until one day he consented to go aloft with O'Flaherty. Enthralled by the first experience on an airplane, he was back out at the field the very next day to take his first flying lesson. The desire to become a boxer was gone. Now his goal was to become a pilot. Initially it was Ted who gave him flying lessons, but it was not enough. Looking for someone who would teach him to fly, he showed up at the ranch of the celebrity female pilot Florence 'Pancho' Barnes. The ranch was a combination flight school and dairy farm. Approaching the ranch owner, Kerkorian said,

"I haven't got any money. I haven't got any education. I want to learn to fly. I don't know how I can do it. Can you help me?"

It appears that no money was needed, nor education, just the willingness to milk cows and shovel bovine manure. Thus, Kirk milked cows and shoveled manure in exchange for flying lessons. Within six months of gaining a pilot's license, Kerkorian heard that the Royal Air Force was flying Mosquito bombers from Canada, where they were built, to the British Isles. He went up there and got hired as a pilot right away. They were paying a generous salary for those years, $1,000 a trip. The flights were deadly and dangerous: Each flight could be the last one, but he took the risk.

Kirk was so smart that he chose the route across the Atlantic, riding an airflow called the 'Iceland Wave' so as to reach the destination earlier. The reason was that the Mosquito's fuel tanks carried the plane 1,400 miles. It was 2,200 miles to Scotland. The airflow blew Mosquitos toward Europe at jet speeds, but it wasn't constant. If it waned in mid flight, the plane would fall into the ocean. On the other hand, the Germans strafed the planes, as England was under blockade. It was in these hard and difficult circumstances that Kirk made money. He was so skilled that he managed to deliver 33 planes from Canada to England, when only one of four pilots made it to the destination.

Having saved most of his salary in this period, Kirk bought a single-engine Cessna plane for $5,000, training pilots and offering charter flights between Los Angeles and Las Vegas, which was, roughly speaking, an air taxi. He was making significant amounts of money on these flights. A gambler named Jerry Williams occasionally hired Kirk's plane. During one of those flights he suggested Kerkorian to invest the money and gamble.

Kirk and Jerry decided to go to a casino to play. They thought they had lost all the money, but Kirk found $5 in his pocket. Jerry suggested they save it for coffee. Kirk didn't like the idea.

"What good is five dollars going to do?" asked Kerkorian, and headed back to the craps table, where he won $700. Since that day, Kirk became known as a high roller, who could in later years lose $50,000 per day. But he didn't entirely got involved in it. He went into the charter end of the business. Later, Kerkorian remembered that the best times of his life were in Vegas.

Finally having accumulated $60,000, Kerkorian purchased a tiny charter line, Los Angeles Air Service, in 1947. He later changed the name to Trans International Airlines, TIA, and offered the first jet service on a nonscheduled airline. The risk was great – Kerkorian was investing all the money he had earned into a dying company. Yet, not only did he manage to set the company on its feet, but he also managed to sign contracts of cooperation with other airlines. He knew at the time that there was no air service between California and Nevada, and he decided to fill the gap. *Seize the moment.*

Kirk took advantage of the Vietnam War, flying soldiers to Vietnam and taking state orders from the US government, at the same time adding to his fleet of planes. Later, he sold TIA to TransAmerica Corporation for $104 million. *Imagine the fantastic investment – bought for $60,000, sold for $104 million. Stunning, bravo to Kirk Kerkorian.*

In 1962, Kerkorian made a deal that Fortune magazine called "one of the most successful land speculations in Las Vegas' history." He bought 80 acres of land on the Las Vegas Strip for $960,000 and then leased it for $4 million to the director of Caesars Palace. In 1968 Kirk sold this area for $5 million. *Again, compare – purchased for $960,000, sold for $5 million.*

In 1967, Kerkorian purchased 82 acres of land for $5 million and began the construction of the International Hotel. The design called for over 1500 rooms and a 'youth hostel', where kids could play while their parents were busy. And this was before anybody's time, as no other hotel in the world took special care of children. Of course, everybody opposed this idea, but Kirk's motto was, "You have to ask a lot of questions and listen to people, but eventually, you have to go by your own instincts."

In addition, the hotel opened with the presence of the best singers and actors, while no one had gone that big on entertainment before. Along with the opening of the hotel, Kerkorian offered the public 17% of the company's stock at $5 per share, but only after a month it was sold for over $50. While enjoying huge success in Las Vegas, Kirk also was studying the Hollywood film industry.

In 1969, he purchased Metro-Goldwyn-Mayer MGM studio and later considered selling it. Alex Yemenidjian was responsible for the sale. A common acquaintance had introduced Alex to Kirk. Alex was then offered a job by Kerkorian and tasked to sell MGM. He was successful in selling MGM and was transferred to Las Vegas to head Kerkorian's businesses.

They sold the MGM/UA conglomerate to Ted Turner in 1986 for $1.5 billion. The sale lasted 74 days — Turner had debt problems — and Kerkorian bought it back for a mere $780 million. In 1990, he again sold the company — this time to multiple investors for $1.3 billion — and in 1996, he again bought it all back and Alex took over MGM's management. Thanks to Emenidjian's efforts, the price of MGM shares grew substantially, and they again sold the company at a price three times higher than they had bought it. Great deal. *They said Emenidjian was Kerkorian's right-hand man and managed his businesses, and again I'm convinced that no one can achieve success alone.* In 2004, MGM was finally sold to Sony for $4,9 billion.

Kerkorian's business approach had the following formula: he bought undervalued companies — occasionally selling off assets to help fund the purchase, added strategic resources to augment and enhance the value of the companies, then sold his stake in the companies at a profit. He exhibited patience in waiting for the value to rise, and he evidenced discipline and agility when it came to knowing when to get in on an investment and when to get out. It is also the case that his choices of undervalued companies were often singular, although eventually, of course, investors would follow where Kerkorian led. But the singularity is notable: Kerkorian would buy planes that could barely move and sell the fuel that made them move; he would buy land in the desert when land in the desert was something people fled from; he would buy a movie studio and turn it into a hotel company. He saw something in each of these circumstances that others did not see. Or he saw the circumstances in unique ways, looking past the obvious to perceive some undeveloped potential that simply eluded others.

On December 5, 1973 the opening for Kerkorian's second hotel was held. The new $107 million mega resort was named Grand Hotel, which was the largest hotel in the world at the time. At 26 stories, it had 2,084 rooms, a 1,200-seat showroom, shopping arcade, etc. In November 1980, a fire raged through the hotel, killing 87 people and injuring hundreds. Kirk was in New York at that time. In two hours he arrived in Vegas. His first question was "Where do we start?"

Many did not believe he could find the strength to rebuild the hotel, but they were wrong. Kirk's persistence was infinite, and after only 8 months it reopened. Kirk went into the casino business after the Mafia had run out of it. Let me point out that the first casino and hotel Kerkorian purchased was the Flamingo, which he bought from Howard Hughes. And it happened when Hughes had already cleared this business from Mafia. This very purchase became the starting point of the casino and hotel business. And now a small part about the strategy of casinos.

We all know that there are no clocks in casinos, but there are no mirrors, either. A casino visitor shouldn't see his real face, so as to imagine he's a hero, because no one feels confident when there are any shortcomings in his appearance. The absence of mirror makes people feel perfect subconsciously. Everything in a casino is red, bright, flashy, and golden. Even the automatic machines, which only have to give banknotes to the winner, are made to sound like falling gold coins to affect people's subconscious.

The absence of clocks is explained that if there's no clock, the player doesn't look at it and subsequently spends more time in the casino. It is clear that, when indulged, a player will spend more money than someone who sits and watches the clock constantly. There are no windows in casinos so that people lose track of time, not knowing whether it's night or day, and feel comfortable in that environment. Besides, passers-by shouldn't see what's going on inside, for they might divert the attention of the absorbed gamblers[1]. Here the environment is structured in a way that if someone wins big, everyone on the floor will know it, it is celebrated with flashing lights

1 http://www.businessinsider.com/how-casinos-make-you-spend-money-2014-8

and noises. A question arises – if they can win, why can't I?

The staff are always smiling. The seats are soft and comfortable. If you want to get some food or cash out your chips, you must go deeper into the burrows of the casino, passing through machines and tables that can capture your attention. It's one more effort to keep you inside the casino and make you try your luck once again.

Everything is done here for people to stay longer in the casino. For example, there are casinos where people are provided with free food, drinks, alcohol. It gives the impression that they take care of people. Drunk people will undoubtedly spend more money[2].

Now back to the hero of Secret 3, who made investments in airlines, real estate, the film industry, and hotels and casinos, and since 1990 he entered the car industry, buying shares in the Chrysler company. However, after the merger of Chrysler and Daimler-Benz, Kerkorian's 13% of Chrysler shares turned into 4% of DaimlerChrysler shares, which he successfully sold for $3 billion some time later. After Chrysler, GM shares became Kerkorian's next purchase, which he sold soon after. Kerkorian's decision to part with GM shares meant that the famous billionaire lost hope to subdue the management of GM on which he had long exerted strong pressure. I should remind you that it was Kerkorian's idea to merge GM with the Japanese-French Renault-Nissan Alliance, with an aim to bring GM out of the severe crisis. In early October, GM and Renault-Nissan stopped merger negotiations, prompting sharp criticism from the investment company Tracinda. The negotiations were stopped largely because of GM management, which announced that the company could come out of crisis on its own.

In 2008, Kerkorian to invest a sum of $1 billion in Ford. But the company suffered losses, as it was during the financial crisis. Kerkorian started selling his 7.3 million shares at $2.43 each, whereas he had bought them at $7.10 each. A very big loss for Kerkorian. What was the cause of it? According to Stephen L. Weiss, the problem was the promise Kerkorian felt for the potential in the auto industry based on the large profits he gained from his investments in Chrysler. But that was in the 90s, and this was the 2000s, with a weak market and crisis. So do not let the previous success outrun the

2 http://listverse.com/2010/02/09/10-tricks-casinos-use-on-you/

present, because all that is already in the past. The present is a new game, a new environment; everything must be evaluated anew.

And last but not least, Kerkorian was a philanthropist. Named after his two daughters, Kerkorian's Lincy Foundation has made huge charitable contributions, much of this to Armenian causes. Kerkorian has donated about $180 million to Armenia through his charity, the Lincy Foundation. Since 2001, the bulk of the money has been spent on various infrastructure projects. Those included the repair of 420 kilometers of major highways and the construction of 3,700 new apartments in the country's northwestern regions hit hard by the catastrophic earthquake in 1988. In May 2005, President Kocharian awarded Kerkorian Armenia's highest honor, the Medal of Fatherland, which carries the title of "national hero" of Armenia.

As Kerkorian gave so much to charity, Alex Yemenidjian asked him why he was against his name being mentioned and having a street named after him in his honor. To which Kerkorian replied, "If you do something and expect an answer in return, it's not charity, it's trade."

That's who he was, a man who never raised his voice, did not go to public events, and, some sources say, had neither e-mail address nor a cellphone. On his days off he played tennis, and his biggest wealth in the world was his children. Kirk's holding company is named Tracinda in honor of his daughters, Tracy and Linda.

Secret 3. Do not be afraid to take risks.

Secret 4

I decided I was either going to be a professor or start a company.

Larry Page

Google (Sergey Brin, Larry Page)

Google's greatest asset is that people use it for free and don't have to get registered. Unlike many companies, where the administration develops strategy prior developing a new product, Google first develops the product, after which the team comes together and discusses how to make it profitable. *Yes, the team, and not only the executives, as it usually happens in many companies. In Google everyone's opinion is taken into account.*

No dress code must be followed by the workers, but most wear jeans. Google also has its own rescue team so that no one drowns in the pool. Employees enjoy such perks as health insurance and free medical care. Google also has a laundry service, a dental center, hairdressers, a car wash service where oil is changed for free, a children's playground, and fitness and massage centers.

People have the opportunity to play beach volleyball, American football, and drive scooters. There are palm trees and soft armchairs, and the employees are allowed to bring their pets to work. For those who come from distant places, the company has special buses with free Wi-Fi, not to let the employees get bored on their way.

As for working conditions, there are around 11 free cafes for the employees on campus, so that they never get bored with the same menu. In them one can find a wide variety of dishes, from Asian cuisine to vegetarian food. Moreover, employees can have three free meals a day.

Investors sometimes criticized Google for the free food, but Sergey Brin explained it in this way, "In any case, the employee must leave the workplace, wait in line till he's served and come back, while the food on-site saves him 30 minutes, which is quite expensive for us." By some estimates, Google annually spends more than $72 million on food. These numbers are justified by the high level of motivation of the staff.

The hallways are lined with whiteboards where the employees can jot down their ideas. Google employees can take courses in foreign languages. Each employee can use free electric scooters and move around Googleplex campus. All employees can go skiing once a year.

You will never see advertisements on the Google home page, as it's meant to be convenient. If you type Yahoo.com and Google.com, you'll see why I say so. Let me point out that Google's simple home page has to do with a very simple fact, which the founders didn't break later. Google's founders just didn't know how to create a web page design.

The multicolored letters of the logo and the snow-white background create a sense of purity, which is so much lacking on the Internet platform.

The company employees are divided into teams of a minimum of three people, and they are entitled to spend 20% of their time on their own interests. Due to this policy, AdSense, Google News, and other projects were born. There are projects that fail; others develop and turn into lucrative products. The principle of 20% was borrowed from the university environment, where the professors were allowed to spend one day on the realization of projects they were interested in.

Anyway, all this aside, we can say the most important and valuable resource in every company is the human capital, and Google has almost no rivals in this sphere. It has left everyone behind, as talented specialists whose work is truly appreciated gather here. Can you imagine specialists move to Google from different universities, as well as such giants as NASA, Bell Labs, Microsoft, and Amazon, as they are eager to work in the dynamic and vibrant environment created by Google. I'm quoting – your well-being depends on the well-being of your staff. Dear readers, so always attach great importance to these lines in management rules. It's interesting that Google creators didn't even know what the ultimate form and goal their project would assume.

Larry Page recalls, "Sergey and I met at Stanford University. When I saw him for the first time, I thought he was pretty obnoxious, but the interesting thing is that he thought the same of me. After the first meeting, we had some argument. Neither of us would yield. But soon we were able to find common ground, because we were both from scientists' families. Sergey is a Jew, and my mother is Jewish. We both belonged to the same generation and went to the same university. We were both fascinated by computers and spent most of our time in front of them."

Stanford, unlike other universities, enables its students to use university resources to implement their plans. Thus, the students were provided with special rooms to pursue their projects. Larry shared Room 360 with 4 other friends. Sergey was in another room, but he spent most of his time in Larry's room. Larry and Sergey were together every day, and even today they occupy one office.

In 1990 the Internet was growing at such a pace that the number of users was increasing day by day. E-mail had facilitated interpersonal connections, and people spent much time in front of computers. During this period two Stanford students, Jerry Yang and David Filo, were defending their dissertation on Yahoo! Yes, it was due to this thesis that Yahoo was created, the most perfect search engine in those years. The idea of a web search engine did not give the two friends rest. Page kept thinking about how to download the entire web to one computer.

At Stanford, Larry began meeting with his doctoral program advisor, Terry Winograd. In search of a dissertation theme, Page considered exploring the mathematical properties of the World Wide Web, understanding its link structure as a huge graph, an approach encouraged by his supervisor. Page was studying search engines day and night. Once, he noticed a peculiarity about the AltaVista engine – the system was fast due to a new function that brought websites by links, one click was enough to get to a website.

Page informed his professors that he had found the way to download the entire web. Professors laughed at him. But Larry's persistence had no borders. In fact, Page had a brilliant idea: If the website had many links, this would increase the probability that it would rank higher in search results.

If you publish certain material or work, you mention the sources of information in the end. The more references you include, the more thorough it becomes. The same can be applied to search engines. The websites link to one another, and, because of those links, it's possible to decide the degree of their usefulness for people. If a website is referenced a lot, it's clear that more people will visit it, as it contains valuable information.

The more important the website is, the more its link has been shared. Larry called his program PageRank, in which Page stood for both the word page and Larry's last name. One of the professors who believed in him was Rajeev Motwani, who was quite supportive of the two friends. Brin, Page and Motwani developed a prototype of a search engine: If the rest of the search engines simply compared the words in the search box with the words on web pages, PageRank ranked the received results in a logical sequence. Finally, computer users could quickly find the desired information on the web.

Sergey's supervisor, David Cheriton, was soon convinced of the uniqueness of the idea. Sergey was also excited by Larry's idea, and together they started working on the idea of links. Page and Sergey worked for hours downloading websites, with no inkling of day and night. They even had their food in front of the computer, and left the computer only in case of need.

When the database had already become outgrown, the two friends decided to buy computers, but they had no money. So they were buying different computer parts, collecting them, and building a ready-made computer, which cost them less. As there was no free space left in Room 360, the two friends moved to Sergey's room, which had turned into a computer laboratory.

In 1997 the initial version of Google, nicknamed BackRub, was created, though the young people didn't quite like this name. They suffered. They asked their fellow students and wrote different words on the whiteboard, but there was no solution. One day one of the guys from Larry's room suggested the word "Googolplex." Larry thought it could be shortened and typed it in as "Google."

He liked it and told Sergey, who also approved of it. They registered it later that evening. They wrote it on the whiteboard, and next morning saw one of the girls had written the following - you have misspelled this word, it has to be spelled "googol." After settling on a name, the two friends determined that there should be no advertisement on the homepage, so that the user won't rush to leave it.

When the guys were running out of money, they would visit their professor, Rajeev Motwani, and ask him to transfer money, because they didn't have flash drives for indexing and storing the websites. They needed to buy new ones. Page's search engine became so popular in the Stanford computer network that Page began to think of a commercial plan. One day the two friends came up to Motwani and told him they wanted to start their company. Whoever heard this would have given the traditional negative feedback, "Are you crazy? There are 37 such search engines, who needs the 38th? It's interesting how you are going to handle it, what are you going to do without money?"

I think you have heard many similar opinions - listen to yourselves. Actually, search engines existed earlier than Google. Google simply proposed a new approach based on links. If you are not the first one, improve the idea and become a leader - this is the principle. From the first day Google realized that the only way to defeat the competition was to produce the fastest and most accurate search product in the world.

Understanding the complexity of the situation, Winograd said to Page, "I don't see how you're ever going to get the money." Larry replied, "Well, you're going to see. We'll figure that out."

There is always a way out. If there's no money, then you should think of finding it. Persistent people reach their goals and do not turn any problem into a reason to quit. If there's a problem, then find a solution. It was Sergey's supervisor, David Cheriton, who provided the first tangible aid. No one achieves results alone; you are always going to need somebody's assistance - in some form - to help you succeed. Remember this.

One day in August 1998, Larry and Sergey sat waiting for the "angel" in

Palo Alto. Stanford Professor David Cheriton had written to his friend, Andy Bechtolsheim, and suggested that he meet with the guys. Bechtolsheim came out of his Porsche and walked towards the guys. Hearing what idea the guys had, Bechtolsheim, the founder of Sun Microsystems, wrote a check for $100,000 without thinking much so the guys could start a company. He asked, "What was the name of your company?"

Brin replied that they had named the company "Googol." But Andy wrote "Google Inc." on the check. But here was the hitch: Bechtolsheim wrote a check to the company under the name "Google Inc.", but it did not even exist yet. So the check was put in Larry's drawer where it stayed for a few weeks, until they legally registered the company under the name "Google." And what does Google mean? It refers to the No 1 followed by 100 zeros. After filling out the check, Andy hurried off to the next meeting. Larry and Sergey were so happy that they went to Burger King to celebrate their success.

The young men decided to leave Stanford to start a company of their own. This made their parents, who wanted to see their sons become professors, very sad. Anyway, when Larry and Sergey left Stanford, they chose Prof. Rajeev Motwani as their advisor. He became one of the first investors with a significant number of shares. Google's first employee was their fellow student, Craig Silverstein, who, like Larry and Sergey, left Stanford and did not complete his doctorate. As money was still not enough, they turned to everyone – their acquaintances, relatives, friends - from whom about $1 million was collected.

The next step was the logo. The Google logo was created by Ruth Kedar, who was teaching design at Stanford University. Unlike other startups, which would offer shares for such services, the young entrepreneurs insisted on paying for the logo. "I had no idea at the time that Google would become as ubiquitous as it is today, or that their success would be of such magnitude," Kedar says. She wishes she had taken payment in Google shares.

Neither Larry nor Sergey had an idea how they'd make money, but they knew that their system was going to be the best of all. They were running out of money. They needed to find a way out, and, in fact, they didn't know what to do with the website. The two friends decided to take the most extreme step – to sell the website. At first they encouraged Kleiner Perkins Caufield

& Byers Company to buy it for $1 million, but nothing came of it. They were rejected for the reason that similar companies - AltaVista, Excite, Infoseek - were rejected. They operated at a loss, and little potential was seen in Google. Their attempts to sell Google failed, as there were no buyers; the two friends deeply disappointed.

Then they met with Paul Flaherty, the founder of AltaVista, and offered to sell him Google. Brin proposed $1 million for their PageRank system, saying that AltaVista was the present and Google - the future. A week after the conversation, the two friends received a letter saying that AltaVista turned down the offer. A long series of refusals began. Let me remind you that AltaVista no longer exists today. Page and Brin visited Excite Company and were turned down again, because the front page lacked advertising. No company wanted to invest, but the young men didn't give up.

They met with Yahoo co-founder, David Filo, hoping that he would buy Google. Filo listened to them and refused, saying that they wanted people to stay longer in Yahoo than in Google. But he advised them not to sell Google and go forward in forming their own company. "When it's fully developed and scalable," Filo said, "Let's talk again." Larry and Sergey did not expect such an answer from Filo, but his advice did encourage them.

Filo was the man who pointed them toward creating their own business, not knowing what a headache it would become for his own business, for the development of Yahoo. The guys could not imagine what a stroke of luck it was that they couldn't sell Google. That's it. The problem should be made into an opportunity, instead of giving up on the dream in the face of the first failure. And they succeeded after Filo's advice. It's clear, success is not achieved alone.

Everybody rejected them. Disappointed in not being able to sell their idea, the two friends decided to improve Google. The period for raising money began. Venture capitalists did not believe in Larry and Sergey and discouraged them, saying that 80% of startups failed. Larry countered that most of them were restaurants, not search engines. The conditions were that hard, rejections from all sides.

The two friends kept turning to venture capitalists. The friends visited two competing companies, Kleiner Perkins and Sequoia Capital, which agreed to finance their further activity and provided $25 million. Everybody was stunned at Stanford, as those two companies had never invested such a large amount of money together, because they were rivals. As surprising as it was, John Doerr and Michael Moritz became members of the company's board.

John Doerr explains, "You could see Google was growing rapidly." Additionally, there was technical excellence; Larry and Sergey wanted to assemble a good management team. They were going after a very large market, and "they had a sense of urgency about them." "They were nerdy white males, dropouts with no social life." *Take advantage of the moment.*

In 1999, by investing $25 million, Sequoia Capital and Kleiner Perkins Caufield & Byers received 20% of the shares, and in 2008 Google's market capitalization had risen to more than $108 billion.

Receiving $25 million from venture companies, Larry and Sergey vowed that they would choose a professional manager who'd help Google grow in the right way. So venture capitalists began to worry, because things didn't go forward, as Larry and Sergey didn't have the necessary management experience. Doerr got involved. He introduced one of the managers he knew, Eric Schmidt, to them, after which Schmidt was recruited to run Google.

According to Schmidt, curiosity and probing play a large part in the management style introduced to Google by their triad. He brings forth the most frequently asked questions concerning Google management style:

How do we make the products we have the most useful?

What is the best long-term path for the company?

What are the next big breakthroughs in research?

How is the competition affecting our business?

"Out of the conversation comes innovation," Eric Schmidt notes. "Innovation is not something that I just wake up one day and say, 'I want to innovate.' I think you get a better innovative culture if you ask it as a question." *Try to hold discussions. Listen to everyone's opinion on the subject. New ideas are born as a result of such discussions.* As Larry often points out, "If you set a crazy, ambitious goal and miss it, you'll still achieve something remarkable."

Another pressure from the investors came regarding ways of earning money, as Google had to be made profitable somehow. Having excluded advertising on the front page, the two friends started thinking about the tools. At first, they had no desire to use advertising, but later it turned out that advertising would become the main source of income. As a result, Google developed two methods of advertising, AdWords and AdSense. The idea that advertising sells best when it is pertinent to search results helped Larry and Sergey develop their business model. Advertisers give preference to the options of advertising that allow them to reach the target audience. On the other hand, users typing keywords in the search box are willing to click on an ad that is thematically pertinent to the information they are looking for on the Internet.

As one of Google's managers says, "I think the beauty of the search model is the one thing we know is your intent. There's a chance that we're going to be able to give you the right information at the right time - the right ad to the right user at the right time with the right outcome – because it's very self-directed form advertising. Google doesn't need to know who the end user is to be successful." *They discarded a common method and created something new. They decided to be different, a really wonderful and effective solution by Google.* Here is the opinion Warren Buffett expressed concerning this, "It's not hard to see that Google is a phenomenal company. The whole idea of search never occurred to me. I never thought of it. Now at Geico, we pay these guys a whole lot of money for this and that key word." *This is a century of ideas – search for that idea.*

Google's growth started in 2000, during the bubble burst, which resulted in massive layoffs in Silicon Valley. Sergey and Larry took decisive actions and increased staff numbers by hiring great professionals. In these years Google hadn't gone public yet and wasn't sensitive to the Wall Street crisis. It had an excellent opportunity to increase its intellectual capital and took advantage of it. *I'll elaborate on this in Secret 5.*

In 2004 Google became a joint stock company, and its founders became billionaires. Before issuing shares, Page had warned everyone that they weren't a traditional company. The company itself indeed behaves independently of Wall Street and refuses to provide advance information to analysts on future financial performance. They have to figure out what quarterly financial performance to expect from Google independently.

Secret 4. Happy people generate the best ideas.

Secret 5

"Hire only people who are better than you in some meaningful way."

Laszlo Bock

Google (Laszlo Bock)

*In the previous secret we got acquainted with the history of the creation one of the tech giants of our day, and now I will talk about the most important point of its strategy, called **human resources.** I was wondering a lot why it's tech companies that create paradisiacal conditions for their employees. Then I realized that this is a century of ideas and that they need smart people. So they must do everything to keep them in the company. And now I'll expand on how the company recruits the bests and what steps it takes to motivate them.* Parallel to the development of the company, Google's human resources department observed a very strange phenomenon; one after the other women were leaving the company.

Like the majority IT firms, Google is mostly staffed by men. The "feminization" of employees became a priority for the company. The giants of this field are always vying to attract the best employees, and Google's position was weakening in comparison with Apple, Facebook, Amazon, Microsoft, and other powerful companies. Each employee's departure means a costly recruitment process and investment in the training of new hires, both of which are time-consuming and have unclear outcomes.

The en masse departures made Google seriously think about creating desirable conditions. They had to make sure that the employees would feel happy after walking through the company doors. That is why there came a man, Laszlo Bock, who completely changed the company's working environment. Bock was interested in why women were leaving. It turned out that the majority were leaving because of family problems. After childbirth, they got 12 weeks of paid time off. Naturally, they didn't manage to take care of the baby in 12 weeks and were forced to leave the company. Bock decided to change the plan.

He prolonged the paid maternity leave to 5 months; moreover, he granted 12 weeks' leave to new dads. If even this was not enough, women could take an additional three-month vacation and take care of the baby. Besides, Google decided that every employee should take a 7-week vacation to relieve work stress. After childbirth the company transfers $500 into the parent's account to help with expenses like household chores, gardening, dry cleaning and the chores that the child's parents won't manage to do.

Another interesting thing organized by Google's human resources department was making an inquiry into whether the workers would prefer a $1,000 increase in salary or a $2,000 bonus. It turns out people preferred to get a salary raise than bonus. After the survey, Google management announced that the salary would be increased by 10% for all the staff. Many employees had written on their pages that it was the happiest day in their lives.

After the death of an employee, Google pays his family half of the salary for 10 years. Why in 10 years and not wholly? Because a long-term money provision is preferred. If an employee dies, his child receives $1,000 per month until age 19, or age 23 for full-time students.

All this is planned to attract the world's most talented people and reduce their flow from the company. Google's entire business is based on human resources, intellectual abilities. At the root of such policy lies Google's desire to attract the brightest minds, and it's natural that extremely attractive conditions should be created for them. Under such conditions people work and create with pleasure. Yet, despite all that Google does, some talented employees leave the company, as they want to start their own businesses. At first, Google really attracted everyone and created those conditions so that the employees would not leave the company, but to no avail.

One of Google's managers says that there are people who must be hired no matter how much they will cost the company. Google takes these kinds of people. Google receives more than 2 million job applications in a year. Today, more severe and harder trials await job applicants than before. Sometimes you can hear questions like: Describe a time when you had to deal with a rude customer? What is your biggest failure in life? Tell me how Target competes with Wal-Mart? How would you get more customers for Wachovia Bank? What challenges will Starbucks face in the next ten years? How would you monetize Facebook?

The applicant's abilities are checked right during the interview, for example, the sales manager has to sell products, the marketing expert is told to write a marketing plan, the lawyer writes a contract, and the programmer writes a program, and so on. Comprehensive development is also crucial here, as the employee from the technical department can be transferred to another department.

In addition, IT companies ask questions that test logic. For example, what number comes next in the series? 10, 9, 60, 90, 70, 66. Don't knock yourselves out with the numbers, in fact the numbers need to be spelled out in the English letters, for example, nine, sixty, ninety, seventy, sixty-six (hyphen doesn't count). It turns out that the figures are arranged according to the number of letters, for example, Ten – 3, Nine-4, Sixty-5, and so on. But ten is not the only one with three letters, for example one, two also have three letters, so here is taken the greater number of them. It is clear that 10 is greater than 1 and 2. This means the next number must be the largest number with 9 letters, which is 96 – ninety-six.

For Google's first five years Larry and Sergey insisted on being included in the interview process for every single hire. Up to this day, Page is the one to approve the hiring of each employee. The two friends got notorious for shooting job applicants the oddest interview questions. Once Sergey Brin asked an applicant who was lawyer to write a contract for him to sell his soul to the devil. That applicant had 30 minutes to draft it and send it to Sergey's e-mail address.

The people who need to work with the candidate if he is hired are also included in the interview process with the HR department. Google believes that the best ones can be selected after at least 4 interviews. An applicant can have up to five interviews with different people within a day. In the end, all the decisions are sent to Larry Page.

Senior Vice President of People Operations at Google, Laszlo Bock, says that in 1998, the company had no profits, and for years the company paid almost the lowest salary in the industry. Coming to Google cost him financially; the head of his department at GE told him to call him in case things did not turn out well at Google, so he would find him a job.

When Bock was employed, Google was growing rapidly, and its task was to hire the best specialists. But here it faced a serious problem. It was difficult to find the CVs of the best applicants. Why? When Google was a small company, it was easy to hire graduates of Stanford, Harvard, MIT and similar institutions. As the company had grown enough to be in need of thousands of new employees a year, it was faced with the fact that many of the best specialists had never attended these elite schools. According to Bock, education means much less than actual achievements. For some posts it does not even matter whether you graduated from a university at all. The important thing is the contribution you make to the company and your achievements.

At the dawn of Google's existence, and many years later, the best source of candidates were those recommended by its staff – the referrals. On the other hand, more than half of the employees were referrals themselves. For example, the Googlers were being asked, "Who is the best financier you have ever worked with?" "Who is the best developer of the Ruby programming language?" But soon this was not enough to satisfy the need for new employees. In gradually solving the hiring issues, they noticed something amazing. The best of the best are not looking for work. They are happy and deservedly rewarded where they work now. Hardly would they agree to be referrals: Why recommend someone who is content with his work? And, of course, the best of the best do not send resumes for vacancies. Therefore, the recruiting system was reconstructed. Google created its own recruiting company to fulfill the task of seeking out and cultivating the best employees on the planet.

Now let's take a look at a few rules by Laszlo Bock to help you to create a powerful team:

1. Trust your people – The companies make extensive efforts to find the best employees, and then they restrict them to make a contribution in something else outside their duties. Be open and honest with your people and give them a voice to decide how things should work. If you have a small shop, make it a rule to ask your employees what they would change so the business went better. What they would do if they were the owners. You should encourage them to behave like owners, as if it's their own company. And the only way for that to happen is to sacrifice a little of your authority. Let people try to lead themselves. If you are part of the team, turn to your boss, "Give me a chance. Help me understand what your goals are, and let me figure out how to achieve them."

2. Hire only people who are better than you – When Google learns about some extraordinary people, it will do anything to get them hired. Former Google staffer Randy Knaflic tells this story, "We knew of this small team of brilliant engineers working from Aarhus. They sold off their previous company and were trying to figure out what to do next. Microsoft got wind of them and was all over them. Microsoft wanted to hire all of them, but they would have to move to Redmond. The engineers said, 'No way.' We swooped in, ran some aggressive hiring efforts, and said, 'Work from Aarhus, start a new office of Google, build great things,'" Knaflic says. "We hired the entire team, and it's this group that built the JavaScript engine in Chrome." This experience with the Aarhus team taught them that sometimes it is more expedient to hire a team on its terms than the company's.

Bock states that whoever he has hired was better than him in some meaningful way. For example, Prasad Setty, Vice President of People Analytics & Compensation at Google, is a more talented analytic. Karen May, Vice President of People Development at Google, is a more effective consultant, partly because her emotional sensitivity is much higher than his. Sunil Chandra, Google's VP for Staffing and Operations, has better work discipline and intuition and can make any process faster, cheaper and better for users. Bock admits that any of them can take his seat tomorrow and that he himself learns from them. What's more, he waited very long before he could bring them to Google. Karen turned him down for four years until he brought her on board. So recruiting exceptional hires takes time, but it is worth it. *Select the best professionals in their fields, the ones who are better than you in some capacity.*

Bock notes that organizations often act as if filling jobs quickly is more important than filling jobs with the best people. Not everyone agrees with him when it comes to the best people, though. The managers hate it that they can't hire their own people. People disagree that the bar should be set that high for every job. Anyway, Bock urges us not to give in to the pressure. Very often you can hear people saying they just need a secretary that will answer the phone calls and organize meetings. An outstanding secretary or an assistant is a strong support for the manager, a person who helps better plan the time, prioritize and organize the performance of more or less important tasks. In addition, this individual represents the manager in the eyes of anyone dealing with him. These are very important responsibilities, in Bock's view, and the difference between an exceptional secretary and an ordinary one is tremendous. He was lucky to work with an outstanding assistant, Hannah Cha.

When Laszlo Bock worked in McKinsey & Company, he had a boss named Andrew, who demanded from Bock to present perfect market analysis for the clients. Though he was not involved in micromanagement, he would explain how each page of the report was to be written and analyzed. He simply set the bar high. In 1999, they were working for a company that provided financial services and was engaged in one of the first e-commerce projects in the company's history. Bock took the project report to Andrew, though Bock knew it was fine. Still, Andrew might find something to improve in it, but instead of editing the report, Andrew asked if he had to take a look at it. Bock decided to take it back and work on it a little more, and when he returned for the second time, Andrew asked the same question. Bock went back again, and repeated the exercise for the fourth time. He told Andrew that he didn't have to take a look at it and that it could be handed to the client. Great job, said Andrew and sent the report to the client, without even looking at it. *If you expect little, you'll receive little. Set the bar high.*

3. Focus on the two tails – Professor Boris Groysberg from Harvard Business School, analyzing the careers of more than a thousand star analysts from investment banks, demonstrated that "star analysts who change firms suffer an immediate and lasting decline in performance." Their earlier success in many cases depended on their colleagues, their former firm's resources, organizational cultures, and networks. Not always do people manage to function optimally in a new environment, so they need support. There are two types of tails: the best ones - the top tail, and worst ones - the bottom tail. About 5% of employees at Google regularly lag behind. These are people who form the bottom tail. As Bock says, they are not looking to fire people; they are finding the ones who need help. So instead of going the traditional route and rewarding the poor performers with a "kiss of death," they decided to take a different approach.

The goal is to explain to all the performers in the bottom 5% that they are in that group. This conversation is not easy one, but this message makes it easier: "You are in the bottom 5% of performers across all of Google. I know that doesn't feel good. The reason I'm telling you this is that I want to help you grow and get better." It's not "shape up or shape out" conversation. It's a talk with an aim to help them improve their performance and grow as specialists. First, Google offers them a range of coaching and training to develop their skills. If this does not work, they try to help the person find another role within Google. As a rule, the employee's personal performance grows to an average level. If not, some choose to leave, and others are fired.

It sounds cruel, but the result of the process is that they are satisfied because the company showed understanding and tried to help them, and eventually they were given time to find another job. People either significantly increase productivity or leave and succeed elsewhere. It happened so that Laszlo Bock had to terminate someone who worked for him. Upon leaving he said, "I'd never be able to do your job." Bock said, "You can, but at a place where the demands are different." Three years later he called Bock to share with the good news: he was promoted to chief human resources officer of a Fortune 500 company. He told Bock the pace of work was a bit slower than in Google, but it fit him perfectly. And due to his measured, thoughtful style he managed to become a trusted adviser to the head of the company.

Jack Welch insists that directly telling the employee about the situation is an act of kindness. Let's consider the example of the companies where the kindest managers let the employees, especially those lagging behind, remain in the bottom tail for years. When a crisis comes, the middle-aged people in the bottom tail are always the first candidates for dismissal. And it turns out that the person who has been working for the company for 20 years has never done his job well enough. Were he told about it earlier, he would be able to find a job in a place where he would have a future. And now that he's already 45 or 50, he has to go into a highly competitive labor market. Now this is cruel. If you believe that the employees know their job and are worthy of trust, be honest and open with them, and this means that you have to inform them if they are performing poorly. The majority of poor performers know that they are poor performers and strive to improve. It is important to give them a chance, to help them acquire the needed skills or find another role. But if this doesn't work, you have to fire them immediately. You shouldn't pity them; they will feel better in a place where they won't be in the bottom tail. *If you notice that people are in the bottom tail, tell them about it. Teach them. Try to help so they improve their performance to average levels. But if they don't cope with the situation, fire them. Perhaps they will be able to flourish in another environment.*

At the same time, the top tail, that is the best employees, feel differently in the company than the average or mediocre. They feel valued and perceive that their work is more significant; they leave the company five times less often than the employees with the worst results. Why? Because the best ones live in the circle of victories, great feedback, new achievements and acknowledgments. Every day they bask in the light of love, so any additional programs you offer them will not make them happier. Much more important is to learn from the best. The best employees in any company are the seeds of its future success.

An interesting experiment that helped to reveal the "bad" and "good" managers was carried out at Google. The engineers could freely move from one project group to another within the year – but they did not know whether the future leader was among the good or bad managers. In 2008, 65 Googlers turned to bad managers from good managers, and another 65 – the opposite. All of them were the most typical staff members who worked well and were content with their company. And the managers mattered. The 65 people who switched to bad managers showed significantly lower performance in 34 areas of "Googlegeist" out of 42. The next year the ones that switched to good managers demonstrated improvement in 6 areas out of 42.

Now they knew their good and bad managers, but they didn't know the difference between their actions. How could what the good managers did to differentiate themselves from the bad managers be determined? And how could this knowledge be turned into a tool for sustained improvements in the quality of Google managers? They took a simple approach: They asked them. The survey helped to find eight common attributes of the good managers:

Be a good coach.

Empower the team and do not micromanage.

Express interest/concern for team members' success and personal well-being.

Be very productive/results-oriented.

Be a good communicator – listen and share information.

Help the team with career development.

Have a clear vision/strategy for the team.

Have important technical skills that help advise the team.

Here you can see what qualities a good manager must have. Take notice of this list, dear reader. The teams with good managers produce the best results.

The teams working with the good managers showed better results in lowering staff turnover. Thus, the quality a manager was the best indicator to determine whether the employees would leave or stay in the company, as a proof of the well-known saying: "People leave managers, not companies." Now there was a guide to create great managers. As Bock put it, "It's actually become harder to be a bad manager." And now, knowing that the manager quality affected employee performance, satisfaction and desire to remain in the company, Google tries to get better with each day.

4. Be frugal and generous – Laszlo Bock's father founded an engineering company that he led for over 30 years. He very much cared for all of his employees, paying them not only with money but also with kind words, advice, and guidance. When any of his employees had worked five years, his father would, in a private conversation, inform them about the company's pension plan for those who worked there for five years, a plan that put money aside for them in addition to their own savings. People were happy. Some would cry or simply thank him. Nobody knew about it prior to that because his father did not want people to stay only for money. He wanted them to stay because they loved their job and the team. He showed generosity when it meant the most for people, and the difference was immense. *Show care for people.*

Errors are easily forgiven here, but often repeated mistakes won't be forgiven. For example, one of Google's vice presidents, Sheryl Sandberg, whose fiefdom included the company's automated advertising system, described the following incident: Once, she committed an error that cost Google several million dollars. Frightened to death, she walked across the street to inform Larry Page. When Larry listened to her, he responded,

"I'm so glad you made this mistake, because I want to run a company where we are moving too quickly and doing too much, not being too cautious and doing too little. If we don't have any of these mistakes, we're just not taking enough risk."

Do not be afraid. Try. The only one who doesn't err is the one idly sitting in his place.

5. Pay unfairly – Remember that in majority cases labor productivity is determined by the power law, no matter what your HR department states: ninety percent or more of the value on your teams comes from the top 10%. Thus, the best employees are worth much more than the average ones, perhaps twice as much as average employees. Bock advises you to make sure they know about it. Even if you don't have as much money to secure a substantially higher pay for the best, the difference will still play its role. Perhaps your B players will be a bit offended, but you can tell them the truth and explain to them why you pay them less and what they can do to change the situation. And be generous in your public recognition. *Celebrate the achievements of teams and do not forget to cheer those who failed and learned important lessons.*

Besides, employees can evaluate each other's work, as they know better than the managers who really contributes the most. Google offers a gThanks platform through which the employees are able to express their recognition of their colleagues' excellent work with "kudos." Why is this system better than the usual e-mail? Because kudos are published in the public domain, and anyone can see them and share via Google+. Compliments bring satisfaction for those who make them and for those who receive them. And it is much shorter than the private e-mail, so gratitude does not require special hardships.

After launching gThanks, Google had a 460% growth in kudos compared to the previous year when the Googlers had to go to a special site. And the new version had a thousand more users each day. As Napoleon Bonaparte said, "I have made the most wonderful discovery. I have discovered men will risk their lives, even die, for ribbons!" To put it simply, public recognition is one of the most effective and rarely used tools of management.

Another element of gThanks is the peer bonuses, which can be seen in the bottom center of the screen. It is important to give the employees the opportunities to freely recognize one another. Every employee at Google can gift a colleague with a reward in the amount of $175 without approval from the management. In many organizations it would be seen as madness. Wouldn't the employees conspire with each other and manipulate the system to get thousands of dollars in extra income? But experience has shown that they don't.

And, finally, Laszlo Bock states that "it's also important to reward failure." Yes, incentives and goals are important, but an act of calculated risk in itself deserves a reward, especially if failure looms ahead. Even the best of us sometimes suffer failure. How you react to it is important. For example, the Google Wave system worked for almost a year but was shut down and given to the Apache Software Foundation. The Wave team worked on the product for two years, spending countless hours to transform the principle of online interaction. "They took a massive, calculated risk. And failed. So we rewarded them," says Bock. Of course, the team did not receive the size of reward they would have if the platform they launched had been a success. They received less than they expected, but more than they expected in the given circumstances. *Appreciate the people who took a risk, even though they failed.*

6. Enjoy! And then go back to No. 1 and start again – Larry Page and Sergey Brin set out to create a company where they themselves would want to work. You can do the same, says Bock, but this isn't a one-time effort. Creating a strong corporate culture and working environment requires constant learning and renewal. But you shouldn't do everything at once. You have to experiment with one or several ideas, learn from the results, amend the plan and try again. A good work environment itself becomes a good motivator and helps to create an organization that is creative, fun, hardworking, and highly productive.

Google's innovations in HR management have been made possible thanks to: visionary founding fathers, the guardians of the corporate culture; deep research; and the creative discoveries of other companies and government agencies. Thousands of Googlers have been building a company where they would want to work. Every year the Google complex is visited by people who want to find out why everyone looks so happy there, what the secret of Google is, and how their companies can progress as well.

In 2013 and in previous years Google has grown by more than 10 thousand people. It means that every year around 5,000 people join Google. To do this, Google considers 1-3 million applicants per year, and it turns out that the company hires about 0.25% of them. For comparison, Harvard University admitted 6.1% of applicants in 2012 (2076 from 34,303 people). It is very difficult to get into Harvard, but it is apparently 25 times easier to get into Harvard than to get a job at Google. In 2013 Fortune magazine ranked Google as the best company to work for in the country, leaving behind Apple, Facebook, Amazon, and Microsoft, which was No. 75. The remaining three didn't even make the list.

Secret 5. Choose and hire the best people.

Secret 6

There is no clear path. We are building it on our way.

Joan Manuel Serrat (Catalan singer)

Inditex Group (Amancio Ortega)

Inditex Group Company (Industria de Diseño Textil) sells the most clothes in the world. The industrial area on the grounds of Inditex headquarters occupies an area equal to the size of 47 football fields. The working rhythm of this company is impossible to assess. As Antonio Abril, the Secretary General of Inditex says, "Everything must have been done yesterday; tomorrow it may be too late." Zara remains an enigma for many: How can things be so inexpensive with the designs so modern and models constantly updated? What is the secret of its success? The answer lies in the following sentence, articulated by one of the company's managers,

"The whole production process is carried out without intermediaries. The raw materials are purchased at fairly cheap prices, and the product is sold at a reasonable price. We prefer to have less income and sell more."

At the basis of all this stands Amancio Ortega – a man who does not have an office and has never had one, a man for whom the work is in the factory and not in the office. He is a person who does not like to be photoed or give speeches. He constantly strives for perfection and goes to work at 11:00, though he used to start work at 9:00. He always chooses the hardest path and is never late for meetings, as he hates missing the meetings. He is someone who is ready to take risks, who knows business from start to finish, and who draws up new plans every day and keeps repeating, "The only way to survive is to grow; if there is no growth, the company will die." He has a very strong memory. He is able to describe each piece in detail, showing how well he knows his business. Whatever Ortega knows is from his own experience - in short, he is a man who has achieved everything thanks to his experience, diligence and risk.

Amancio Ortega was born March 28, 1936 in Busdongo de Arbás. Now, I'll continue Ortega's story:

Ortega's father earned 300 pesetas per month. That's more than 2 euros nowadays. There were four kids in the family, and his father's salary was not enough for them. Ortega well remembers the day when he went for food with his mother. He was young. His mother usually came to take him from school, and they went to the grocery store together. The store was so big that he could see nothing behind the shelves, but he could hear a man's voice saying that he couldn't keep giving her credit to buy the food that she needed for the family dinner that evening. Amancio never forgot these words. Being only 12 years old, he decided that such an incident would never happen again to his mother. He had to find a job. He left school at the age of 13 or 14 and decided to find a job, no matter what.

The first clothing store where Ortega was hired to work was Gala. While working in Gala, he did everything: cleaning the floor, packaging products, selling, and communicating with customers, as he liked his job. He loved learning. Then he moved to LA Maja, where his sister Pepita and brother Antonio worked. Due to his commitment and management talent, Amancio was soon promoted.

Saving 2500 pesetas, Ortega started his business in 1963, naming the company GOA Confessiones (GOA – Gaona Ortega Amancio). At first, he rented a small workshop, where his wife, sister, brother, and friend worked. They tailored women's dressing gowns. By reinvesting the income in business, Ortega made the workshop stand on its own feet; he focused on the clothing industry, while an intermediary company dealt with the wholesale trade. There were no positions in the company; they knew their duties and did whatever was required. In 10 years, Ortega's business capacity grew by 500 times, and he took both the distribution and sales into his own hands.

Ortega was near 40 years old when he began to do business. Of course, at that age he had already mastered the whole business cycle: production, purchase, working with suppliers, sales, etc. Ortega came to realize that it was more profitable for him to sell more, but at a lower price. The buyers were content because they could buy clothes for 30 euros, which was worth 100 euros in another place. Modern, high-quality stores providing affordable price and good service are the key to Spanish success. According to Ortega, the customer forms the market, and if you want to achieve success, you must know the customer, watch his behavior, and take care of him.

It's important for Ortega to set an aim and do everything to achieve it. When he started out, he was preoccupied with the idea of creating something that did not exist in the market. He could clearly see the free zone in the textile industry. *Always think of some new idea where you'll be the first and the leader.* Ortega points out that his company does not produce different designs in accordance with the "styles" of 80 countries but rather creates things that suit the inhabitants of 80 countries. Ortega has entirely devoted himself to his work and has never been satisfied with what he achieved. He maintains that being satisfied with your work is a big mistake because when you are satisfied, you do not move forward. And if you do not move forward, how are you going to achieve your goals? He and his team never sit still; they have worked with the same perseverance today as when they started out. He's of the opinion that you must do something better today than yesterday, because you need to be under a strain to overcome difficulties. *To weaken and lose vigilance means to go back. We need to constantly think about moving forward, realizing new ideas – this is how we progress. Never stay in the same place.*

At first they were working with middlemen, but there came a time when Ortega felt discontent because they could not enter into relationship with the customers and understand their needs and taste. So he decided that, to be closer to the customer, the whole process should be managed by his company. The product cannot be sold just because of its price. First and foremost, the customer must like the product, and for that reason they had to make out what the customer needed. If the product is on the mark, success is a matter of time. *Be close to your customers as much as possible.*

Ortega never gave up, never lost energy, and worked nonstop. *I am convinced that such a hard life strengthens the urge and ability to solve problems. A man who abandoned childhood at the age of 12 and undertook the burden of keeping the family!* He had no time for education because he was working from morning till evening, but he had a clear idea of what he wanted to achieve. The only thing he regrets is not learning English; now he realizes how important it was to learn it. Whatever he was not able to learn through education, he learned by listening to people and analyzing their moves.

At first Ortega did everything by himself. He visited different countries and cities. He negotiated and explored the stores, but now he assigns others to do all this. His policy is that you must do whatever is possible by yourself. For example, the store is the heart of Ortega's company, and if it doesn't work, there will be no result. He insisted that certain stores be opened in certain places and did not take into account how much money the rent cost because he felt that it was the most convenient place for the store. He spends quite a lot of time visiting various departments, as he is interested in how everything is going. If Ortega is not in the workshop, he's at the designers' department. The work of the artists attracts him most of all.

Antonio Abril recalls an incident when he and Ortega travelled to Israel to explore the market. When they returned, Abril went home and Ortega instantly headed to the factory, saying that he never went home earlier than 10:00 in the evening. True, he doesn't travel a lot now, but he is always aware of what is going on in his empire. When an employee returns from a foreign country, Amansio asks him a torrent of questions on what products sell well or what products do not sell well in that country, why, and so on. *Always keep track of your business. Travel and ask the staff.*

But one incident changed the whole course of business. Coming to El Corte Ingles to sell his products, Ortega saw that the wholesale buyers were demanding products that the customers did not quite like. That is why he started thinking of his own stores. *This means that when there is a problem, you should solve it and not adapt to the situation.* The first store had no connection with the present Zara, but some time later, Ortega focused on high-speed production, which became his trump card. The first Zara store opened in 1975. Initially, everything was manufactured at the company's factories, but as Zara grew, some part of manufacturing was outsourced to other factories.

In the 90s Zara appeared in Europe's major cities and created a great stir. Knowing that one brand was not enough to satisfy all the consumers, Ortega decided not to stop only on Zara, whose consumers were middle class women and brought in the 78% of the revenue. They began to expand the assortment, but now with different names. This was quite a correct step because each brand was aimed at a separate segment. In 1991, Ortega founded Pull & Bear, aimed at young people, and then he purchased Massimo Dutti, aimed at both women and men who had above-average incomes . In 1998, Ortega decided to attract teenagers and created Bershka, and then he bought Stradivarius. The strategy is simple – don't put all your eggs in one basket.

Since the creation of GOA, Ortega's main passion has been to give the consumers what they wanted faster and at more attractive prices. Prior to his appearance in the textile business, a completely different business approach prevailed in this sphere. The collection was planned and prepared within a year. It was manufactured in three or four months and then provided to the distributors, who delivered the products to the stores twice during the season. There were two risks in such an approach:

A large amount of unsold goods accumulated

The product prices were not competitive any longer

As for Ortega, he would not be able to predict which product would be a greater success, but he was able to understand what people liked. From the start of his business, Ortega knew that the most important person – the customer – was not given much attention. Ortega's business model was to merge design and production so that the chain ended with the distribution and selling in his own stores. In such a case, the consumer became the main source of information. He was interested in what the customers demanded and tried to adjust the whole production process to their desires. Ortega realized that if he manufactured clothes preferred by the customers, he would avoid the unsold, leftover goods. Zara's success lies in the fact that the company gives the consumers what they need. It maintains a competitive edge in a strong competitive environment.

The whole business is built on a sentence – the buyer is a queen. And how is the business organized? The first step of the whole process is the discovery of trends. The designers in the Barcelona office watch fashion progressions and react as fast as possible. The discovery of trends is realized by three steps:

The first step is that the employees travel around the world and see what people wear on the streets. Later, they present their findings at the gatherings in Arteixo. The second step is that the designers gather special information on what interests the customers. They visit New York, Paris, London, Milan, or, say, Tokyo to have an understanding of the current trends of what is going on in the famous fashion capitals. They closely watch the dominant colors, materials, and clothing details. And finally the third step is that information is gathered from fashion magazines, research on collections from the catwalks, TV shows, and famous stars walking on the red carpet, etc.

If Ortega feels that people will like something, he does it by all means. He doesn't have to go and see catwalk shows. On the contrary, he gets great ideas by observing the images in the streets, magazines, and films. For example, once while he was standing at a traffic light, a man walked past him in a denim jacket with badges. He liked the idea, called their designer and described what he had seen. After two weeks, the badged denim jacket was already being sold in the company's stores. *Seize the moment.* Ortega advises designers to be observant in the street because it's a wonderful runway. For example, if his friend Armani or other talented people are closed in a room so that they see nothing, they will stop being creative.

It's indeed a major advantage to be close to the customer because the world changes, and we need to be as close to the customers as possible. There was a time when the fashion industry operated according to the system of presenting a new collection twice a year. No one was interested in the street or in what was going on outside, as the designers had no idea what people thought of their collections. This was really a big change because now it was not the designers who dictated their will, but the customers. Ortega's skill is that he doesn't force people to shop but suggests what they would like to have.

There is also another method of gathering information – that's the information obtained from Zara stores, where the managers call the head office and report on the clothes their regular customers have bought from abroad. All data are digitized and updated every day. In order to achieve maximum effectiveness, the store manager must have a direct connection with Arteixo.

After collecting all this information, the designers make the prototypes of clothes with the artists – more than 22,000 copies per year. The prototypes are tested on mannequins, real people, and children. When the model is ready, it is displayed to the colleagues, customers, and suppliers. It is a common occurrence in Arteixo when designers communicate with employees and in effort to find flaws.

The moment the choice of clothes is coordinated with the marketing department, different factories are allowed to bid. The factory that offers the most suitable price, deadline, etc. is chosen.

Then the process of distribution begins. The interesting thing is that in the beginning Ortega established warm relations with the suppliers of raw materials. At the initial stage of business, Ortega constantly visited the suppliers with his brother and convinced them that his project was the best. Today, everything has changed and the suppliers are sending numerous offers themselves. Conditel sends Inditex 65% of Zara's raw materials beforehand, and the remaining 35% is sent when the collection's design is ready. Each distributor strictly follows three rules – low price, fast delivery and high quality.

After the production, the clothes are included in special catalogs so the store managers can see the assortment and prepare their order through the PDA system. If 20,000 units of product have been produced, it's ok if fewer than that is ordered, but if the order is more than that, the operator will have to coordinate with the managers. If the item is popular, the production cycle begins once again, even though it may not always be so, because the collection might be going out of fashion.

The unsold items are destroyed after a set time, but according to unofficial information, sometimes they are sent without label to small stores in Latin

America and France. The company is quick to respond to the situations it faces. For example, if some product is not sold, it will be transferred to another store, as the unsold products must not be neglected. Steps must be undertaken to sell them. If there is a delay, the first one is delivered to the top 500 stores, and then to the rest.

Logistics plays a big role in Inditex and is concentrated in La-Coruña, Zaragoza and Madrid. The goods are collected and sent out to the stores from here. The shipping is mainly done over land, but by air to the United States and Latin America. The Asian stores are supplied by sea, a time consuming practice.

The stores - where the buyers shop and dictate what will be produced in the future - are the last point of Inditex. The stores are run by managers who usually have up to 120 employees. There are managers whose annual salary reaches 240,000 euros. The managers are the people who place orders by catalog and send information to the head office as to what works and what doesn't. They organize the work of the store, though everything inside the company has long been planned as to how the display windows should be arranged, with what details, and so on. The stores place the orders, and the product is there in the shortest period of time. Statistically, 3 out of 10 visitors make a purchase. You know what is the most intriguing aspect of these statistics? The visitor knows that if he doesn't buy it, the next day that model might not be there any longer. There is nothing accidental here. The music, furniture layout, the place of the checkout – everything is pre-planned.

At the beginning of each season Zara demonstrates its new collection, and from that moment on they watch what the customer wants and continue producing the products that are in demand in the market. Day by day, the information is analyzed so the customer gets what he wants. Ortega liked to stress that the customers have expectations and that these expectations must be accommodated.

The location of the stores and the internal and external structure are defined by professionals who send the final look to Ortega. Ortega makes the final decision because, as the team of architects points out, no one knows better than him. If you work for the best retailer, you had better ask him what he thinks about the project.

The peculiarity of the stores is that the assortment is updated frequently. The customers know that in all cases they will come across a new range of clothes or will not see the clothes they had tried on a few days before, because the assortment is updated every week in certain stores or two times a week in European stores. This means that if people see some clothing they like, they must buy it at once, or else they will not find it. That's an interesting method of increasing the sales that makes one shop on the spot. Yes, create scarcity in your sales, as one of the company's former leaders says. For comparison, let me mention that in Spain the customers visit Inditex stores 17 times per year, while they visit other stores less than 4 times per year.

What makes people want to visit this store? The reason is location: The stores are located on the main streets of big cities, areas that provide a large influx of customers. The most difficult part for the company is to secure flexibility, as it's the rapid distribution that gives such impressive sales numbers. Each shopping center offers the best conditions for Inditex stores because the sales are bountiful here. Amancio always prefers to go his own way, and, for example, if the experts are against the opening of a new store in Venezuela, and Amancio is for it, then the store will definitely be opened.

Most interesting is that Zara stores are never empty – from Mexico to Jerusalem, from New York to Paris, from Bilbao to Vienna you will see people gathered at the checkout counters. As one of the managers says, the female buyer is a queen here, and their goal is to make her happy. Many seller consultants mention that Ortega visits the stores from time to time and asks them not to pay attention to his visit. He goes to the stores not to see what the situation and things are like, but to motivate his employees.

The problems in Inditex are solved in this way: If there is a problem, several departments offer solutions, and when they arrive at a unified solution, they send it to Ortega. When Ortega affirms it, the responsibility is placed on the employees, and each is assigned to solve the problem or carry out the decision. On one occasion, for example, the owner of Sephora Company wanted to sell his business to Inditex. Ortega had agreed to conclude the deal. But some time later the company was taken over by LVMH Group. The reason was that Ortega's employees were against the deal, as the company specialized in perfume and cosmetics, whereas people at Inditex were not well-versed in that business.

Ortega is always open to innovation and pays much attention to people's opinions. He is always looking for people who keep asking questions and are searching for something, people who think outside the scope. People like these bring to life the most daring ideas. Ortega always likes plain and simple ideas, and he likes to solve the problems quickly. In fact, he doesn't like the long, technical discussions and always asks why this or that idea is better. As Ortega says, "I always listen to my employees. I thank them for the good job. If they make some mistake, I point it out so they fix it." Ortega often repeats that if there's something he's proud of, it is those people who work with him. He keeps telling his managers,

"You should love the people with whom you work. You must be with them, take care of them, understand who they are, and know how their work is going. If you don't love them, you will not achieve any results. I remember when after the meetings many employees would tell me that I took care of them and they took care of the company. If you want all to come together around a common aim, take care of the employees, and you will get what you wanted. It's no good to say proudly that 'I did it.' The right thing would be to say 'We did it.' I am proud that my employees do their job and treat it like their own. I don't have an office as such. I prefer walking inside the whole building to see how the work is done with my own eyes. That way I can see how the quality of our products improves."

"When I hired an HR manager, the first advice that I gave him was as follows: 'You should love people.' We need to concentrate on people – this is of the most important points of my philosophy. The second most important factor is being close to people. I spend most of my time with different teams, discussing ideas, expressing my opinion, and listening to their suggestions. The product we create must simply be perfect."

As a result, Ortega manages to gather the type of people around him that realize his ideas and work devotedly. Another peculiarity of Inditex is that there are no stars on the team. The teams are created in a way that if someone leaves, no big problems arise and the work goes on as before.

According to the manager of Mercado de Capitales, Mark Lopez, at Inditex each worker receives 50 shares for every year of work, depending on his position. For example, the fabric painter who has worked in the company for 20 years receives 1000 shares, (20*50), and the manager who started working in the company yesterday receives 50 shares. A truly unique and generous gift to the employees! On May 23, 2000, Inditex released its shares. Some shareholders accumulated considerable wealth, even Ortega's former wife, who had 7% of the shares.

Many employees start from the bottom and rise to the top here. For example, one of the truck drivers heads the department of men's shirts. Elena Perez is a woman who has led one of the stores in Madrid for many years. Perez says that she loves Ortega because he is a leader who works shoulder to shoulder with his workers in both the stores and factories. And, if need be, he comes to work earlier and goes home later than anyone else. Ortega is a perfectionist. Everything is a challenge for him – if there are problems, the first step is to solve the problems. He never raises his voice, but uses his reputation and sees that the assignments are done on time.

Elena was travelling for many years and helping to open stores around the world. The overloaded work had left her exhausted, and she needed a rest. When she applied to the HR department for holiday, Ortega himself called Elena and told her that he was aware of the situation and that the work of others needed to be organized in a way that Elena would have free time. When Ortega asked Elena what she needed, she explained that she would at least like to rest on Saturdays as well to be able to recover. Ortega agreed and gave Elena the opportunity to rest one more day.

Elena continues, "Promotion is a very important factor. The employee that works hard and has the necessary skills will be promoted. There are many positions in the company that can be reached. For example, 90% of the company's managers in Madrid started from seller consultants."

According to one of the Inditex employees, Ortega is demanding. He makes people work to the max. She says Ortega sometimes gives tasks that seem impossible, but you try doing them because he trusts you. The director general of Zara Home, Eva Cárdenas, says the following: "Ortega is able to lead people, help them, give assignments and allot the responsibilities, allowing them to make decisions and be responsible too. There have been many cases when I asked Ortega for his opinion, to which he answered, 'And why are you here? You should learn to make such decisions.' In fact, he always wants to move forward and do even better, and still better." *Strive to constantly improve. Today you must be better than yesterday, and tomorrow you must be better than today.*

There is no such phrase for Ortega as "people don't do it like this." He would often repeat,

"Yes, perhaps people don't do it like this, but I intend to."

The international expansion began in 1988 when the first Zara store opened in Portugal because there was no competition in that market. Then slowly the company spread to France, Belgium, Netherlands, Greece etc. Three or four stores opened in the United States in a year, while at the same time 400 stores were opened in Europe. The reason is that Zara does not have such a strong position in the USA. Imagine that Amancio doesn't like to fly and travels either by train or by car.

1989, New York

In 1989 the first chain of stores opened in New York. Ortega explains,

"I reached one of Manhattan's shopping streets where the first store of our chain was located. When I saw how many people had gathered in front of our store, I could not believe my eyes. Women of all ages went in and out just like in our Spanish stores; they tried the garments, looked in the mirror, touched the fabrics and patiently waited at the checkout counter. The seller consultants could hardly manage to pay attention to everyone. I went to the toilet so that no one saw the tears in my eyes – the tears of happiness."

Bea Padín, who runs one of the company's departments, has summarized what she has learned from Ortega over a period of more than 20 years:

- Decisions must be based on logic.

- Be objective with people and always try to put yourself in their place.

- Management is not a qualification. It means teaching, but by example and support.

- If you want to judge something negatively, then you must come up with an alternative.

- Always use the plural when talking about work. Never say: "I did this."

- Concentrate on details. Keep your eyes and ears open.

- Treat suppliers with a great deal of respect.

- We are surrounded by competition. Never underestimate anybody, as very large companies have managed to crash.

- Decisions must be flexible so that the core business doesn't suffer. It can't be allowed to fail.

Secret 6. Speed keeps the business young. Be fast and constantly try to update the assortment in the way it is done at Inditex. Always submit a new proposal, as people love novelties.

Secret 7

I believe that money is, in some respects, almost immaterial to Sam Walton. What motivates the man is the desire to absolutely be on top of the heap. It is not the money.

Charlie Baum

Wal-Mart (Sam Walton)

Sam Walton was often asked how he managed to build such an empire, to what the modest American would respond, "Friend, we just got after it and stayed after it."

At a young age, Sam Walton's father had him play on different football teams, and he realized that only a team can achieve serious results. It never crossed his mind that someone could beat him. It's this kind of thinking that becomes a trump card for each person.

In the morning he delivered newspapers. After that, he worked as a lifeguard in one of the pools, and in the evening he waited tables. While doing all this, he still managed to graduate from college with a bachelor's degree in economics. In those years he was sure he'd become an insurance salesman. In 1940 he joined J.C. Penney as a management trainee and was paid $75 per month. From that day on he stepped into the incredible world of the retail business. Walton's first problem at work had to do with his handwriting, as it was really terrible. His wife, Helen, always mentioned that there might be only five people in the world who could read his handwriting. Penney's had a regional supervisor named Blake who would say to Sam when he came to Des Moines,

"Walton, I'd fire you if you weren't such a good salesman. Maybe you're just not cut out for retail."

For two years Walton worked at J. C. Penney, when World War II broke out. He was supposed to join the Armed Forces but was turned down because of heart problems. This course of events left him disappointed, but he had already resigned from J.C. Penney, so he had to find a new job.

He got a job at a DuPont munitions plant and was introduced to the oil business. The plant was based in Prairie City, where he went out for walks in the evenings and bowled. During one of the games he met Helen, after which they were together all the time. They got married in a year, and the first thing Walton faced was the need to make a living.

He wanted to get started in the retail business, and he was sure he'd succeed. The passion to win was killing him: he visited libraries, found books on retail business, and read avidly. He wanted to master all possible nuances. Helen came from a rich family, and her father wanted Sam to work with him. But Helen said something that completely changed their life,

"Dad, I want my husband to be himself, I don't want him to be L. S. Robson's son-in-law. I want him to be Sam Walton."

I just have no words to describe this woman, who, having rather a big fortune, believed in Walton. Let me go on with Sam Walton's and Wal-Mart's story. Most importantly, Helen believed in her husband, and Walton wanted to go into the retail business. They found a place in Newport, Arkansas, which had a population of 7,000. The young man who had opened a variety store in that area wanted to get rid of the store as soon as possible, as it grossed a meager $72,000 in sales per year. Walton was 27 years old and didn't know anything about land lease contracts.

He purchased the store for $25,000 and signed a 5-year lease. He made the biggest mistake of his life. By the way, he had $5,000, and the rest he borrowed from his father-in-law. And his dream came true: Walton had a variety store called Ben Franklin, a franchise of the Butler Brothers chain, where he sold their products. *Remember, you can rent a property. Your customers will get used to the location, and one day the owner of the property will force you out under the terms of the lease. Therefore, my advice to you: Sign a long-term lease.*

Upon acquiring the store, Walton noticed the Sterling Store across the street. It was run by John Dunham and grossed $150,000 per year, twice as much as Walton's store. Walton checked on Dunham's store every day and studied the business as closely as possible. It's worth mentioning that he learned lots of nuances about the retail business from Dunham. Every day he looked at his prices and his displays. He was ready to learn and improve every day.

Walton worked all day in the shop, then closed it in the evening. When he could, he drove around the neighboring states in his pickup truck. In Tennessee he found a supplier who was selling at lower prices than Ben Franklin gave him. He decided to sell those goods, too, which he priced at a reduced level, as he had that opportunity. As a result, the goods from Tennessee were just vanishing from the store shelves. His own experience taught him a simple rule, which completely changed his business model.

"Here's the simple lesson we learned ... say I bought an item for 80 cents. I found that by pricing it at $1.00, I could sell three times more of it than by pricing it at $1.20. I might make only half the profit per item, but because I was selling three times as many, the overall profit was much greater. Simple enough. But this is really the essence of discounting: by cutting your price, you can boost your sales to a point where you earn far more at the cheaper retail than you would have by selling the item at the higher price. In retailer language, you can lower your markup but earn more because of the increased volume."

By using this method, Walton reached substantial results and paid back his father-in-law's $20,000 loan after two years. He kept thinking of how to increase the number of customers. He set up a corn popper in front of the store, which justified itself. If the corn popper worked, they could also put an ice cream machine and sell outside. Walton took a $1,800 loan from the bank to buy a soft ice cream machine. $1,800 was his first bank loan.

These two devices indeed attracted people, who crossed the streets to visit the store. This tactic was an innovation, as no one had tried to attract customers in this way this before. The first year they had $105,000 in gross sales; the second year they had $140,000; the third year the sales grew to $175,000. Within only three years they managed to outperform John Dunham. Walton was beside himself with happiness, as he had won the competition.

The important thing was that they caught up in sales with Dunham and surpassed him. *Find someone who is ahead of you, and try to surpass him. You get stronger when you play with the strong. Remember this.*

During his triumphant days, Walton overheard that Dunham was going to expand his store by buying out the lease of the Kroger grocery store next door. No, Walton wouldn't let his rival expand his store. Wasting no time, he found the owner of Kroger and bought the lease ahead of Dunham. "I didn't have any idea what I was going to do with it, but I sure knew I didn't want Sterling to have it." He decided to open a tiny department store and called it the Eagle Store, but it wasn't very profitable. Walton preferred to have a small income, but not a strong rival. Now he had two stores. If goods didn't sell well in one, he transferred them to the other.

Walton and his team did all the work themselves: They would sweep the floors, clean the windows, and do the sorting, storing, and packing of the goods. The small store already had a turnover of $250,000 per year, with $40,000 in profits. But in only five years the landlord decided that the lease had expired, and they had to leave the place. He refused to renew the lease and offered to buy the franchise, fixtures and inventory. Walton had no choice but to sell everything and walk away.

The world came crashing on his head, he had made a mistake, but it was useless to think about defeat. He was in an emotionally difficult state, because he was already achieving serious results when he was stabbed in the back. But this is life. He had to go forward. Walton had built the best variety store in the whole region. He provided people with comparatively inexpensive products but received such treatment. He determined not to make such a mistake anymore and to adjust all the points of the lease in his favor hereafter.

Walton could set up business for the second time with the $50,000 he received from the sale of the franchise, and this time he knew what he was going to do. He drove around with Helen's father in Bentonville to find a suitable place for his store. There were already a few stores there, and there was no space for a new one, but Walton loved the competition. With the help of his father-in-law, he managed to find a suitable area and signed a ninety-nine-year lease. Only 3,000 people lived in the city, half as many as in

Newport. In the first year the store grossed more than $32,000, as compared to the $250,000 of the Newport store. But this figure didn't bother him much, because he had big plans.

When Walton launched the store in Bentonville, he provided large discounts at once to attract people to visit the store and get used to the place. The interesting thing was that this tactic helped him understand which products people bought most of all and sell more of them later. In the store, children were given balloons, and the adults were given discounts. True, although it operated as a Ben Franklin franchise, and Walton purchased products from them, it was a 'self-service' store. After the first store, he thought of opening a new one. He found a suitable store abandoned by Kroger in Fayetteville.

But he had two serious rivals in Fayetteville, Woolworth and Scott Store. Walton recalled that when he was busy with the store interior, people were saying that the store would be closed in just two or three months. He never cared much about others' opinions, so it was pleasant to hear all that and think to himself: We will see who'll be closed.

It might sound surprising, but Walton opened up the first Wal-Mart at the age of 44. And with the expansion of business, he needed good managers. Without remorse, he started hunting for talented specialists. Don't ask where, of course. It was among his rivals. That's how he found Williard Walker. He visited TG&Y and had an hour's talk with Walker. Now a question will arise: How was he able to attract the managers of different stores? Of course, by stakes. He offered them stakes in the store. If the manager knows that he has a percentage of the profits, he'll be more caring and try harder to boost overall sales. Walton worked equally with the managers every day. The example was contagious, and everyone worked with him. Over the initial period, Walker would even sleep on a cot in the storeroom. This is how the great business was being built.

Walton broke all the rules, and nobody liked him. All aimed at destroying Sam. Why? There was a consensus among retail outlets in the USA - you don't cross my border, I don't cross yours. But Walton did not care about what they had planned. He could simultaneously solve problems caused in the stores in four states. As David Glass says, two things distinguish Sam Walton from almost everyone else he knows, "First, he gets up every day bound and determined to improve something. Second, he is less afraid of being wrong than anyone I have ever known. And once he sees he's wrong, he just shakes it off and heads in another direction."

Since the stores were based in different states, Walton couldn't physically visit them all. An airplane would be a solution. After acquiring a small, used airplane and learning to fly, he would visit the stores and by airplane and save time. They would instantly invest the profits of one store in the opening of the next one. Walton gave stakes to all store managers, and if he contributed $50,000, the store manager would have to contribute $1,000, so that his stake wouldn't exceed 2%.

Walton's achievements were small compared to his desires. So he decided to go around the United States and understand how other retailers organized trade in other states. In Dallas he met an amazing young man, Herbert Gibson, whose stores followed a "Buy it low, stack it high, sell it cheap" strategy. His prices were the lowest Walton had ever seen. And much to his surprise, he learned that Herbert was going to open a franchise near Fayetteville. Walton felt that the future belonged to Herbert's model, which was called a discount store, in other words, retail sales at lower prices. He had made up his mind to convert his stores into discount stores, as the future belonged to them.

In one of the towns in Arkansas, Rogers, Walton couldn't open a store, since there already was a Ben Franklin variety store. He had to choose another name. That was the first Wal-Mart store, for which Helen and he pledged their house and land, in short, everything they had.

In the spring of 1962, they were flying over the Boston Mountains with Bob Bogle. Walton pulled a card out of his pocket with a few store names written on it and stretched it to Bob. Bob gazed at it and said,

"Well, you know, Scotch as I am, I'd just keep the Walton name and make it a place to shop." He scribbled W-A-L-M-A-R-T on the bottom of the card and added, "To begin with there's not as many letters to buy. This is just seven letters."

That's all. They settled upon this new name of the store, Wal-Mart. The name was written on the front of the store, on one side of it they wrote "We

Sell for Less" and "Satisfaction Guaranteed" on the other side. On July 2, 1962 the first Wal-Mart opened. The facilities of the first Wal-Mart were simply awful. The shelves were made of the cheapest steel. Some goods were piled on the floor. In short, the conditions were no good. But the prices were 20% lower than those of others, and people were visiting because the cost was decisive. Ben Franklin's strategy was that some goods were sold at low prices, while the rest at higher prices. Walton wanted to sell all the goods at prices as low as possible.

Everyone wanted to enter the discounter's industry. When the number of Walton's stores reached 19, they had $9 million in sales, while K-Mart already operated 250 stores with $800 million in sales. Walton declared war on K-Mart. When the third Wal-Mart store opened in Springfield, he started selling antifreeze at cost. He did the same with Crest toothpastes. They had an uncontrolled flow of shoppers; the crowd was so big that the fire department made them open the doors for five minutes, then lock them until shoppers left.

Walton kept repeating that everything must be done to reduce expenses. The hardest part was the lease issue, which he had solved by keeping his rents below a dollar a square foot. Their stores didn't even look like stores; they rented an abandoned Coca-Cola bottling plant for the eighth Wal-Mart store. They didn't have systems, ordering programs, a basic merchandise assortment, any sort of computers, a warehouse, and other resources required for retail business. Only the prices were low, and it was all that counted; "When customers thought of Wal-Mart, they should think of low prices and guaranteed satisfaction."

They had no regular distributors. When they ran out of a product, they'd have to fill its place by another product till the distributor came. There was no credit system of payment. The salesmen were coming to the front of the store and offering their products. Sometimes it was difficult to get bigger companies like Procter & Gamble to call Wal-Mart, and if they did, they would dictate how much to sell and at what price. For instance, Procter & Gamble, provided a 2 percent discount if the stores paid within ten days. If not, they took the discount right off. The conditions were really difficult.

Walton had recruited all the managers from his rival stores. They had become a great team together. They all worked together. Everyone had freedom of expression; they turned all reasonable ideas into reality.

Walton constantly held competitions between his store managers; the winners were the ones who sold the most and were the quickest, or the ones who sold the largest amount of the same product. Such inner competition boosted company growth. *Create an environment like this, and see what outcome it entails. In striving to be the first, everyone thinks of innovative strategies.*

One such interesting strategy was implemented by one of the managers, Phil Green. Green was sent to Hot Springs to open Wal-Mart number 52, where one of the K-Mart stores operated, and he decided to beat the rival. Green negotiated with Procter & Gamble, placing an order for Tide detergent of 3500 cases - the largest order for Tide ever. Such a large volume of purchase enabled him sell a box of Tide for $1.99, while K-Mart sold it for $3.97. Walton got angry to learn about this, as it wasn't reasonable to accommodate such a large amount of products in the store. But how much more surprised he became when he saw a pyramid of Tide detergents. The pyramid had caused a sensation, and it was sold just within a week.

Walton required all store managers to turn in weekly and monthly reports. The point was that he could track what was selling and what wasn't, what and when to order, and what to mark prices. In short, the report was a perfect source for his decision making. If certain products didn't sell well, he'd pay a visit to find a solution. Every week all the managers joined together and engaged in self-criticism. They compared their purchases and expenses, and they drew up plans for the sales of different products.

They were deciding what to order and in what volumes. When somebody made a gross mistake, they spoke to him, discussed it, solved it, and moved forward. Whatever Walton did, he required the same from his managers. If he was checking into his rival's stores, then they had to do so. He would mention that they should observe their rivals and not concentrate on their faults. He was not interested in what they were doing badly. He was interested in what they were doing well in order to apply it himself. *You should also do the same. Study your rivals and take the best of it. Everyone can see the bad.*

Walton's children worked in the store; Rob was cleaning the floor; Jim was carrying boxes; Alice was cleaning the shelves, etc. His children received a salary and invested it in obtaining Wal-Mart shares. Sometimes his wife and children were upset by his actions, as when they were on vacation, he'd visit stores and spend hours examining them. HIs children would even ask him to drive farther from stores. But winning was Walton's passion. He wanted to get to know his rivals.

Only in this way you can succeed in the retail business.

Between 1976 and the 1990s, 76 out of 100 discounters vanished in the USA. The reason was that they didn't take good care of their customers, and it's the employees who take care of the customers. So first motivate your "associates," as Walton liked to call his employees. He borrowed money from banks, individuals, and insurance companies for all the Wal-Mart store additions. He could hardly recall a day when he wasn't in debt. But it's business. You must nurture it with finances all the time. He wanted their stores to grow, to work by special systematized programs, to track the assortment in different stores, and to know which goods needed to be ordered or refilled.

Wal-Mart didn't have a stable relationship with the distributors, and the store managers ordered goods from different merchants. It needed a centralized distribution system and regular distributors. Some of the stores were too small for an adjacent warehouse, so Walton, to have centralized distribution, rented a warehouse somewhere between these stores. Large volumes of loads were delivered to the centralized warehouse, from where they were shipped to the stores in turns.

When the number of stores had increased, he decided to appoint Ron Mayer as the CEO of the company. Ron improved the distribution system a lot. He worked out a plan by which the centralized warehouse collected the orders of all the stores and passed them on to suppliers. Afterwards, the suppliers delivered the orders to the centralized warehouse from where they were distributed to the stores. Ron also introduced a truck-warehouse-truck concept. The delivery truck made its way to the stores after being unloaded at one end of the warehouse and loaded at the other end.

In those years K-Mart mainly opened stores in towns of 50,000 people. Walton knew that they could easily conquer towns with 5,000 people, as nobody would disturb them there. If there's no competition in a field, go into it and as soon as possible.

He chose the location from the air. It may be surprising, but from the air they could better evaluate the places with a more intense flow of people. With the small airplane they flew over the town, picked out a spot, then started scouting real estate. A good location is one of the most important conditions in the retail business. At first, Walton did the scouting of real estate and negotiated the deals. Later his son, Jim, was entrusted with the task.

Walton visited Wal-Mart stores himself, inquired about the situation, and worked with everyone equally, but later he put that responsibility on the district managers. So he began to seek and invite people to whom he could entrust responsible positions. He gave the management the freedom to make decisions and, at the same time, correct their mistakes. He wouldn't remain silent in case of mistakes. He'd criticize them and give advice.

Every Saturday morning Walton would visit the head office to keep track of the week's sales numbers. Reviewing the numbers, he could assume what the situation in the stores was like, what problems there were, and how they should be resolved. He recorded the meetings with his associates, if there were any "great ideas," he'd have them recorded. He always carried a yellow pad with him to take notes during my store visits.

The district managers would leave Bentonville for their territories. For four days they visited Wal-Mart stores and the rivals' stores. On Friday morning they all came together in Bentonville to discuss the situation. If one of the district managers discovered that a certain product was selling well in his district, the other stores would send certain volumes of it to his store so that it was not missing from the shelves.

Each district manager had to suggest some new idea or solution to cover the flight costs. Thus, they paid for the trip with a new idea.

When the district managers came back, senior management would pile into the airplanes to see different stores. The purpose was to get them closer to trade so that they could to know what was selling well and what wasn't - that the dried fruits were more required in Wisconsin, and the milk in Kansas, etc.

Create an environment in which the senior management will communicate, get acquainted, and understand what volumes of goods each store needs.

For Walton, the staff was the biggest issue, since the company had to recruit and train them as fast as possible. His rivals, for instance, wouldn't give promotion to someone with less than 10 years of experience. And he would just hire a good person, even someone who had no idea of trade at all.

If someone was to gain knowledge about distribution, layout, or the service sector, Walton would appoint him as the manager's assistant. It'd been a long time since he realized that the more he shared the profits with his associates, the more income they'd get.

For example, in this case, the management treated the employees better, who, in their turn, treated the customers well. If the customers are treated well, they come back to Wal-Mart over and over again. Since 1971 Walton has been implementing the following profit-sharing policy; if the employee has worked for Wal-Mart for 1 year and worked at least 1,000 hours per year, he receives a small percentage from Wal-Mart profit either in cash or Wal-Mart stock. To date, Wal-Mart's employees have $1,8 billion in profit-sharing.

A truck driver named Bob Clark recalls, "I went to work for Mr. Walton in 1972, when he only had sixteen tractors on the road. The first month, I went to a driver safety meeting, and he always came to those. There were about fifteen of us, and I'll never forget, he said, 'If you'll just stay with me for twenty years, I guarantee you'll have $100,000 in profit sharing.' I thought 'Big deal. Bob Clark never will see that kind of money in his life.' Well, last time I checked, I had $707,000 in profit sharing, and I see no reason why it won't go up again. I've bought and sold stock over the years, and used it to build on to my home and buy a whole bunch of things."

If you are familiar with the retail business to some extent, you should know that theft is a serious problem in this field. In 1980 Walton decided to find a solution to this problem. It was this: If the company shared profits with its employees, it would do the same with the losses. If the level of theft was going down in a store, that store got a $200 bonus, and if not, it got none. At the end of the year, the bonuses constituted a pretty substantial sum.

Walton treated his employees like kings, because he loved them. He rewarded them for each new idea, and this was what was leading the company to success. Employees knew that if they wanted to grow in Wal-Mart, they'd have to be ready for a journey. If a new store opened, and you were told about it via phone call, you'd have to pack your luggage and go. That was the rule.

Once Walton overheard Phil Green advertising a TV set he would sell for 22 cents in their Fayetteville store on George Washington's birthday (February 22). Shocked, Walton instantly got in touch with Phil. It turned out that Phil had hidden the TV set and the first person who found it could buy it.

On February 22, Phil was unable to enter the store in the morning because of the crowd in front of it; some even had slept in front of the doors to get in the first. When the store doors opened, 600 people jostled into the store to search for the 22 cent TV set. Phil sold an unprecedented number of products that day, but unable to control the crowd, he decided to abandon the idea of product hiding.

Kmart had interested Walton ever since 1962. He spent a lot of time wandering around their stores and talking to their employees and customers, trying to figure out he could take from them and make it better. He looked forward to meeting Kmart head on. And Walton had this opportunity in one of his best stores in Little Rock, Wal-Mart number 7. When Walton noticed Kmart being aggressive towards them, he told his manager to do whatever he wanted, but never let them win the sales of any product. It didn't matter what product it was, Wal-Mart would be the winners.

Walton recalls the manager of Wal-Mart 7 calling him once and saying that he had significantly reduced the price of Crest toothpaste, because Kmart had reduced it, too. In those days, Wal-Mart's prices were 5 cents lower than Kmart's, so they couldn't offer any lower prices.

The competition makes you stronger. None of Wal-Mart's rivals treated it seriously. So they ignored it while it was developing. For instance, Herb Fisher of Jamesway, Herb Gillman of Ames, Dale Worman of Fred Meyer and others would constantly visit Wal-Mart stores to figure out how they worked. They criticized the signs, useless low prices, lack of price tags, dirty walls, rudimentary shelves, etc.

They were being criticized, but Walton was happy, because due to their criticism, they could solve those problems and achieve results. Taking those criticisms into account, the company focused intensely on improvement. The discount competition was getting more and more intense with each day. Their rivals provided the customers with better service and were cleaner. They had better displays, but none of them could work on such a scale and as efficiently as Wal-Mart. None of them could cut expenses like Wal-Mart.

To boost the overall sales, Wal-Mart employees, including the management, practiced a "Volume Producing Item" contest; each chose an item of merchandise they'd like to promote in a creative way. Then they observed who was selling more. The emphasis was particularly on the sales volumes. People did all kinds of crazy things just to sell more. One would pick an item and hang it all over a tree filled with stuffed monkeys in the middle of the store. Another one drove a pickup truck into action alley and filled it with car-washing sponges. Sales exceeded all records. This was the story of the creation and growth of the largest retail chain in the world.

Secret 7. Study your rivals and take any good strategy they implement. Don't copy them though, but make it better and apply in your business.

Secret 8

If you dream big and take risks, impossible becomes just a word.

Richard Branson

Virgin Group (Richard Branson)

Sir Richard Branson is a man whose adventurous and risky nature has no boundaries. I won't describe it, though, instead I'll tell how he created his empire and how he withstood the tough attacks of British Airways. Many of you may have seen this broad-smiling man's interviews, not knowing what hardships it took him to endure to achieve success. Richard Branson was born on July 18, 1950. I'll continue from his perspective.

Richard admits that by the age of eight he still could not read. He had problems with his eyes, but nobody cared about the fact. Everybody thought that Ricky did not want to learn. He was considered the laziest and least intelligent student in the class. Despite the problems in education, he was successful in sports. From an early age, he became the best football player in the school and the team captain.

He was the one to raise all the trophies, and this filled him with some kind of passion towards them. It was the only way to stand out, to show that they had rushed to give him the label of a slow and weak pupil. But a sad thing happened that completely ruined his sports career. A knee injury during one of the matches forced him to say goodbye to a sport he loved.

After the injury, Richard was sent to a boarding school, where he had to study with disadvantaged pupils. There he would have to experience quite hard times. On leaving school, his headmaster told him, "Branson, I predict you will either go to prison or become a millionaire." At that time Branson didn't take these words seriously. Somehow he managed to pass the exams and leave the school and move to another school where something most interesting was awaiting him.

In the new place Richard got acquainted with a guy named John who was thinking of changing the whole school system. Richard was also taken with this idea, but how to change? They decided to launch a magazine. The most painful part began - choosing a name. He was writing different names on paper "Today", "1966", "Modern Britain", "Interview", but nothing worked. Finally, they settled upon "Student," which became the name of the magazine.

The next step was to decide their target group, who the magazine was meant for. At that time there was a period of student sit-ins, occupations and demonstrations at universities. This was a source for great material. Thus, the name was decided - same for the target - but they needed money to get the undertaking done. What to do? Richard asked his mother for some money to pay off phone and mail expenses, and Jonny's father helped them with paper. Richard picked up the telephone book and wrote out the names of all the possible companies.

Richard started to call everyone and inform them about the magazine, after which he asked them if they would like to place their advertisements in it. He asked the school headmaster to provide a phone and a room to run his business from. But he was turned down. He had to make the calls from the phone boxes outside, but it was expensive, and he didn't have the money. Soon Richard discovered an interesting trick. When he called the operator of the phone boxes and said that the machine had eaten his charge and that his call had been cut off, they'd give him a free call. You can imagine how many such telephone boxes there were in the city. Having a free call from each helped to save money.

He was calling potential advertisers on his list, but to no avail. Nobody wanted to place an advertisement in an unpublished magazine. Everybody refused, and he was looking for an alternative. For instance, he would call National Westminster bank and tell them that Lloyds Bank had already taken out a full-page advertisement in their magazine. Would they want to advertise alongside Lloyds Bank? The desire to have advertisements was so great that Richard even called Coca-Cola and said that Pepsi had just booked a big advertisement and that only the back page of the magazine was still free. He was doing the same with the Daily Telegraph and Daily Express. Often his voice trembled during the conversations, and he, through great effort, pulled himself together so that nobody could guess it was a 16-year-old boy talking to them.

Richard admits that if he were a student or at an older age, his hands sure would tremble to call such companies and offer advertising, but at 16 he didn't know what failure was. He wanted it, and that was all. Because of a lack of money, they worked from the basement of Jonny's house. He spent days in front of the phone trying to persuade companies to place ads in the Student magazine and famous people to give interviews.

Richard persuaded famous people to meet for an interview, and Jonny carried it out. Even if they saw some famous person visiting a nightclub, they would keep track of him, find him, and ask questions on the spot to include in the magazine.

Richard's mother and sister also helped him by distributing the magazines around the city. His mother visited tour agencies and handed out the magazines one by one. They needed the magazine to be widely circulated, because it would build trust in their advertisers. The Vietnam War became a salvation for the magazine.

First, nobody went to Vietnam to broadcast news on the war, and newly-graduated journalists were thirsty for information. That moment had to be used. Richard called the Daily Mirror and said that they had a journalist who was eager to cover the Vietnam War but couldn't afford him. They agreed to finance the journalist under an exclusive contract. One of the persons working with Richard left for Vietnam and was frequently reporting news to the Daily Mirror and the Student. This helped Richard to earn money; otherwise, he would become bankrupt.

The other option was to earn money on advertising, and he managed to convince 9 companies out of 300. That is, only 3 out of 100 became his advertisers. The money earned from the advertising and the Daily Mirror was enough for 30,000 magazine copies. When the printing had started, news about them started to spread. Wanting to know about them and their magazine, different newspapers visited Richard and Jonny, and what did they do to make an impression?

When famous newspapers visited them, Richard sat at the main desk, and his friends stretched the phones towards him, interrupted the conversation, as if he were talking to different famous company representatives and newspaper journalists. All this was repeated several times to show how busy they were. Once, Jonny passed the phone to Richard and said it was Mick Jagger of the Rolling Stones. This is how they managed to throw many into confusion, and as a result, various newspapers started talking about them.

But a small fact caught Richard's attention – people could stay half-hungry, but buy Bob Dylan's records. Why not take advantage of the moment? At the same time, he observed that all the record shops sold records at a high price and never offered discounts. It was a suitable moment, he said to himself. He decided he would sell records at a low price. But they had a problem with the name: He didn't want to name it Student, as it was a magazine. When thinking of names, they were about to settle upon Slipped Disc, when one of their team members said, "What about 'Virgin'? We're complete virgins at business."

"Great, it's Virgin," Richard exclaimed, and Virgin became the name of the company.

They spread an announcement through Student that each buyer could order records and receive them via mail at a lower price. The plan was that the client sent the money and name of the record via mail, while they bought the record from retailers and sent it back by mail.

This is how Virgin Mail Order was founded. That is, they took the money beforehand to be able to buy the record and send it. Since Richard couldn't manage it all alone, he invited one of his friends, Nicky. Success is not achieved alone.

After some time, however, a postal strike began in England. It was terrible. They were going bankrupt and had to find a way out. They decided to find a shop and do the selling from the shop, though none of them was competent in sales. They rented a small shop and installed a sofa, soft pillows, and headphones to create a cozy environment for people. Richard studied the rivals and noticed that people were made to leave the shop right after shopping.

They did the opposite. They provided the customers with the latest issues of New Musical Express and Melody Maker magazines, free coffee, and a chance to hear different styles of music. Richard's employees pointed out that this approach caused each customer to visit Virgin twice a week. *And what measures do you undertake for your customers' convenience?*

Having forgotten about the magazine, Richard completely immersed himself in the new business. But an unexpected occasion utterly changed the direction of his business. Once, one of his relatives, Simon, visited his house. Simon was music mad and had exquisite taste. Learning about his music preferences, Richard invited him to a café to persuade him to work at Virgin together.

His duty was to decide what songs were to be sold in Virgin shops and who would be recorded in their studio. The salary was £20 per week, as they were all getting as much. Simon's musical taste guaranteed Virgin's success. *One more tip – select experts in the field for the growth of your business.* Richard didn't quite understand what music should be played in the shops or even how loudly, while Simon was developing one by one the lists of songs to be played in the shop.

Before Simon came, Richard was only selling the records of British singers, and Simon suggested importing records from the United States. By this means, they had a wider range of records to offer than the rivals and thus gained a serious competitive advantage. *If you have massive sales, offer the customers a reasonable variety, not just quantity. Offer them quantity wide enough for choice.*

Afterwards, they sent information on the new records via mail, and orders literally came pouring in to them. In this way, they could figure out which singers or records were in higher demand. Simon managed to select hits that attracted people. He made excellent choices of bands and songs. He predicted which songs would have success, and his predictions were being fulfilled.

Richard admits he could do nothing without Simon. Virgin was slowly becoming popular. No earnings were spent without purpose. They were scraped together for the opening of new stores. Distribution was no strong point in the record business. For instance, the latest album of David Bowie could be sold out in a few hours. If a store didn't have the best-selling records in stock, the customer would go to the rival. So they had to be flexible. *If you have a product that is selling well, always have it in stock, because if you don't, you'll lose both sales and customers.*

But they had problems with sales. They needed to have sufficient numbers of records. Certain companies refused to supply them, as Virgin sold records at low cost, thus hurting their retail business. Others doubted their ability to pay. Thus borrowing was no option either. After a long search, they found a small shop, Pop-in, which was ready to buy records from others and transfer them to Virgin.

They gave 5% of the profit to Pop-in. By this trick they managed to find a way out of the situation. They gave the names of the important singers for them; Pop-in bought the records, and Simon delivered them to all Virgin shops. True, this was a way out, but Richard was losing significant money, so they had to think of something new. After some time, Virgin's financial situation was good enough to quit working with Pop-in and buy records without intermediaries.

They decided to set up their own recording studio in addition to record shops, as it would be more sensible to have the singers recorded right at Virgin and sell their records through Virgin. This idea gave birth to Virgin Music. The first person Simon wanted to record was Mike Oldfield. Mike didn't cooperate with any record companies at the time. He didn't have money, so they offered him an initial salary of £20, what all the employees at Virgin received. Richard was worried because he had no idea how they could make money by Mike's music. But it's business; he had to give it a try.

Mike was recorded and, naturally, would have to do a concert to become more popular and have potential buyers of his music. After the recording, Virgin started selling his records and getting ready for the concert. But suddenly, on the day of the concert, Mike panicked and said to Richard he couldn't do it. Richard was shocked. Everything was already prepared.

Richard pulled over his old Bentley, which was a wedding gift, and took him on a ride, as he knew Mike loved Bentleys and thought it would be easier to convince him during the ride. All along the roads there were ads for the concert, but he looked at them and kept repeating that he couldn't go on stage. It annoyed Richard, so he stopped the car and said,

"Would you like to have this car as a present?"

"A present?" asked Mike.

"Yes, all you have to do is to drive it around to the Queen Elizabeth Hall and go up onstage tonight."

"It's a deal," Mike agreed.

Mike's performance was very important for them, and Richard made the sacrifice for the sake of their cause.

The concert was a success - standing ovations, shouts of "Bravo, Mike" - and tears filled Richard's eyes. He had won. Those were sweet moments. Mike was a new star. That night only, several hundred copies of the record were sold. Mike Oldfield's "Tubular Bells" became the album of the year. This success brought Virgin Music recognition, and money was flowing into its pockets.

For a sales increase, Virgin next turned to Island Records. Island Records' advantage was that it had large advertising budget and could promote Mike Oldfield's records. As Richard expected, Island Records rejected the offer, because it was already working with Virgin's rivals. But in the end it couldn't refuse Virgin's tricky offer – Island was offered 18% of the total sales; 5% was for Mike, 13% for the company. As surprising as it was, Island Records agreed, and without realizing the seriousness of it, helped one of its most serious rivals, Virgin Music, grow. Mike's album sold millions of copies, which brought Virgin Music huge amounts of money.

As I already mentioned, Virgin spent the income on opening record shops. Day and night, Richard was discussing some business on the phone. His wife told him they had no private life. But he had a goal; he wanted to expand worldwide. In 1974, Virgin Music faced some serious problems. After Oldfield, they needed one more talented musician to shake the market.

In those days the name of 10CC was being circulated, whom Virgin Music wanted to recruit, as they met Simon's requirements. Their previous album sold 750,000 copies. It was clear that in order to sign a contract with them, Virgin would have to give a considerable advance. Richard met their manager and offered £100,000, but that number was quite low compared to Phonogram's offer.

The manager exacted an advance of £200,000 from Virgin. Richard was certain they would have great success with 10CC. They urgently needed money, and he called everyone who could help, starting from Virgin shops in France, Germany, Netherlands, plus the USA. One day before signing the contract, Richard wrote to all Virgin's managers, telling them to buy champagne and get ready to celebrate the new contract they had concluded.

Yet, when he called 10CC' manager to meet, the latter answered that they wouldn't sign a contract and that there was no point running after them. The contract was cancelled; moreover, they had already gone to Virgin's rival, Phonogram. Richard lost control of himself. At that time he was taught an important business lesson. Do not celebrate before the outcome is certain. The sad thing was that 10CC's new album sold several million copies. Richard was going mad. He had lost the game. *That's life - one day we win; one day we lose. Whatever happens, we should learn lessons and continue the journey.* In addition, it didn't work out with the Who and Pink Floyd. He had no other option but to take the risk and call Rolling Stones' manager, Prince Rupert Loewenstein.

Prince Rupert Loewenstein asked for £3 million and added that Virgin was a small company to have it. To attract his attention, Richard said they would pay £4 million if they were given the permission to release the older albums as well. The 4 million had to be on Prince Rupert Loewenstein's desk on Monday morning.

It was Friday, and Richard was in a desperate situation. He was on the run again, contacting the distributors in France, Italy, Germany, Sweden, Norway, Netherlands, he collected £250,000 from each. The rest he borrowed from Coutts Bank on Monday morning and visited the Rolling Stones' manager.

Prince was taken aback by Richard's persistence, but he lost again since

EMI paid more, £5 million. Just imagine how it felt: Money in his hand, he failed again. But failures only made him stronger, so Richard did not step back but determined to keep moving forward. As Oscar Wilde said, "There is only one thing in life worse than being talked about, and that is not being talked about."

The next unsuccessful contract was with the Culture Club, whose album sold 8,000 copies, once again a failure. Not giving up, they tried again with the Culture Club. Richard believed in them, and his faith was justified, since their next album sold more than 4 million copies. Most surprisingly, their sixth song became a worldwide best-seller, which made the company a worldwide phenomenon. After this success, Virgin's financial state significantly improved, profiting £2 million. The company had a turnover of £50 million in 1982 and a turnover of 94 million in 1983, with 11 million of net profit.

When funds were flowing into the company's budget, Richard started thinking of alternatives; he didn't want to depend on one field. *In other words, Branson practiced business diversification. That's when business people invest in several fields, thus reducing the risks of being dependent on one sector.* He didn't want to put all his eggs in one basket, for if it dropped, all the eggs would break. He had already reached considerable heights and was looking for challenges.

Secret 8. Don't be satisfied with what you acquire. Always look for further ways to develop your business.

Secret 9

If somebody offers you an amazing opportunitybutyouarenotsureyoucandoit, say yes. Then learn how to do it later

Richard Branson

Virgin Group (Richard Branson)

The story of Richard Branson continues.

It was 1984 when Richard Branson was first approached by a young American barrister, Randolph Fields, with the idea of owning an airline .

The proposal was unusual for Richard; he decided to spend some time studying it. Randolph's idea was to serve only business class passengers. And what about the days when businesspeople are on leave, Christmas, New Year, public holidays, working days? This point had to be resolved. He was thinking of an airline that would serve only tourists and business class passengers. And why not? Why not take advantage of the moment? The aircraft would be leased for a year. If it didn't work, he'd retreat and return the plane. Weighing all this, he went into action. The first thing to do was to discuss it with his friend Simon. Simon's reaction was not the most approving one. He thought Richard was mad and suggested giving up the crazy idea. *How many times have you talked about your idea, but given up on wonderful business prospects because of such reactions?* Richard didn't further discuss it.

The next morning he checked the phone number for Boeing and called them. They were rather bemused to hear an ordinary Englishman asking for purchase conditions of a passenger airplane. All night long Richard talked to different staff members and found someone who could help him. It turned out Boeing did lease aircraft. When he told Simon about this, the latter categorically spoke against the new venture. He told Richard he could waste money as long as he wouldn't engage them in it.

It was decided that Virgin Music would be a separate company. Branson had agreed with Boeing on the airplane leasing. He also estimated they would lose £2 million per year if the airline proved unsuccessful. They had millions in their hands, and he thought they could try to invest for only one year. Richard could buy an airline, but most of all he relished starting a business from scratch.

Branson realized that he put everything at risk, but it was a challenge he wanted to accept. He didn't want to take a step back, and going forward meant running the risk. He was ready for it. Since the flights were going to be across the Atlantic Ocean, from Great Britain to the USA, he decided to name it Virgin Atlantic. Branson knew absolutely nothing about the business, so he had to gather information from experts in the field.

He visited Freddie Laker, whose work he had always admired. Freddie explained to him all the nuances of the airline industry - the service rules of business class passengers, and its philosophy and pricing policy. During the conversation an interesting idea was born - meeting business class passengers with limousines. Freddie also warned about the competition with the established giant of the industry, British Airways.

He encouraged Branson to beat BA, which had destroyed him. Another thing he warned Branson about was the stress, as the airline industry was the toughest of all businesses.

One more tip – if you are a startup in a business, get acquainted with consult the best professionals in the field and learn all the processes.

They'd agreed with Randolph: Branson made the investment, and Randolph ran the company. Randolph had already invited two key people from Laker Airways. One of them was David Tait. When asked what he thought of the name "Virgin Atlantic," Tait said it was a bad name from the point of view of branding.

But Branson was adamant. If it was a matter of perception, people would get used to it. They rented a warehouse near Gatwick Airport and started the recruitment of the crew, pilots and attendants. The other team headed by Tait worked on flight schedules, ticket distribution, and computer programs. To get money from Coutts & Co private banking service, Branson offered the firm certain management privileges.

But hardly had the company started operating when Randolph had issues with the staff. He didn't treat them well. Branson decided that the tumor must be removed at the first symptoms. And so he removed it. Randolph was fired from the company. Branson didn't go home for days. The company was deciding on the attendants' uniforms, colors, and the menu. It was studying a 96-page lease agreement with Boeing.

Nothing worthwhile comes easy in this life. Before the airline's first flight took place, David Gate, the head of the New York office, had decided to launch a teaser campaign. Skywriters had to festoon the sky with the words "WAIT FOR THE ENGLISH VIRGIN" to make people talk about them. But when the idea was realized, what could be seen in the sky was WAIT FOR THE ENGLISH VIRGI, as the last N did not appear. Thus, the Americans did not understand what it was all about.

David's next step was to ensure ticket sales through agents, who sold 90% of the tickets. That is, if you go into the airline industry, you don't have to open special offices and spend money on the image. It is better sell through agent networks. Branson was working at the other side of the operation, negotiating with Boeing for the aircraft. Within two months, they reached an agreement, leaving Boeing surprised by their persistence.

One of Boeing's representatives even mentioned that it was easier to sell 20 aircraft to an American company than 1 aircraft to Virgin.

The day of Virgin Atlantic's inaugural flight came. When the airplane took off, Branson cried tears of joy. Suddenly, the plane lurched to the left and a massive flame shot out of one engine, followed by a long trail of black smoke. Branson broke out in a cold sweat. One of the employees said that a flock of birds had been sucked into one engine and that it happened with planes. The engine was damaged during the first flight, and the plane was uninsured. A bad sign, Branson thought to himself. But he didn't give up. A photojournalist from the Financial Times was there to cover the flight. He had noticed smoke and got a shot of it. After landing, Branson did not understand what had happened and what dark clouds were gathering over his head, when the photojournalist approached him and said,

"I'm sorry. I saw the flames and smoke pouring out of your engine. I actually got a great shot of it." And then he continued,

"Don't worry, though. I'm from Financial Times; we're not that kind of paper."

He opened up his camera and handed Branson the film. He didn't run the story, or else it would have been the end of Virgin Atlantic before it had even started. Branson felt indebted and grateful to the journalist, to that kind person. The replacement of the engine required £600,000. What bad luck. With great difficulty Branson went to Coutts & Co to get a loan. After the engine was repaired, the plane was tested again, with civil aviation authorities present, and made a successful landing. On that day, they received a license. The same day the plane took off again, as they were returning to London to celebrate the victory. Dozens of boxes of champagne, chocolates, records, in a word, everything for dancing and enjoying themselves. Halfway, they started to watch a movie, during which the attendants treated everyone to chocolate ice cream, laying the basis of an important tradition – treating passengers to chocolate ice cream when watching a movie.

Now Virgin Atlantic needed to attract public attention. Branson kept thinking of ways to do it. The company didn't have as much money as British Airways to spend on advertising, so Branson understood he had to turn himself into a public figure and become his company's brand image. His friends and family avoided the media, but he knew it was important for success. If no one took their airplane, they would become bankrupt. He built the public relations policy of the company around his personality. Almost every day he gave speeches and participated in different events. He was becoming more and more of a public celebrity.

In the meantime, Branson made another mistake. They got £30 million when the company's shares started to be bought on the stock exchange. He had big problems with the shareholders. They demanded dividends, while Branson wanted to expand the business. He wanted to pursue refinancing, which was typical of the Japanese business model, but the English thought otherwise. Before entering the stock exchange, he was confident, because he made all the decisions himself without any obstacles, and now his position was weakening, as the shareholders would take control of his moves. They were more interested in short-term profits, while Branson preferred the longer term perspective. Anyway, he had to adapt, the mistake was made; Virgin Atlantic was a joint-stock company.

While Branson was busy with such operations, his rivals were not having a rest. BA managed to acquire the shares of British Caledonian, and absorbing this company significantly increased its market share. As unpleasant as it was, BA was the market leader. It had destroyed all rivals and had now focused on Virgin Atlantic, which had to be ready, for its existence was at stake.

Branson would have never imagined he'd fall into such a tough competition. Under the Bermuda Agreement, two British airlines had the right of flights to the US and Japan. The unification of British Caledonian to BA gave Virgin Atlantic the opportunity to enter the US and Japanese markets. In other words, Virgin Atlantic was entitled to apply for the routes that British Caledonian had served.

In 1987, Virgin Atlantic had two aircraft. For Los Angeles and Tokyo flights, Branson took the risk again, leasing two more aircraft. In such a difficult situation the shortest way to obtain money was to sell Virgin Atlantic's shares, because of huge debts. But Branson didn't want to sell the shares to the British, so he sold 10% of shares to Seibu-Saison for £36 million. He chose the Japanese because they were interested in capital increase and not the quick return of dividends. Branson once heard that a Japanese investor had required a company to show its 200-year business plan, surprising as it is.

Since Branson had started working with the Japanese, he also wanted to have a branch of Virgin Music in Tokyo. Mike Inman, a Virgin Music employee, visited Tokyo. He introduced Tokyo to Branson as an inhospitable city for people from abroad - as it was difficult to find areas that secured an influx of people, as everything in Tokyo was identical, and as real estate was too expensive.

But there's a rule in business that Branson always applies. If you can't do it yourself, cooperate with others. They decided to join Marui clothes store and launched the first Virgin megastore on Japan. Why Marui stores? The first reason was that the clothes were for young people; the second was that they were near the bustling railway station and busy stores.

Business in Japan had been growing until the day Branson heard about the Iraqi invasion of Kuwait on the news.

The price of a barrel of oil had risen from $19 to $36. Aviation is the industry that depends on the number of passengers and fuel prices. Fuel accounts for almost 20% of airline expenses. They had to carry out flights when 3000 tickets were returned in the first week. Upon hearing the news, Branson staggered nervously, wondering how many more passengers were going to cancel their flights.

During the chaos, many refugees had crossed into Jordan and lived without shelter, water and clothing in extremely hot days and frigid nights. Branson wouldn't miss this chance. He contacted King Hussein to ask how he could help the refugees. All the staff of Virgin Atlantic supported Branson's idea. Gathering needed supplies for the refugees, they flew to Amman and returned with a number of British nationals who had been stranded in Jordan and wanted to come home. This caused a stir in Britain. Everyone was talking about Virgin Atlantic. When Branson was already in London, the Red Cross representative stated that the head of British Airways, Lord King, had said they should have done it all, not Virgin Atlantic. Branson had made a major move in the strengthening of his company's image.

The next week British Airways rushed to Jordan to help refugees and flew back some British nationals stranded there. Many Britons said they had been asking BA to provide an aircraft for years, but remained unanswered, while Virgin Atlantic was by their side at the first opportunity. The decision had a positive impact on the image of the startup airline. Branson had an aircraft at his disposal, and he wanted to help people. This move became critical for him, because Lord King didn't like it at all, and he couldn't wait to kick Branson out of the market.

British Caledonian provided aircraft maintenance for Virgin Atlantic from the start. After BA gained control of British Caledonian, the Civil Aviation demanded that it continue providing the aircraft maintenance. In 1988 Virgin Atlantic increased its number of aircraft, and something cruel began. BA increased its hourly maintenance costs from £16 to £61, because it knew Virgin Atlantic was dependent on it.

There was also a commitment that if one of Virgin Atlantic's planes needed repair, BA had to provide them with a spare aircraft for a while. Once, when a Virgin Atlantic aircraft was under repair, they turned to BA. BA rejected them, saying that the no aircraft was available because it was also under repair. The incident took place in August, the peak period for flights, while Virgin Atlantic was waiting for its aircraft, which wasn't being repaired. In despair, Branson picked up the phone and called the chief-executive of BA, Sir Colin Marshal.

To Branson's accusations of bad aircraft maintenance, Colin Marshal answered that such issues were a norm in aviation business, but Branson wouldn't accept this. Such conduct would not have happened in the music business. Marshal added that BA would repair Virgin Atlantic's plane when they considered it appropriate.

Branson was shocked. His company was losing money, and the aircraft was still not there. To come out of the difficult situation, Virgin Atlantic was forced to move its aircraft to Ireland, where Aer Lingus Airline was to carry out the maintenance instead of BA. The expenses were huge, and the rival's blow was quite strong. Virgin Atlantic was still running at a loss and had debts. But this was not all, British Airways held other unpleasant surprises for them.

Lord King didn't miss an opportunity to stress that Virgin Atlantic was heading towards bankruptcy, could hardly survive, and was unreliable. Branson could do nothing, as British Airways was an established market leader, with influential shareholders and politicians behind it. The whole state system exclusively made use of British Airways, as it was the national airline. Everything was permitted to BA, but Branson had his say, which was still something.

At last, Branson decided to hit BA where it hurt and conquer Heathrow - the primary hub for British Airways. The access to London's largest and busiest airport would enable Virgin Atlantic to have more flights and beat British Airways, because it was the only airline flying out of Heathrow.

No British airline had successfully flown exclusively out of Gatwick: Virgin Atlantic would have to get to Heathrow to survive. No one from Gatwick would be able to compete with British Airways, but they could compete from Heathrow, so Branson hit the nail on the head – either they were going to die or enter Heathrow. This was their way out. After years of campaigning, Virgin Atlantic was granted the right to fly out of London's main airport. If you can't fight face to face, then hit from the side. Branson couldn't believe his eyes. They had won, but the worst was yet to come.

BA refused to provide spare check-in desks, while Virgin Atlantic didn't have desks to serve the passengers. Only after the intervention of Civil Aviation did BA provide them with check-in desks. Each success was given to Branson with much difficulty, but he was ready to fight to the end. It happened once that one of the passenger's didn't like Virgin Atlantic's service and wrote in the visitor's book,

"No wonder your boss travels around the world in a balloon."

When Branson saw this piece in Sunday Telegraph, he was shocked, as Lord King was among the executives of that magazine. Another nuisance that could be used by British Airways against them, and BA did use it. That phrase was broadcast on TV as well and became a real headache for Branson. He immediately demanded to see the visitor's book for the previous fortnight, thinking there was something wrong about it, as they generally received so few passenger complaints. He found the entry in the visitor's book. It read exactly as noted above, but the punch line was missing, which read: "But seriously, I had a great time."

Not that Branson avoided criticism, he appreciated sincerity, but the Sunday Telegraph didn't introduce it fully. Branson found the passenger who said that he had a great time and that it was all a joke. Then Richard criticized the Sunday Telegraph for its misinformation, but the damage had already been done to the Virgin brand. A journalist from the Sunday Telegraph gave Branson a cynical answer, "Oops, I'm sorry about that misquote. I looked over a neighbor's shoulder, and that's all I could see."

Another episode had to do with BA's poaching of Virgin Atlantic's passengers. Virgin Atlantic realized this was happening when BA representatives had called two of Virgin's passengers and persuaded them to transfer to BA. Besides, Virgin Atlantic's employees had observed that BA representatives came to the terminals and persuaded the passengers that Virgin's planes were unsafe and that they'd better switch to BA. By such tricks, Virgin Atlantic was being pressured by BA.

One of Branson's friends, Ronnie, ran a limousine service in New York. He sent limousines to the airport and transferred passengers to their hotels. For many years they worked together, as their target was the business-class passengers. Ronnie's drivers had noticed British Airways employees approaching Virgin's passengers and offering them discounted tickets before they got into the limousines. Learning this, Ronnie clashed with them and forbade them from approaching his limousines.

British Airways was unbearable. It was openly poaching Virgin's passengers. The management of British Airways didn't pay attention to Branson's warnings; its self-confidence had no limits. Branson didn't want to go through a judicial process, but he had to, because he didn't accept the "dirty tricks" as competition. He worked 18 hours a day and really had no desire to go to court. The winter of 1991 ended with great losses for Virgin.

The banks demanded debt repayment, and Branson knew British Airways was waiting for his bankruptcy. But an incident changed everything. One of Virgin's passengers was sitting at home when someone called him, introduced herself as a Virgin employee, some Mary Ann, and announced that the flight on the sixteenth was overbooked. She then suggested using British Airways instead. She asked to be waitlisted for her flight and asked Mary Ann to call her the next day, but she didn't call her, just as it was with "Bonnie" from Virgin in August, who had said that her flight was delayed, and "Larry" from Virgin in September, who had said that all nonsmoking seats were full. Being a loyal customer, she was displeased and surprised as to why Virgin had such sloppy service. Finally, she called Virgin and asked Mary Ann to the phone, but it turned out there was no such employee at Virgin.

"Then who called me yesterday and said that I was bounced off the October 16 flight?" the vexed passenger asked.

This episode led to the start of a long judicial process to put a stop to the dirty competition. Thanks to the passenger's testimony, Branson won the case, and distributed the £500,000 compensation among his staff, who had gone through the ordeal together with him.

All those that start a business with limited financial resources have to know that they're going to face either collapse or success. Such conditions never allowed Branson to indulge in luxuries. He invested all the money in business. After that year, no banks could tell him what to do, because he had achieved self-financing. No matter how many difficulties you have, always remember, if you endure, you will win. Branson was always confident that Virgin must be unique. So he called Boeing's chairman Phil Condit and asked if it were possible to install seatback TVs in all seats if Virgin Atlantic bought 10 Boeing 747-400.

Phil was shocked, since no one had turned to him with such a proposal before, and he agreed. Branson said the same thing to the head of Airbus, Jean Pierson. As a result, Virgin Atlantic became a lucrative, powerful airline with a significant number of aircraft.

Customer service is the number one priority in Virgin; everything is done to keep customers loyal. For example, what does Richard Branson do for the customers so that they are satisfied with the service of Virgin Atlantic? When customers call Virgin Atlantic and Call Center employees fail to respond in time, the customers hear Richard Branson's voice,

"Hello, my name is Richard Branson; I'm the owner of the airline. Now all operators are busy. This is a disorder. Let's proceed as follows: After 18 seconds if no one answers, you will receive a discount of 450 pounds. I'm starting the countdown – 18, 17, 16, 15 ..." And you can imagine that the customer does not think anymore that he has not been answered, but gets into the game and passionately wants only one thing – that the operator does not pick up the phone. Irrespective of whether they are answered, Branson knows the way to convey positive emotions to people. *I assume many of you have read about Branson's fun ways and billions, but few of you know what fierce competition he endured to achieve such results. Do not give up.*

Secret 9. Think of something the customer will enjoy even when waiting.

Secret 10

If you have to ask how much it costs, you can't afford it.

John Pierpont Morgan

JP Morgan and Chase (John Pierpont Morgan)

Morgan was one of those people who didn't produce a single product in his life, but built a financial kingdom. Not holding any public office, Morgan managed to control the huge capital inflows into the USA from Europe. This person is the hero of Secret 10. The bank he founded was later expanded by the fusion of Chase Manhattan Bank, J.P. Morgan and Co financial institutions.

John Pierpont Morgan was born on April 17, 1837, in the United States, into the family of a rich banker. As a child he was weak and sickly. His parents had to interrupt his education and send him to the Azores to recover. Being a weak child, he created problems for his financier father, who worried about having an heir to his wealth. After spending some time in the islands, his father sent him to Switzerland to complete his education.

His father, Junius Morgan, had big ambitions. If the Rothschilds managed to create a banking empire in Europe, the Morgans could do the same in the US. In 1854, Junius Morgan traveled to London and met the Rothschilds and Barings, who had great trouble entering the US market. Junius Morgan assured them that their money would be in safe hands overseas. The deal was made. Now he had to prepare his son.

The first rule: No speculative investment. The second lesson flowed from the first: A man prone to speculation cannot be trusted with the capital of others, because, ultimately, trust is built on character and reputation.

After the first venture, John Morgan had losses. In 1850, Morgan made his first serious steps. He ventured into five shares of the Pacific Mall, each for $63. His father was against buying the shares, but John was adamant. He again bought a large number of shares of the same company, but in a few months had to sell them for a loss of $1500. But he was not discouraged; he borrowed money from his father again and bought shares in a railway company in Michigan. After only a month he sold them for twice the price.

These two rules became Morgan's initial lessons. After studying in Europe, Morgan returned to the USA, where the war between North and South had started. This very war became the basis for Morgan's "brilliant" career. The Morgans, father and son, were among those who provided the warring parties with all the necessary supplies. The first deal sealed was the purchase of weapons from the South and their sale to the North. In fact, they were defective, but the North didn't know about it. Morgan did not care about the result, but the deal.

Soon John Morgan opened a joint bank account with Edward Ketchum and started drawing gold. The partners borrowed money and secretly obtained large amounts of gold. After accumulating gold for $1.15 million, they sold it to England. A fever of gold started in New York, as there was not enough gold. Creating an artificial shortage, Morgan and Ketchum caused a rise in gold prices.

As a result, the partners, by selling gold in England, profited $160,000. That is to say, these people made money out of thin air. Having no startup money, they borrowed money, bought gold, and exported from the country. This created a deficit, and as a result, considerable amounts of money were accumulated by sales. Morgan's father didn't accept such deals, but he was already powerless to stop his son.

Morgan's key success was that his bank became the only financial institution linking the Old Continent and the USA. Can you imagine how much money has flowed between these entities? So you observed where Morgan's wealth emerged – the initial capital of his father, the sale of weapons during war, the sale of gold sale, the investment of funds from Europe, foreign currency exchange, and later, the operations involving the shares of large companies. Now I'll expand more specifically on where those finances were invested and by what mechanism this was done.

Morgan did not build a single kilometer of railway and never owned a single line. He was solely engaged in the "organization" of the railway business, its financing and received profit. From his point of view, Morgan was right - the risk was relatively small and the profits were huge. In 1867, railroad construction was growing at full speed. Investment capital was needed. The moment had to be seized. Morgan did use this moment to his advantage. He took money from Europe, particularly from the Rothchilds, and invested in the railroad construction. Morgan's management style was peculiar in that he wouldn't invest and leave. He supervised the work meticulously. If there were a defect, he'd fire the director, update the personnel, control finances, and change the organizational structure.

He controlled everything without missing a single detail. He carried a dozen notebooks with him, and when his business grew so much that one person could not keep track of everything, he replaced the notebooks with as many assistants. He was always accompanied by assistants, who recorded the details of each transaction Morgan made, because he physically was not able to remember or write them all down. Morgan was able to select the right staff. As a rule, those were talented and enterprising people who would carry out the boss's assignments and, at the same time, could show personal initiative.

Morgan led business like he led war: He was Morgan engaged in business as if waging war: He would spy, start the battle, and smash the weakened enemy. Morgan was a farsighted man and always tried to smash the enemies by tactical tricks. In 1869, a fraudulent American businessman, Jay Gould, wanted to take over Albany & Susquehanna Railroad from municipal authorities. (I'll touch upon Gould and Fisk in the topic about Cornelius Vanderbilt.) But the head of the railway, Joseph Morgan, did not agree and turned to John Morgan for help. Morgan was not well-known among the narrow financial circles of the time, and it seemed like a good opportunity. A part of Albany & Susquehanna Railroad shares was owned by the city authorities, and Gould and James Fisk started illegally buying their shares of Albany & Susquehanna, and sometimes they made direct attempts to annex the company to themselves. Morgan answered by all methods: to an attack he answered by an attack; to the hiring of lawyers by the hiring of lawyers; to stock fraud by stock fraud. And finally he sued Gould and Fisk. He won the case, and, through these events, his reputation grew even more.

After Albany & Susquehanna it was the turn for New York Central Railroad, which was owned by William Vanderbilt and was a rather effective system in the country. Cornelius Vanderbilt had died, and his son was running the company on his own. After the lengthy dramatic strikes of railway workers in 1877, public opinion rebelled against the owners of railways, who were accused of exploiting not only the workers but also the passengers. The New York State Legislature started an investigation on the Vanderbilt case. Morgan immediately came to his aid. Morgan met William Vanderbilt. The meeting was strictly confidential. After the meeting, Morgan became a member of the directors' board of New York Central Railroad and managed to distribute company shares overseas. Such was his plan: Of the 400 million shares of "New York Central" Vanderbilt sold 250,000 – of course, with the banking services of "The House of Morgan." For about $25 million, Vanderbilt bought government bonds, bringing a good income. This way he got rid of the burden of being the railway's sole owner while retaining a significant stake and full control over the railroad.

Attention, Morgan obtained one share for $120 and sold it for $130 in England, earning more than $3 million from this deal. If Cornelius Vanderbilt had been alive, things might have proceeded differently, but the son, who surrendered quite quickly, was not like his father.

All the weak railroad companies pressured by Morgan disappeared over time. In 1893, one more economic crisis occurred. Among the bankrupt entrepreneurs, traders and bankers appeared certain railroad owners. Such major companies as "Baltimore and Ohio," "Erie," "Northern Pacific," "Union Pacific," and "Santa Fe" declared bankruptcy. Now Morgan could use all his capital and show all his talent! His representatives examined the financial situation of the railroad companies that had gone bankrupt and presented a plan of "reorganization" to the boss. Here Morgan acted as a banker who "saves" railways from total disaster. By a strange coincidence, all his steps were directed to further increase his influence on railway companies.

While taking over different railways or in search of mechanisms to establish financial control over them, Morgan, as if reluctantly, was also becoming the owner of coal mines. When the railway company "Philadelphia and Reading" was in a difficult situation, Morgan offered it his "help": First, he engineered a collapse in its shares, and then purchased them on the cheap. Together with the railway line, Morgan bought the large coal mines in Pennsylvania belonging to the company.

Unappeasable in his hatred, Morgan never forgot and forgave disrespect; he could be easily offended. Distinguished by an iron will, he walked firmly to the destination, and if needed, trampled people. Among the many examples Morgan's biographers cite, I'll mention only one. In 1893, when George P. Morgan was vigorously engaged in the "reorganization" of railways. All of a sudden it turned out that the chairman of the board of one of the railway companies, a certain Archibald A. McLeod, did not want to accept the dictates of the billionaire and instigated a resistance among the miners. It should be noted that McLeod was at the head of "Philadelphia and Reading," the same one that owned coal mines. McLeod's obstinate behavior led Morgan into a rage: He could not tolerate any resistance. The billionaire instructed his subordinates to start speculating in the shares of this company on a major stock exchange. The result was almost immediate: Within a few days, "Philadelphia and Reading" did not withstand the attack and declared its bankruptcy. McLeod had to leave the stage, and the company was taken over by Morgan. This is how Gustavus Myers characterizes Morgan at the time he was securing the leading position in the railway industry:

For Morgan, power meant dictatorship, as any other model of management did not exist for him. He had finances and people, and he constantly demanded obedience. "He was a truculent, aggressive financier, with a domineering, even fierce, personality and great power in his own field, that of banking. His mind was of that resolute, masterful order declining to be balked by any man or set of circumstances, and his methods were not distinguished by delicacy. His method of treatment is drastic, and the holders of junior securities have made many a wry face, but the method has seemed to be efficacious."

Thus, you saw it yourselves with what flexibility Morgan gained control of almost the whole railroad sector of the United States. The ones who invested in Morgan Bank began receiving huge dividends, due to which Morgan's reputation was spreading. There was a great rivalry between John Rockefeller and John Morgan, as both wanted to take over Carnegie Steel. Rockefeller was the first to go to Carnegie, which required $250 million, and Rockefeller refused to pay.

But on December 12, 1900, the New York bankers J. Edward Simmons and Charles Steward Smith hosted a gala dinner at the University Club in New York. Charles Schwab, chairman of the board of "Carnegie Steel Company" was a guest of honor. Among the other eighty guests was John Pierpont Morgan. After the dessert and coffee, Schwab gave a speech.

The tycoon started by unfolding the tempting picture of the American steel industry. He said that the American technology in this area was the best in the world and that the prices of the steel products could be reduced if the demand for them was increased. According to Schwab, the path to this was to concentrate all the steel industry in one giant trust that would immediately eliminate competition and require each subordinated trust company to specialize in one area. The audience could notice John P. Morgan carefully listening to the words of the speaker; he had even set aside a lit cigar. When Schwab finished his speech, Morgan came up to him, took him to the corner of one of the salons, and had a confidential talk with him for half an hour.

This was followed by Morgan's offer. The wily Andrew Carnegie was the only one with such a strong company. He was independent. That is, he had his own money to invest in transactions, rather than take loans from banks or shareholders. Carnegie offered $480 million, and Morgan had to agree, as he was interested in the increase of capitalization. This matter caused Carnegie a lot of suffering, because if you say a price and the buyer agrees at once, it always seems like you said a cheap price. Morgan bought Carnegie Steel and renamed it United States Steel Corporation, and the company became world's first corporation worth $1 billion in assets.

After a few months, when Carnegie met Morgan on board the ship, he said that he probably had made a great mistake and should have required $100 million from him. Morgan was sincere to answer that had Carnegie wanted more he would still have paid.

After buying Carnegie Steel, Morgan faced yet another problem. Carnegie had taken out a lease from Rockefeller on one of the most important mines, and Morgan didn't want to depend on Rockefeller, so he invited him to his office for a meeting. In response to Morgan's invitation, Rockefeller said he didn't visit downtown in general, and invited Morgan to his office instead. Morgan had to agree. Visiting Rockefeller, he immediately started talking about business.

Smiling, Rockefeller said he had already passed his business on to his son. Morgan was waiting for Rockefeller Jr. angrily. When he arrived, to Morgan's question as to how much he sold the mines, Rockefeller Jr. responded that he had no idea his father intended to sell the mines and wished Morgan good luck.

Infuriated, Morgan left, but made up his mind to take over the mines at any cost, so as not to be dependent on Rockefeller in any way. And he reached his goal through his employees, even at rather a high price. For him, the most important thing was to achieve his goal.

As is known, Schwab assured everyone that the concentration of the entire steel industry would inevitably lead to lower prices. But Morgan acted differently. In fact, one of the first steps of the new trust was to establish fixed prices on rails: Instead of the previous 23 dollars 75 cents per ton now the price was 28 dollars. The price increase was all the more unreasonable given that the cost price of rails was only 12 dollars per ton (about which the consumers learned many years later, when the private letter of Charles Schwab were published). But the exploitation of workers and the maintenance of high prices corresponded to the life philosophy of John P. Morgan. The creation of the "U.S. Steel" trust became his third source of millions of profits, along with the banks and railways. As in the railway business, Morgan was no manufacturer, no merchant, but only an organizer and financier.

The other element of Morgan's success was that he was looking for talented people, contributing to the implementation of their ideas, and giving them the opportunity for self-expression. It's natural that, having a share in each transaction, he gave others the opportunity to get rich. Morgan was the first to pay attention to Edison's inventions, providing Edison with an office, an appropriate amount of money, and a laboratory for his experiments. Because of all this, Edison created Edison Electric Company, and Morgan became the father of this American giant. Thanks to Edison, Morgan's Wall Street office was the first to be illuminated. In 1892, Morgan bought Edison Electric and

Thomson-Huston Electric Companies, on the basis of which General Electric came to be formed.

Morgan's principle was not only gaining profit, but simply winning the game. Once a month Morgan would leave business and devote himself to rest, as he followed a simple rule, "Rest is an extremely necessary thing. I can do all the work within nine months, but not twelve."

Morgan is known as America's financial king, because he rescued the world - and the USA in particular - from financial collapse three times. In 1893, the US government had to have $100 million in gold in its reserve fund to support its internal costs. In those years the number mentioned was reduced to $38 million, and this caused the USA fall into a difficult financial situation. The market started to panic. The US president asked Morgan to find a way out. Morgan provided the government with $62 million in gold, thus making it dependent on him. When the New York Stock Exchange was about to close, and only $20 million was needed, Morgan gathered the leading financiers together in his library and said they needed $20 million in the next 10 minutes, vowing that no one would leave the place until the money was pledged.

Had someone else done this, it might have seemed unconvincing, but Morgan's reputation and character for forty years spoke for themselves.

Morgan provided large amounts of loans to the Entente countries, which, in their turn, bought ammunition and fuel from Morgan's friends, who were setting prices with each other. They had even planned in his bank how to restore Germany's economy and made a serious contribution in this regard in the financial terms. *What was Morgan's secret of success? To be in the right place in the right time.* So many presidents consulted with Morgan and then made financial decisions.

Another distinctive feature of Morgan was his way of interacting with people, as he would leave a strong influence on the interlocutor. It was said that looking into Morgan's eyes was the same as standing and looking at the train lights rushing towards you. Morgan would make his interlocutor talk, while he'd only answer yes or no. If somebody rejected Morgan' proposals during negotiations, he would earn a severe rebuke.

If someone rejected his statement, he'd receive a tough answer. For example, one of his colleagues once opposed Morgan's proposition and said he wanted to leave the syndicate. Morgan gave a terribly cold and sharp response. He told him that he could leave but that he would never again be able to work with them.

As to Morgan, he had little interest in public opinion and the preservation of at least a semblance of decency. His conversation with a legal counsel and prominent lawyer Elbert Gary is well known. To his lawyer's remark that the deal could not be done without breaking the law, Morgan answered,

"Well, I don't know as I want a lawyer to tell me what I cannot do. I hire him to tell how to do what I want to do."

If he addressed his teammate in this way, imagine how he treated his opponents. In fact, none of Morgan's colleagues knew what he was thinking about. He would not ask anyone for advice, and would always direct others on how things should be done. Just by being a closed person, he aroused interest in his personality. They say that during times of important issues and problems, Morgan wouldn't speak to anyone but take two packs of cards and close himself in his office.

Here he would shuffle the cards over and over until he found a new interesting solution to the problem. Being fond of reading, he financed and opened the Morgan Library. Thanks to him, it became the most visited library in the United States. John Morgan always repeated, "Go as far as you can see; when you get there, you'll be able to see farther."

John Morgan passed away on March 31, 1913. All the flags on Wall Street were lowered that day. After his death, Morgan's fortune was estimated around $80 million. Learning about this, Rockefeller said one of his most famous quotes,

"And to think, he wasn't even a rich man."

I very much like this anecdote related to John Morgan. Frankly, I don't know if it's real or not, but I will share with it because it's a great motivational story. At some point, a young, unknown businessman started sending letters to John Morgan. For about a year the stream of letters wouldn't stop. In his letters the young man pleaded with Morgan to receive him for at least for 10 minutes.

But in response he would receive a sharp "no."

After a year passed, the young businessman started asking for only a 5 minute meeting, "5 minutes that will change my life," he'd write in his letters. But Morgan responded to them with refusal as well, "My time is too precious, I can't allow myself to spend it without benefit." This rejection also didn't stop the young man. He stubbornly kept writing new letters. "Allocate me the time you spend to reach the car from your bank doors," he wrote.

Morgan's bank was based in Wall Street, and his car was always parked on Broadway. The daring young man knew about it and understood that if Morgan agreed he'd have several minutes at his disposal. After receiving the serial letter, the magnate was shocked at the young man's persistence and determination. Morgan decided to meet him and agreed to his latest proposal. On the appointed day and time the young man approached the bank doors.

He met the master of Wall Street with a calm smile. He introduced himself, and together they walked down the street to Morgan's car. During the whole walk, the young man would only look at Morgan, would slightly nod at times and smile quietly, without uttering a word. Reaching the car, surprised, Morgan was about to go into the car, but curiosity won. He asked,

"For more than a year you were going out of your way to meet me, now that you did it, you keep silent. How shall I understand it?"

"I don't need anything else," answered the young man, "tomorrow the whole Wall Street will talk that we were walking together, fondly smiling at each other. This means that all banks will agree to open unlimited credit accounts in my name."

By the way, John Morgan was of the same opinion. He did not reproach the young man for "cheating" him. On the contrary, he praised him for his wit, persistence, and attempts to find his place in life. He understood the boy - the boy was like him.

Secret 10. Do not sell your business or resources, but try to expand and take over the competitors' resources.

Secret 11

My first message is: Listen, listen, listen to the people who do the work.

Ross Perot

Examples of Motivating the Employees

Every company needs successful and loyal employees since, according to the heads of the companies, people are the biggest asset of the company. The best service can be provided only when you treat your employees well and fairly. People spend more time at the office than at home, and they want to get personal and professional satisfaction from it. And it is not just about money. They want to have the opportunity to grow, develop, and improve. They want their contributions and achievements to be recognized, and it is important for them to have a goal in their work and see meaning in what they do.

Companies do not realize that it is not enough to carry out activities for the recognition of the employees' contributions. It is not important for people to see signs stamped with their names or a title like "the vendor of the month" on the wall. What matters is how people are treated on a daily basis. Note that when you smile or greet people, then people, as a rule, smile back at you. Smiling is contagious. Try it. It's simple and it works.

I have included various examples of motivating the employees in the book (Google, Zappos, etc.), and I still have selected a whole range of examples in this secret as well. Here they are:

*1. **Praise your employees.** Praise is an important tool in helping the employees be loyal to the management and the whole company. It won't take too much from the management to say an additional "thank you" to an* *employee for the work he's done. In nearly all companies the employers notice their workers when they make mistakes. But why? We should notice the good work too, appreciate it, and say "THANK YOU."*

I really enjoy saying these words to my colleagues and employees every time they achieve something or do a good job. These words simply motivate all of us. Even if the employees make a mistake, it doesn't mean you have to offend, hurt or fire them. You have to explain their mistake and give them one more chance. As the chairman of Sony, Akio Morita, who would say, try again, because there are no infallible people.

According to an anecdote, IBM lost about $10 million because of a VP whose development project had failed. As the VP stood in Tom Watson's office expecting to be fired, this is what Watson, the CEO of IBM, told him, "You are certainly not leaving after we just gave you a $10 million education."

Of course, there are companies that are not as rich and won't turn a blind eye to such large numbers, but the idea is that everyone makes mistakes. Sometimes employees need to be given a chance.

2. Address the employee by name. In small companies, the managers know their employees by name. But with the constant increase in the number of employees there may be some difficulty remembering the names of all employees. The head of LiveInternet.ru portal Herman Klimenko recommends fixing the employees' names in the diary in case you are having problems remembering them all. The employees typically have worked in his company for 15-20 years, and experience shows that nothing sounds more pleasing to the ear than one's own name.

The CEO of luxury retail Mitchells/Richards/Marshs, Jack Mitchell, says that a good friend of his told him an instructive story. Once, the CEO of some company was inspecting the floor of a store where his friend was the head of a department. The CEO was looking for the supervisor and found her talking with one of the employees. She warmly welcomed the boss, who returned the greeting, then, without a glimmer of recognition, he glanced at the other employee and asked if he was new there. The employee had worked for the company for seven years. Can you imagine what he felt?

Before he was hired, that person passed the job interview in the CEO's presence, treated him with great respect, and worked hard, hoping that his contribution would be recognized and that he would be given a chance to grow and climb the corporate ladder. At that moment, he completely lost his motivation and simply felt crushed. Within a year, he resigned from the company. But things could have turned out differently had the boss said, "Hey, Bill, nice to see you! How are you?" Such cases are not uncommon in many companies.

Obviously, the management of a big corporation is not able to remember the names and interests of all employees who work for it. However, in order to create a cohesive and loyal work team, senior executives should pay far more attention to this issue than they usually do. A manager ought to know 100-150 employees personally. Actually, 250 is also not such an inflated number. Whatever happens, the names of these employees must be remembered, they are:

- your immediate supervisor;

- your direct subordinates;

- employees on whose work the realization of your plans largely depends.

The more people you know, the better. In this sense, the senior vice-president of human resources at General Electric, Bill Conaty, is a champion when it comes to remembering the names of the company's employees. GE's worldwide network includes 625 top executives, and Bill said he knows almost everyone. Bill personally knows the heads of the company's 185 offices, as well as their wives and children. And, of course, he is aware of their personal interests. Wow!

3. Provide extra holidays. *Many managers can confirm how important extra rest can be for employees. Effective managers grant compensatory time off, offer employees an opportunity to come to work later, or allow workers to leave earlier. These privileges are not always available for everyone – employees need to earn that right.* For example, the editorial staff of the "Director General" magazine allows the author of the week's most popular post on Facebook to leave earlier on Friday. Motivating the staff in this way has proven to be an excellent practice.

Certain companies, such as Google, which I already mentioned, or 3M, give their employees free time to engage in their own research. For almost 65 years 3M has given its employees the right to spend up to 15 percent of work time on their own projects. 3M believes that creativity needs freedom. That's why it encourages its employees to spend up to 15 percent of the paid time on their projects. They are allowed to use the company's resources, form special teams, and follow their intuitive insights in finding solutions to problems. On the basis of this program, such well-known projects as Post-it Notes adhesive and Trizact abrasive were created.

4. Give the employees the opportunity to express their opinions and be heard. *It is important for the employee to perceive the importance of his contribution in the overall development of the company. In addition to motivating the employees, this approach allows you to get quite useful ideas and recommendations from the employees, because they are much more familiar with what is working within the company, as they work directly with the clients. This approach will help management identify the company's weaknesses .*

The employees of the Virgin Group know the phone number of the company's owner, Richard Branson. Any employee can call him personally to offer a new idea. And there are around 35,000 employees in the company. This practice has been applied in the Virgin Group for a long time now. There's the case when in 1989, the airline's first in-flight beauty therapist, Jane Breeden, approached Richard Branson with the idea of offering the passengers on-board massage and manicure. The service was a success and became popular, and soon Breeden and Branson opened a beauty salon Body and Soul in London's Heathrow Airport.

It is advisable to show interest in the opinions and ideas of the employees. Many employees may really have useful and effective ideas, but no one seems to be interested in them. Although the majority of managers want their employees to share relevant thoughts and ideas, not all the managers know how to ask them to. They mostly just interrupt the employee and reject his initiatives, depriving the employee of self-confidence and motivation. To solve this problem, it is better to get a notebook, file, or other documents and note the ideas of the employees. Through such an approach, the leaders soon begin to listen to the staff, which can offer pretty good ideas.

In Disney there's a program called "I Have an Idea." If an employee offers a creative idea that turns out to be effective for the company he gets a bonus of about $100,000. *When the entrepreneurs don't listen to their employees, hundreds of ideas die; listen to each of them. Encourage the propositions. Accomplish them. Western and Japanese experience shows that the majority of new ideas are proposed by the employees. The examples, facts, and ideas of each employee helped me in making a decision. So consider their propositions.*

5. Give unexpected bonuses. Jack Mitchell says that many of their employees come to them not because they are sure they will be happy in the new workplace, but because it was bad at the previous workplace. The new employees confess that they worked hard for the company but were not appreciated. And they, in turn, did not experience any warm feelings towards the previous workplace. That's why if the employee has stood out as a good specialist (or simply because they believe that it's the right thing to do), they pay him a bonus even before the person has worked for six months. We are not talking about some dizzying sums. This bonus can be one hundred or three hundred dollars. But the joy one feels when receiving it is not comparable to the size of the sum. The thing is that no one expects to receive a bonus so early. Usually companies start paying bonuses at least a year after a worker has started. Therefore, any earlier bonus becomes a pleasant surprise.

6. Thank publicly. For example, the general director of the store chain "Favorite Children" goes around the offices in the central office every day, marking and thanking the employees who successfully handled their tasks. *It turns out that gratitude is much more important if it is supported by a useful gift. Public thanks is pleasant for the staff member.*

For instance, Stew Leonard's chain of supermarkets has the concept – Super Star of the month. All the employees gather in the store for the best one. They get balloons, which are thrown into the air. They clap, and the star is officially attached to the employee's garment. The best employee gets additional vacation days and bonus payments.

The Convention and Visitors Bureau travel company would conduct a survey with each tourist group to know which worker treated it friendlier and more courteously. And the best ones were rewarded by baseball, football or, say, American football tickets for the match of the week. At the end of the year, a lottery was held among all the best employees. The winner travelled to the Hawaiian Islands with his family.

7. Give awards. All employees expect to receive a variety of gifts, bonuses and premiums from the employer at the end of the year. These can be given for the achievement of the goals and plans, and they can enhance employee motivation. Jack Mitchell says that sometimes his company gives a gift certificate for dinner at a restaurant or for a game of golf. Tickets for sporting events might also be given. And the company always take into account the interests of the gift recipient. They have developed a bonus program for all the employees 2-4-6-8. The program is simple: If in the period from 10 November to Christmas the store sales increase by 2 percent compared with the same period of the previous year, all the employees receive a fixed bonus X, equal, say, to $250. If the sales increase by 4 percent, all the employees receive twice more, i.e. $500, and so on. Everyone receives a bonus - tailors, purchasing agents, employees at the reception desk. This stimulates the whole team.

The employees of Smith & Hawken, in addition to the monthly salary, receive dividends, as they have a significant number of shares.

In Sewell Village Cadillac, $100,000 is divided among the best mechanics. The chief executive of Next, Simon Wolfson, received a $3.6 million bonus for outperforming his planned yearly indicators. He then divided the money among the employees who had been in the company for 3 or more years, since it was due to their efforts that the company had overcome a crisis.

In the Four Seasons Hotels chain the employees are entitled to free accommodation at any of the hotels (even the most expensive ones) and a 50 percent discount on food. The length of stays, however, depends on the length of service. For example, the employees who have worked at Four Seasons for more than 10 years can stay at any hotel for 20 nights.

8. Celebrate the memorable occasions. Celebrate victories together with your employees with pizza, cake, or, say, champagne. Oleg Tinkov explains,

"Always celebrate success. If you have a victory, celebrating it enhances the team spirit. We celebrate every big occasion. For example, when Tinkoff Credit Systems released the millionth plastic card, we went to one of the most expensive islands with our managers and spent a good time with Richard Branson.

I have rewarded my employees since the years of khinkali production; we travelled to different parts of the world together, Jamaica, Sicily, Hawaii and more. All this removes people their sad, everyday lives and fills them with energy. Once again, I repeat, celebrate every occasion, be it the first customer or the ten millionth. No matter what reason it is, if there are any such occasions, then celebrate them with your team. It invigorates them."

Another great opportunity is the employee birthdays. Jack Mitchell says that when a team member's birthday approaches, he sends a personal greeting card to that person's home address, and on the day of birthday celebration, a cake appears at the store. They blow out the candles and eat the cake. That's why people come to work with them and stay with them, and, for all that time, the smiles do not leave their faces. *Be sure to celebrate the occasions.*

9. Show by your own example. Sometimes you need to serve as an example yourself. When the chairman of Louis Vuitton, Bernard Arnault, goes and starts sorting clothes at a store, things swing into high gear. Or let's say the same scene takes place Inditex when Amansio Ortega visits the stores. *When I was the head of a sales team, I personally met customers together with the sales professionals; seeing their manager selling invigorated them even more. And we indeed recorded a significant increase in sales.*

Jack Mitchell says that the best way to get people to do something is to do it together with them. Doreen Nugent in accounts payable likes to tell about one Christmas season when they had a huge influx of buyers and not enough sellers. Russ Mitchell asked Doreen to assist in sales. She was frightened. She had never sold or packed goods or even wrapped gifts in her life. Nevertheless, Doreen bravely agreed to help. Russ thanked her for that and asked to wrap the gifts. She paid attention to the fact that Russ was standing behind the counter serving the customers and wrapping the purchases and being part of the whole pre-Christmas rush. Doreen liked it very much. Russ taught her how to pack things. She realized the difference between working for someone and working with someone on the team. This helped her to better understand how Mitchell family's business worked and to build relationships with the employees she hadn't worked with before. And all that because she was asked and not forced to do it.

It's worth mentioning that at Mitchells' all are equal and all have responsibilities. No one gets a privilege just because his name is Mitchell. There's no rigid hierarchy: There are no reserved parking spaces or a special tables for the executives – because there are no such rooms in a regular home. The employees have offices that can be used by their colleagues while they are away on a business trip or vacation. Ed Mitchell would teach his sons to take out the trash and serve people coffee at the store just as if he were at home. Jack and Bill Mitchell and their sons live by this rule. The employees notice this.

10. Give people an opportunity to make independent decisions. *All the trainings and professionals of the service sector stress one important factor – allow your employees make decisions. The fact remains that the first employee who communicates with the client must meet his needs, serve, represent the product, leave a friendly impression etc. This means that the decision should be made during the first contact so that the customer receives quick feedback.*

The employees of Barnett Bank of Florida have been given such opportunities. Many decisions that were discussed and adopted by the head staff in the past are now made by the bank employees. Imagine the motivation of employees when they know that making the final decisions is up to them and that they do not depend on anyone.

Another interesting variant of motivation is implemented by the Merck Sharp & Dohme pharmaceutical company. The employees of the sales department are free to manage their time. The vice president of the company, Jerry Keller, explains, "Salespeople can take off early if they want to. But, in return, they routinely give their home phone numbers to physicians and stand ready 24 hours a day to answer questions or to fill emergency orders." *I'll address this in detail in Secret 55:*

11. Create a warm atmosphere. It is important for each company to create a warm environment inside. For example, Japan General Estate Co offered a cash prize of $3,000 for the manager who would establish the warmest relationships with the team. The conflicts were eliminated and the general atmosphere improved.

Toshiba periodically holds conferences where the staff members speak their minds without hiding anything. An interesting idea was developed in

Google and LinkedIn called "Take Your Parents To Work Days." The essence of this event is that the parents of the employees can visit their children and see where they are working and what they are doing. Another interesting technique is applied by Hyatt Hotels. It's called "Hyatt in Touch day" when company executives work alongside line employees - from president to mail room clerk - and carry bags, bus tables, make beds, etc. The purpose of this strategy is to be as close to the staff as possible and raise the corporate spirit. A *warm atmosphere can be achieved thanks to nice people, a topic I will present in more detail through Jack Mitchell's example.*

The principle of Jack Mitchell's attitude towards the staff is about being nice to them, trusting them, instilling pride in them, including them, and generously recognizing them. When thinking of their company's approach to work, Jack Mitchell quotes Nicholas M. Donofrio, Executive Vice President on Innovation and Technology of IBM Corporation, who says that at the end of each day he asks himself what good he did and how he made himself useful. Every morning Jack Mitchell would hear something similar from his father. The Mitchell's entire team is good towards one another and is used to making people feel good. While communicating, the managers and employees use the words "sorry," "please," and "can I help you?" On the whole, they use a lexicon of positive words in order to be attentive and nice to one another.

Jack Mitchell highlights the importance of behaving politely towards one another all the time and not on a case-by-case basis. It is much more fun to work with nice people, he believes, and it's much easier to behave politely and nicely in the presence of polite and nice people. That is why at Mitchell's people are hired primarily based on such personality traits and social skills, not their professional knowledge and love for the product. They will never hire a person with superb professional skills if he does not fit into the framework of the company's culture. They are of the opinion that nice people can usually acquire professional skills in the learning process. Nice people can be noticed at once: They act thoughtfully and are friendly and sincere. They smile, offer help to others, and take responsibility (without blaming others).

Hire nice people. During one period in my career I worked in a company where I did all kinds of work, including hiring people. For a month I couldn't hire anyone and the management started pressuring me. The reason was that

I couldn't find the nice person our team needed. Finally, after a long search, I found that nice person who didn't have the deep professional skills but was the one I was searching for. After the trainings he, indeed, performed excellently, and he has been working in that company for already three years . Let's keep discussing Jack Mitchell's experience.

Jack Mitchell believes that your feelings will guide you in deciding whether this or that person is nice. When asked where they find all those nice people, the answer is that many of them came to the company themselves because they wanted to work at Mitchell's. And many of them came on the recommendation of their best employees. The clients with whom they mingle often toss around ideas about candidates for new employees. The Mitchell team is constantly looking for good sellers when some other store closes. When Grossman, the main shoe store in Greenwich Village, closed, it let the staff learn about it just a week before closing. The Mitchell team quickly hired several people from among their best salespeople. In addition, the suppliers- friends of the Mitchell Company - always keep Mitchell aware of the young talents on other teams, thus expressing gratitude for the Mitchell's good treatment of them. No one is obliged to pass any type of probation period here. If the Mitchells hire a person, then that person is hired.

Usually from the first day of work, Mitchell's pays the employee more than he could receive from another employer. This already makes new hire feel good. Mitchell's has fewer employees as compared to their competitors, but they are all exceptional, their performance is higher than that of the competitors', which allows Mitchell's to pay its employees more with each year. And this scheme has operated successfully so far. Each time when Mitchell's compares its statistics with the statistics of the industry, Jack Mitchells divides sales by the total number of the employees and sees that his company is the most effective of all. If some are disappointed with the result, the Mitchells listen to them, explain the reasons, and change their goals and expectations. Only once in the whole history of the store, between 1989-1991, the Mitchells went through a difficult period when they had to freeze the wages and not pay bonuses.

Jack Mitchell recalls the meeting with the tailors when he was explaining to them why no one would receive any bonus or a raise. One of their tailors said that they trusted him and his family and understood that when the situation changed for the better, they would not only have a job, but a pay raise. Jack Mitchell is grateful that the employees understood and supported their policy, and that's because they had invested in them a lot. If tomorrow the company undergoes an economic downturn, Jack thinks that the majority of the team will support him in the same way they did in those difficult times. *It's this warm atmosphere that creates a strong connection between the employees and the employer, and they will definitely support the employer even in difficult times.*

12. Congratulate the new hires. Once you accept a new employee to work, it is important to do everything possible to make this person feel at home. *Imagine that you've just been hired and you receive congratulations from the management. Of course, you will get pleasant emotions.* Charles Geschke recalls how in Adobe's humble beginnings he and John Warnock would hand-deliver a bottle of champagne to the newly-hired employees. If the employee was a woman, they'd deliver a bottle of cognac for her husband, and if it was a man, they'd deliver a bouquet of roses for his wife.

Jack Mitchell sends congratulations to make the new hires feel good on their monthly, two-month, and three-month "anniversaries" in the company. They like it immensely. From time to time he wakes up in the morning with a desire to write a nice letter to one of his employees via e-mail.

The newly-hired correspondents at the New York Times have, as a rule, their "editor-partners." They select a staff member for this "position" who is, most of all, positively disposed towards the new colleague. The partner should invite the new employee to dinner, for which, of course, the company pays. In addition, the partner should answer all the questions that arise in the working process. If, say, the new employee is not from New York, the partner should explain the difference between the metro line W and the line 4, where you can buy the most delicious pizza, and who's the snub-nosed guy on TV reporting the national news. This is a most apparent example of showing attention to the person, who then starts to really feel part of the team and feel the care of the colleagues.

13. Create a sense of pride. Nevertheless, there is nothing that helps create loyalty as much as pride. It must be constantly maintained. Studies show that, after being hired, the employees feel proud for the initial period but that with time this feeling disappears. Companies often do not strive to maintain this sense of pride in their employees, even though that's what motivates them to continue working in the company and building a career in it. So how can a sense of pride in the company be built and maintained?

Sharon Behrens, director of customer service at Nike, has found an amazing and creative way to evoke a surge of pride in employees by using the history of their famous brand. She came up with the idea of hanging the posters of Nike's history and heritage between 1957-2006 in the resting rooms. On these posters one can see the important dates for the employees along with names that made Nike one of the most successful companies in the world. Imagine what the employee must feel at the sight of his own name and the date he started in the company next to the date when Michael Jordan signed a promotional contract with Nike.

There's a laudable tradition that exists in the Federal Express. Every time the company replenishes its air fleet with a new aircraft, it is given the name of a staff member's child. The name is chosen by drawing lots. Here's a good way to recognize employee achievements. The child is convinced once again that his mom or dad is the best, and it's so pleasant for the employee to see his or her child's name on the fuselage of the aircraft!

Now my question to you: What are you doing to motivate your employees?

Secret 11. Celebrate every significant event to raise team spirit.

"The world looks at me and says, 'Srikanth, you can do nothing.' I look back at the world and say 'I can do anything.'"

When Srikanth was born blind, the villagers in his community advised his parents to smother the baby. It was better than the pain they would have to endure throughout their lifetime. He was a "useless" baby without eyes. But his parents showed the utmost care and love and brought him up against all odds.

Since the nearest school in his village was five kilometers away, the blind boy had to make his way there mostly on foot, crossing all the muddy puddles when it rained and trying to avoid the vehicles. He did this for two years. At school he would often be pushed to the last bench, and no one would acknowledge his presence. He could not participate in the PT classes. He felt like the poorest child in the world, and it was not because of lack of money but because of loneliness.

Yet, Srikanth excelled in studies and finished his tenth grade with the highest results. He then decided to take up science but was prevented from doing so. The only stream blind people could take up was Arts. He filed a case and had to fight for nearly six months and was eventually allowed to pursue science. With the support of a teacher who converted all the lessons into audio clips, Srikanth scored an impressive 98 percent in his exams.

But his rejections didn't end. This time he was denied admission by the Indian Institutes of Technologies because he was blind. This did not break Srikanth either. He applied to schools in the United States and managed to secure an admission in Massachusetts Institute of Technology (MIT), where he was the first international blind student.

He launched Bollant Industries on his return to India and now employs more than 450 people. Bollant Industries is an organization worth millions that employs uneducated disabled employees to manufacture eco-friendly disposable consumer products and packaging solutions.

Srikanth also promoted Braille literacy, a digital library, and a Braille printing press/library to provide tutorial services for students with disabilities. Through it, he himself has mentored and nurtured over 3,000 students so far.

Angel investor Ravi Mantha was so impressed with Srikanth's business acumen and vision for his company that he decided to mentor him and also invested in Srikanth's company.

Srikanth Bolla, I am proud of you. You are indeed a strong-willed man and an example for all of us. Dear reader, create your own success story, nothing is impossible.

Vahagn Dilbaryan

Secret 12

"Success in any field, but especially in business, is about working with people, not against them."

Keith Ferrazzi

Keith Ferrazzi (Ferrazzi Greenlight)

People who have achieved success in a field of activity are well aware that it is possible to achieve perfection if only you have a good mentor. This applies to the world of business as well. In Secret 1, I talked about this. Success is not achieved alone. Now, through the example of Keith Ferrazzi, I'll illustrate in more detail how to network, what steps should be undertaken for that, and why nothing is impossible without connections.

Keith Ferrazzi was born in a town of steelworkers and miners. His father worked in the local steel mill, and his mother cleaned the homes of the doctors and lawyers in the nearby town. His mother would pick him up in their beat-up blue Nova, while the other children ducked into limos and BMWs. Being constantly teased about their car, about the clothes he wore and about his fake Docksiders, Ferrazzi was reminded of his life status daily. This life experience made him angry to be poor. He felt like an outcast in society, but these feelings pushed him work harder than anyone else around him. It was this hard work that allowed him to get into Harvard Business School.

Ferrazzi's father dreamed of a different life for his son. He knew that his son could live better and would not fail when it came to providing for the family's needs. One incident Ferrazzi recalls was when they were driving down the road to their home and his father spotted a broken tricycle in someone's trash. He stopped the car and came up to the house where the toy lay and knocked on the door:

"I spotted this Big Wheel in your trash," he told the owner, "Do you mind if I take it? I think I can fix it. It would make me feel wonderful to give my son something like this."

"Of course," the woman answered, explaining that her children were grown and no one needed the toy.

Now he had a "new" tricycle to ride. The hostess was left with a wonderful feeling in her soul that only benevolence gives. And his father taught Keith Ferrazzi a lesson that nothing should be feared. The father taught him that the worst anyone could say was no. Ferrazzi confesses that nothing in his life has created as many opportunities as a willingness to ask, whatever the situation. He recalls an incident when he was an anonymous attendee at an economic forum in Switzerland. He got on the hotel bus once and saw Phil Knight, the founder of Nike, who was like a rock star for Ferrazzi. Was he nervous? Yes. But he immediately jumped at the opportunity to talk to him and sat next to him. Later on, Knight became the first major client of his firm YaYa. And this is how Ferrazzi acts in any situation.

Sometimes Ferrazzi fails. He's got a long list of people with whom he tried to establish relationships, but they showed no interest. Ferrazzi's advice for creating an enriching circle of trusted relationships would be to be *out there,* in the mix, all the time. Up to now he feels a sort of fear of being rejected when he has to call or introduce himself to someone he doesn't know. But in these moments he remembers the tricycle his father gave him and pushes ahead anyway. *Not trying means being in a state of uncertainty; trying allows you to know whether it works or not. So do not be afraid to go ahead.*

One's circle of communication largely determines what a person will become. Harvard professor David McClelland studied character traits and personal qualities of the most successful and prosperous people and came to the conclusion that a person's circle of communication is one of the key factors in that person's future success or failure. In other words, if you come into contact with successful people, your chances for success increase significantly. *It's like visiting a perfume store. You walk among the shelves and choose a perfume. When you leave, your clothes smell of perfume. If, say, you went into a store selling leather clothes, you smell of leather as you leave. The same is with communication. Diffusion and interpenetration happen. Mingle more with successful, positive people and you will be enhance your own energy, enthusiasm and self-confidence. Do you want to be confident? Mingle with the confident people or read their biographies. Want to make money? Mingle with the rich. Do you want to have fun? Mingle with cheerful people. You'll understand at once that any conversation, movie, or song affects your mood and psychological outlook.*

As a kid, Ferrazzi worked as a caddie at the local golf club, carrying the bags of the wealthy homeowners and their kids. During this period he often wondered why some people succeed in life and others do not. And he made an observation that changed his world view. He was observing how these people who had reached professional heights his parents couldn't dream of were helping each other. They found one another jobs; they invested time and money in one another's ideas; they helped their kids to get into the best schools and get the best internships, and, ultimately, the best jobs. All this made Ferrazzi more convinced that success breeds success and that the rich get richer. He realized that poverty is not just a lack of financial resources but isolation from a certain circle of people who can help you realize your own abilities.

He came to believe that life, like golf, is, in a sense, a game. People who know the rules well play the best and achieve success. And one of the most important rules of life is that by knowing the right people and being able to utilize these connections, you can become a member of the "club" even if you started out as a caddie. He realized that intelligence, talent and where you come from matter less. Of course, they are important, but they mean little if you don't understand one thing: "You can't get there alone."

Ferrazzi first realized the great potential of human relationships through Mrs Pohland. Being her caddie, he did everything possible so that she won every tournament. Early in the morning he would walk the entire course to mark all the tough pin placements; he would test the speed of the greens. Soon Mrs Pohland started winning right and left. Ferrazzi did such great job for her that she began to brag about him to her friends, and they would also request him. For several years, he actually became a member of the Pohland family, spending entire weekends with them and visiting their house almost every day. *Many would just do their job, but Keith did more than was expected of him. Whatever work you do, exceed expectations and you will have the desired result.*

Mrs Pohland introduced Ferrazzi to all the club members who could assist him, and if she noticed that he was slacking, she'd tell him about it. He helped Mrs Pohland on the golf course, and she helped him in life, appreciating his efforts and care for her. From her he learned a simple but important lesson about the power of generosity: "When you help others, they often help you."

Successfully applying the power of human relationships in his career for many years, Ferrazzi came to understand that connecting is one of the most important skills in business and in life. The reason is that people are more willing to do business with those they know and love. A career in any field is built on the same principle. So according to him, even our well-being and happiness, as shown by multiple studies, depend on the support, guidance and love we get from the community we build for ourselves.

Today, Ferrazzi has phone numbers of more than 5,000 people he can call any time. They can offer him expertise, jobs, help, encouragement, support, and even care and love. The most successful people he knows do not always stand out by some special talent, education or personal charm. But each of them has a circle of reliable, talented, and inspirational advisers who they can call upon. But as Ferrazzi points out, to create such a circle of friends, you have to work hard. He understood this as a child, working as a caddie. For this, one needs to think not only about himself but also about others. So before getting something, you must give something. And it's not necessary to keep score of the good things you've done. If your relationship is based on generosity, the reward will not make you wait too long.

Ferrazzi draws attention to the idea accepted in business that your best customers are the customers you have now. The highest returns don't come from new sales; they come from the customer base you already have. As they are part of your network, it's easiest to reach out to those people. The biggest hurdles in networking arise when you have to deal with the unknown. However, your first step in forming a circle of useful contacts does not have to do with strangers. Ferrazzi recommends connecting with the people you already know.

So first we should focus on our immediate network: friends of friends, old acquaintances from school, and family members. Do we ever ask our cousins, brothers, or brothers-in-law if they know anyone they could introduce us to who could help us in some way in realizing our goals? Ferrazzi makes it clear that everyone from our family to our mailman is a portal to an entirely new set of folks. So we shouldn't wait until we're jobless or think of opening our own business. We should start building network before we need it. Executives of large companies are well aware that if they want to achieve something in politics or business, they need the help of like-minded people. And the more influential and the richer they are, the more can be achieved through joint efforts. *No one succeeds alone.*

Mentoring became important for Ferrazzi early in his career. He was in his second year at business school. The consulting company Deloitte, where he had been interning during summer, was having its annual end-of-the-summer cocktail party. And he saw "this big, gruff, white-haired guy" surrounded by a bunch of partners and senior staff.

Ferrazzi went up to this man standing in the center, introduced himself, and asked straightforwardly, "Who are you?" He said he was the CEO of the firm with a tone signaling that Ferrazzi should have known it.

"Well I guess I should have known that," Ferrazzi responded.

"Yeah, I guess you should have," he said. He introduced himself as Pat Loconto.

"Loconto?" Ferrazzi said, "That's a good Jewish name, isn't it?" He laughed, and they spoke the little Italian they knew. They talked about their families; there were a lot of similarities in their biographies.

That night he stayed up late with the senior partners. Ferrazzi was natural, without pretending to be someone he wasn't. His parents had taught him to speak as little as possible in these situations. After all, the less you say, the more you hear. From an early age these rules of conduct were instilled in Ferrazzi.

Only in this way can you learn something from others and notice nuances in the course of the conversation that will help later in establishing deeper relationship with them.

After graduating from the business school, Ferrazzi interviewed with different companies, and his final choice was between McKinsey and Deloitte. Everything changed when Pat Loconto called him and convinced him to accept their offer. Finally, Ferrazzi agreed. At the beginning he still had doubts whether it was the right decision; McKinsey was much more prestigious than Deloitte in those days. But with time he understood that it was the best move in his life. First, at Deloitte, he was given more responsibilities, and he learned more about consulting in eight years than many manage to learn in twenty. Secondly, he had direct access to the senior partners. Third, he realized that finding a talented and experienced mentor who was willing to invest his time and effort to help him develop as a person and professional was more important than high salary and prestige.

Working with Pat Loconto and his right-hand man Bob Kirk was easy. They taught Ferrazzi many valuable lessons: "that bold ideas weren't enough if they couldn't be executed, that the details are as significant as the theories, that you had to put people first, all people, not just the ones above you."

Ferrazzi admits that Pat should have fired him a few times. But instead, Pat spent his time and effort to make Ferrazzi a good executive and leader. And, yes, he did this for the firm and for the sake of his role as a mentor. This requires some reciprocity. It can be expressed by the hard work or loyalty that you give in return. Ferrazzi admits he owes much to Pat Loconto. He wouldn't be the man he is without Pat.

"The best way to approach utility is to give help first, and not ask for it." Following Ferrazzi's principle, if, say, you need someone's knowledge, find a reason to be helpful to this person. Consider the person's needs and think about how you can help. If you can't help personally, you can try to contribute to the person's company, charity or social activities. You should be ready to give back to your mentors for all the good they have done for you, and let them know about it from the outset. Before Pat agreed to invite Ferrazzi to Deloitte, he was to hear that the young man would be committed to his company. This allowed Ferrazzi to establish a trusting relationship with him from the outset, a relationship that later grew into a friendship.

Becoming responsible for marketing at Deloitte, Ferrazzi now had many employees. Yet instead of treating his employees as partners with whom he could achieve his long-term objectives, he saw them as called upon to carry out his tasks. The tasks that, in his opinion, could be completed in a few hours took days. He realized that something must be undertaken, and so turned to an executive coach, Nancy Badore. Ferrazzi asked her what a real leader should be like. When she spoke, it struck him to the core:

"Keith, look at all the pictures on your wall. You talk about aspiring to become a great leader, and there's not one picture in your whole office of anybody but you: you with other famous people, you in famous places, you winning awards. There's not one picture in here of your team or of anything that might indicate what your team has accomplished that would lead anybody like me to know that you care for them as much as you care for yourself. Do you understand that it's your team's accomplishments, and what they do because of you, not for you, that will generate your mark as a leader?"

Her words just floored Ferrazzi. He knew she was absolutely right. He wondered why he hadn't ever shown concern for the lives of his employees outside of work or why he hadn't made them part of his plans. From the first day he devoted all his attention only to the bosses. At that moment he realized that his long-term success depended on the people around him and that he worked for them as much as they worked for him. And he changed his attitude.

Ferrazzi's career was taking off. After leaving Deloitte, he became the youngest chief marketing officer in the Fortune 500 at Starwood Hotels & Resorts, after which he became CEO of Knowledge Universe, a video game company, and then he created his own company, Ferrazzi Greenlight, a sales and marketing consulting and training firm to the most prestigious brands around the world. As Ferrazzi says, he zigged and zagged his way to the top, but every time he thought about his next moves or needed advice, he turned to the circle of friends whom he had himself created around him.

According to Ferrazzi, connecting is a philosophy of life. Its main principle is that every person is an opportunity to help and to be helped, as no one gets ahead in this life without help. There's this interaction he had with Hank Bernbaum, the CEO of High Sierra, a small firm that manufactures bags. Hank had read about Ferrazzi in the magazine Fast Company, so he called him and said, "The article on you was excellent." Now he had Ferrazzi's attention. He went on telling that he owned a small company that had the best duffel bags in America, but no one knew it. Their revenue and market size was a quarter of what it should be. So he asked Ferrazzi to help them with marketing, even though they didn't have much money to offer.

One of the things Ferrazzi likes to do is connect two people from different parts of his life who might benefit from knowing each other. Hank needed a consultant, and his bags needed exposure. Ferrazzi called Peter, a consultant and great marketer who had worked with him at Starwood. Then he called another friend who was head of marketing at Reebok, whose bags didn't sell as well as its other products. So Ferrazzi thought that they could exchange experiences and ideas and that would both benefit from it. He arranged a meeting and brought Hank along to introduce them to each other.

Then he asked Hank if he'd ever had any publicity. It turned out he hadn't. Ferrazzi sent a couple of Hank's products to Alan Webber, the editor of Fast Company. After a few months, the magazine did a piece on High Sierra products. Hank was delighted. But the story is not over yet. Ferrazzi told Hank that the calls he was doing on his behalf had to be done by Hank himself. "Do you belong to the Executive Club in Chicago?" he asked.

"I've been thinking about it. Why?" was Hank's answer. Ferrazzi told Hank he needed to meet people and stop thinking of himself and his company as an island. He said that there were a lot of CEO's and smart people in the Executive Club who could have done for him what Ferrazzi was doing years ago. He said that making these connections was a necessity.

Shortly thereafter, Hank began to form his own network of contacts. His products were superb. He just lacked the network. Ten years later, a major manufacturer of bags and suitcases, Samsonite, bought Hank's company for $110 million. This story benefitted Ferrazzi's former colleague Peter too, who used the experience to build the confidence he needed to start his own business. Today he has a thriving consulting firm in New York. And the CMO at Reebok was grateful for a meeting that might help him boost his bag business. All this started with one man and one problem and ended with many solutions for several people.

Ferrazzi's point in all this is that "Real power comes from being indispensable." You share contacts, goodwill, and as much information as possible with as many people as possible in as many different worlds as possible. For this purpose, Ferrazzi quotes Dale Carnegie: You can be more successful in two months by becoming really interested in other people's success than you can in two years trying to get other people interested in your own success. *Create connections, and those connections will help you solve problems. No one achieves success alone.*

We talked so much about the importance of connections. And now a question arises – where to start? This is what Keith Ferrazzi advises. First, you should concentrate on people who are already part of your existing network. You might not even have an idea how vast and widespread the list really is:

Relatives

Friends of relatives

All your spouse's relatives and contacts

Current colleagues

Members of professional and social organizations

Current and former customers and clients

Parents of your children's friends

Neighbors, past and present

People you went to school with

People you have worked with in the past

People in your religious congregation

Former teachers and employers

People you socialize with

People who provide services to you

Get to know the players in your field. When Ferrazzi started working at YaYa, he used to read all the trade magazines having to do with advertising and games. When there was someone who fell into his categories mentioned in an article, he would write out his name and find contact information. For instance, some newspapers and magazines do rankings all the time. Even before Ferrazzi became one of Crain's "40 under 40," he used to rip out that list for years. He would include in his list top CEOs, most admired marketers, and progressive entrepreneurs. Ferrazzi advises not only to get to know the players in your field but also to be recognized as one of those players.

There's one more category that can be added to this list. Ferrazzi calls them "aspirational contacts." These are extremely high-level people who don't really have anything to do with the business you do right now but are interesting to you. They can be heads of state, media moguls, artists, actors, etc. Ferrazzi has a separate list for them. For instance, you could find the contact information for Richard Branson on it, chairman of the Virgin company. Ferrazzi doesn't know him yet, but would like to.

As Winston Churchill said, "Preparation is – if not the key to genius – then at least the key to sounding like a genius." Before Ferrazzi meets new people, he researches who they are and what their business is. He tries to find out what's important to them. It can be their hobbies, problems, and goals both in business and in personal life. Usually Ferrazzi or his assistants prepare a one-page summary on the person he's going to meet. It includes anything that can characterize his personal qualities, interests and major achievements in life.

You should be up-to-date on the person or a company you're going to establish a relationship with regarding things like their quarterly performance and new products. Ferrazzi points out the fact that it's human nature for people to care little about anything beyond their own business, and if you are informed enough to step into their world, it will be much appreciated, especially since doing such research is easy these days. You can get information about the person using search engines like Google or read his brief biography. You can learn about his work experience in LinkedIn, etc. In their biographies in LinkedIn, people indicate the professional achievements they are most proud of. That will probably be helpful to you to get a notion of the person's goals. Also, pay attention to their recent activity on the site, and so on.

To establish connections you need contact, and for contact you need to take initial steps. That is, you need to know what to do to when you come into contact with an unfamiliar person. This is not that easy, because everybody is busy.

Here are the steps advised by Keith Ferrazzi:

1. Warming the cold call – *On the B2B platform, one of the most important conditions for a successful deal is the meetings; in many fields it's needless to talk of sales if there are no meetings. The most important factor in having a successful meeting is talking with the right person, i.e., the decision maker.* Calling a stranger can lead even the most balanced people to a state close to neurosis. Ferrazzi says he can even relate to those people. You will always have some percentage of fear, because no one can rule out the possibility of being rejected. And there are always a hundred reasons to procrastinate. So you should just plunge right in. If you don't believe in the result you want to achieve by the call, then you probably won't. So his advice for you is to be brave, "You have to envision yourself winning to win." The calls to unknown people are often called "cold calls." But as Ferrazzi says, he never calls cold; he has created strategies that ensure his calls are always warm.

He gives the example of his friend Jeff Arnold, the founder of WebMD. A while ago they had bought out the rights and patents for a technology that puts digital content on a miniature DVD for a unique delivery. In talking with Jeff and his partner, Ferrazzi learned that they had just closed a deal with a movie theater company and wanted to work with Sony. But because they didn't know whom to contact at Sony, they came to Ferrazzi for advice.

He had met the Howard Stringer, CEO of Sony, several times, so he put a call into his office. Even without waiting until Howard contacted him, Ferrazzi decided to find other paths as well. At the time, he had no one else at Sony who could hook him up with someone entitled to make decisions. He decided to contact an agency that serviced Sony and found out that a marketing agency named Brand Buzz counted Sony among its top clients. It then turned out that the agency was headed by Ferrazzi's close friend, John Partilla. *If you can't find specialists you can contact, try to reach their partners. You may find common acquaintances and find the contacts more easily.*

So Ferrazzi called him:

"Hey, John, I've got two things for you. One, I want you to meet a buddy of mine named Jeff Arnold. He's the guy who founded WebMD, and he's started a new company, Convex Group, which may need your services down the line. And two, Convex is putting out this incredible technology that distributes digital content in a new way. I think Sony would appreciate being aware of it."

In fact, he was offering John two opportunities: first, to meet a person who could be useful for him in the future; second, to look good with his business partner, Sony, by revealing new prospects for the company. John was happy to make the connection. He knew exactly the one they needed - the head of Media and Internet strategies at Sony, Serge Del Grosso. Now John was just as interested in Ferrazzi's meeting with Serge. Serge was busy though, and Keith wouldn't get any answers after several e-mails. In this case, Ferrazzi's advice is, "You have to put your ego aside and persist in calling or writing." Sometimes, setting up such meetings takes time. And you must be the one to take the initiative.

Having received no response after several weeks, Ferrazzi called Sony information and got Serge's direct line. Whenever he calls someone he hasn't spoken with before, he's prone to do it at an unusual time. The reason is that they are more likely to pick up their own phone if you call, say, at 8:00 A.M. or 6:30 P.M. In addition, at this time they will be less stressed than during normal working hours. *A pharmacist in a pharmaceutical company had achieved significant results in sales and performed better than his 650 colleagues. When asked how he achieved such a result, he answered that at the end of each working day he would make an extra call because he wanted very much to be the first. He usually made all the calls in the morning, but every day before going home, he would put on his coat and make one more call to set up a meeting. Thus, at the end of the week, he had greater number of meetings than his colleagues. Now that's an effective method, one also used by Keith Ferrazzi.*

So Ferrazzi called Serge early in the morning but got Serge's voice mail. He then called Serge's direct line at around 6 P.M. This time Serge picked up the phone himself and Ferrazzi spoke about his proposition:

"Hi, Serge, it's Keith Ferrazzi. John's talked highly of you for some time and I've finally got a nice excuse to give you a call. I'm calling for my friend Jeff Arnold, the founder of WebMD, who has a new, very powerful way to distribute digital content. With some of the new products you'll be launching this quarter, it could make for the perfect partnership. I'll be in New York next week. Let's get together. Or, if getting together this trip isn't convenient, I'll make room in my schedule for whenever it's more convenient for you."

In fifteen seconds he used his four rules for "warm calling."

He conveyed credibility by mentioning a familiar person or institution - in this case, John, Jeff, and WebMD.

He stated his value proposition - Jeff's new product would help Serge sell his new products.

He imparted urgency and convenience by being prepared to do whatever it takes whenever it takes to meet the other person on his or her own terms.

He showed willingness to offer a compromise that secures a definite follow-up at a minimum.

Secret 12. If you need someone's knowledge, or some help, then find a reason to be helpful to this person.

Secret 13

Spectacular achievement is always preceded by unspectacular preparation.

Robert Schuller

Keith Ferrazzi (Ferrazzi Greenlight)

The next week Ferrazzi was in Serge's office. Although his budget didn't allow a short-term application, he clearly understood its opportunities for his audience. Below are some rules Ferrazzi follows when calling someone for the first time.

A. Draft off a reference.

Establishing credibility is the main thing that you should do during the first contact with the person. Nobody is going to buy something from you unless they trust you. If you have a mutual friend or an acquaintance, you will no longer be considered an absolute stranger. If you call on behalf of the president, you can be sure the person on the other end of the line is going to listen to you attentively. Drafting off personal references of organizations helps a lot to overcome someone's initial reluctance.

But most of us can't boast of the fact that we work for Microsoft or know the company president we want to reach out to. In this case, Ferrazzi's advice is to go through our network of communications – friends, family, customers, neighbors, classmates, associates and church members - and see who can help us find a path to the person we want to meet. When we mention a mutual friend in a conversation, all of a sudden the interlocutor has obligation not only towards us but also to the person we both know.

Ferrazzi gives the example of "six degrees of separation." You might have heard of it. It presupposes that, theoretically, information can be conveyed to anyone on the planet through a chain of six acquaintances. This idea was put forward by social psychologist Stanley Milgram in 1967. He conducted an experiment that proved that our big world is actually quite small and friendly. He sent a package to a few hundred arbitrarily selected individuals in Nebraska asking them to forward the package to an anonymous target person in Boston. Each of the participants was allowed to forward the packet to only one of his acquaintances, who, in his opinion, stood closer to the target person.

About a third of all letters reached their destination after an average of six mailings. When all those chains were analyzed, it turned out that a majority of letters passed through the hands of three residents of Nebraska. This points to the fact that if you want to create an efficient network of connections, it is best to know just a few super-connectors. Such people can be found in every profession, but Ferrazzi singles out seven professions where they mostly congregate (restaurateurs, headhunters, lobbyists, fundraisers, public relations people, politicians, journalists). Each one them is a link for him to a new world of people, ideas, and information that makes his life more interesting and his business more successful.

In 1999, the journalists of the newspaper Die Zeit decided to carry out an experiment in order to check how small our world really is. To do this, they wanted to know how many "handshakes" are shared by two randomly selected people raised in totally different cultures in different countries with different living conditions. To make the experiment more effective, they chose an owner of a simple diner selling kebabs in Frankfurt as point A, and chose his favorite actor, Marlon Brando, as point B. The search took several months, but as a result the chain of acquaintances turned out to be remarkably short. The owner of the diner – his friend that had left for California – his friend's colleague – the colleague's girlfriend – her friend from college – her father, producer of the film Don Juan DeMarco in which Brando starred. The owner of a small kebab diner who had emigrated to Europe from Iraq was separated only by six "handshakes" from one of the greatest actors in the history of cinematography.

A database research of 720 million Facebook users, completed in 2011, identified the magic number 4.74. In LinkedIn that number would be 3. Like it or not, we are all at a distance of a few mouse clicks from one another.

B. State your value

When someone has agreed to listen to you for thirty seconds, you need to manage to tell them that you can be useful for them. We'll have little time to explain to the other party why they shouldn't get off the phone as quickly as possible. What's more, before contacting people, the first thing to do is to gather information about the company or industry they work for and about the products they offer the consumers. When Ferrazzi finally had the chance to talk to Serge, he already knew that in the following quarter he was preparing to launch new products and would need help. He also knew that this production was aimed at the customers going to the theaters. And he used that fact.

C. Talk a little, say a lot. Make it quick, convenient, and definitive.

You must insist that your encounter take place as soon as possible. This is how Ferrazzi would finalize the conversation, "I'm going to be in town next week. How about lunch on Tuesday? I know this is going to be important for both of us, so I'll make time no matter what." Of course, you should give the person enough information about your value proposition. Another important factor is not to forget that it is a dialog, not a scripted monologue. Ferrazzi left time even for interjections like "ah, huh, yes" or "hmm," in his fifty-second intro to Serge, because the person must be given time to come along with you.

What's important to remember, according to Ferrazzi, is that in most cases, the purpose of the cold call is not to close a contract, but to get an appointment where everything can be discussed in more detail. In his experience, deals, like friendships, are made only one-to-one, face-to-face.

D. Offer a compromise.

On this point Ferrazzi suggests that in any informal negotiations you will only win if you demonstrate a willingness to compromise. Ferrazzi finished his telephone conversation with Serge by suggesting that they meet, given their mutual friend's admiration and respect, even if he didn't want to hear anything about digital content. One example to illustrate this point concerns Boy Scouts who are trying to sell raffle tickets; people often turn them down, but when the scouts offer candy bars instead at a lower price, customers buy the candy, even if they don't need it at all. By conceding, people feel as if they are fulfilling their social obligation to others. So to settle for what you really need, Ferrazzi advises trying for a lot first.

Sometimes one of the hardest obstacles we face during cold calls is the secretary. The role of the secretary within the company is important, but it becomes even more important when you have to seek access to the company from the outside. It happened so that about twenty ad salespeople wanted to meet with Ferrazzi at the same time to make a sale. Among them was Kent Blosil from Newsweek. Ferrazzi had a special media buyer at the agency who took those meetings for him, so Ferrazzi never met with ad sales representatives himself. But Kent was not like the rest. He knew what authority a secretary has in an organization. Kent would call Jennifer once a week. From time to time he would bring a box of chocolates or a bouquet of flowers for her. However, Ferrazzi saw no reason to meet with him. Kent was scheduled on Ferrazzi's calendar more than ten times without Ferrazzi's knowledge. Ferrazzi would cancel it every time. But Jennifer wouldn't calm down, and she kept supporting her friend, because she believed that he was different from the others and had a more innovative approach. And once Jennifer said.

"You're going to meet with him. You can take five minutes out of your day. He's very nice and creative and worth five minutes."

Ferrazzi gave in this time. Kent was indeed a nice man. And most importantly, he had come to the meeting prepared with an excellent understanding of Ferrazzi's business and with a value proposition. The first words he uttered were,

"If it's ok with you, I would like to introduce you to the top three senior editors of *Newsweek*. Would you be interested in that?"

"Of course," Ferrazzi said.

"By the way, we're having a conference in Palm Springs where some other CMOs are getting together with our editors and reporters. It's going to be a really good conference about media strategies in the New Economy. Can I put you on the guest list?"

It was really a value proposition for Ferrazzi, as many of the participants of the conference could become potential Deloitte customers.

"Yeah, I'd like to go to that."

"Also, I know your media guy has been evaluating a proposal we put in a few months ago. I'm not going to waste your time with the details. I just want you to know that it would be great if we could do business together sometime." This is how the five-minute meeting with Kent came to an end. During this short time he managed to present the information that contained 98 percent gain for Ferrazzi and two percent for him. After he left, Ferrazzi called his media guy and told him,

"Go to *Newsweek*. Quote them a fair price relative to the other magazines we were considering, and give them our business in this segment. Make it work."

So what is the moral of this story that Keith Ferrazzi tells us? Always respect the power of secretaries, or gatekeepers, as Ferrazzi calls them. In this case, all the doors and offices of decision makers will be open for you. You might ask what it means to show respect to them. It's about acknowledging their help, thanking them by phone, flowers, a note. And then he adds that there are times when niceties and small gifts are not enough. At times, in order to get a meeting, you'll need to use street smarts. The next method is about mailing, how to write a letter to a stranger.

2. How to warm your e-mail – A question that bothers many of us is how to write to someone for the first time. Many people avoid telephone conversations as a means of communication in general. They say that e-mail is much more effective. Of course, it's not so. But people still think so because it's become a habit for them to waste time checking e-mail. The first rule of the first contact is to communicate with the person in a manner preferable for that person. If e-mail is preferred, then send an e-mail.

A. Carefully consider the subject line. If you fail to express it clearly, your letter will likely remain unread. State your value proposition for the recipient or mention an acquaintance uniting you. Awaken interest towards you.

B. Choose the right time. There are different opinions on this point. Ferrazzi prefers to send letters at a time when his addressee is most probably checking his mail. As a rule, that is the beginning or the end of the working day, as well as lunch.

C. Be concise. Write your draft. Then cut it in half. Yes, our perception of our interestingness has to be shortened by half. Your letter should fit on the screen. If the person has to scroll it, he'll lose interest before he gets to the point.

D. Clearly express a call to action - What kind of action do you expect from the recipient? Rather than simply suggesting to stay in touch, ask for a telephone conversation of fifteen minutes. Rather than offering to meet in the near future, suggest meeting at a specific place and time. Cut corners wherever possible, and do not make the other person guess what you wanted from him.

E. Read the letter aloud. – One of Ferrazzi's assistants always read her letters aloud before sending them. He would laugh at this. But he admits that she did a wise thing. She listened to her own words to make sure that the language of the letter was simple and not too formal. In addition, she took the time and shortened the letter, so that it'd take not more than 45 seconds to read.

F. Check your spelling. – Typos and grammatical errors are not allowed in a letter. Ferrazzi has written two books, and his name is used in his domain name, and all the same people write his name with one r, "Ferazzi." Of course, this leaves a bad impression.

3. Go to conferences. – Those who get the most out of conferences stand head and shoulders above their colleagues in the industry. While some sit quietly at the conferences, taking some notes and drinking free water, others arrange meetings and use the conference exclusively to mingle with people who can change their lives. And if you give a speech at the conference, then you get a special status that helps you connect with people. All participants have a desire to talk to you or just to greet you. You begin to be respected, and when you stand at the podium, your words are treated with great respect.

A. Draft off a big kahuna - If you're not familiar with the most popular member of the conference – the one who knows everyone and whom everyone knows – then get to know him. These people can be among conference organizers, speakers, heads of large companies, and other professionals. Check the conference program for the names of the key figures. Ferrazzi's advice is to talk with the speakers before their speech on the stage. Very often inconspicuous people at the breakfast table will become celebrities after their speeches the next day. So find such people before they've gained celebrity status. In this case, you have a better chance to meet them. If you don't know the people by sight, you can ask the organizers to point them out.

B. Know your targets – You are ready to make contact with the person. Now you have to determine with whom exactly. At each conference Ferrazzi keeps a list on a piece of paper in his pocket of three or four people he'd most like to meet. Then he makes notes in front of their names about what they talked about and how he's going to contact them later. And throughout the conference whenever he meets one of those people, they find themselves chatting again and again.

4. Find your "anchor tenant" – Each one of us has a certain well-established social circle. But if you have dinner parties with the same people over and over again, your circle of relationships won't grow. On the other hand, if you invite random people to your parties, especially those who stand higher than your usual circle of friends in prestige and experience, it is unlikely to produce a positive effect. Such people prefer to communicate with their equals in origin, experience and social status.

There's always that person amongst our acquaintances who falls out of the core circle of friends. Each of us, in varying degrees, maintains relationships with older, wiser and more experienced people. They are often our mentors, friends, parents, teachers, pastors or bosses. Ferrazzi calls them "anchor tenants." They mingle with different people and have a different set of experiences. So one can learn a lot from them. Having found such a person outside your core group of friends and inviting him to dinner pays terrific dividends. He will allow you to reach out to people beyond your circle next time who wouldn't normally come to you.

5. Follow up or fail. – If you meet a person you later want to maintain a relationship with, then you must at least undertake something so that your image is not immediately erased from his memory. For instance, when Ferrazzi was in Florida at an awards ceremony of his college fraternity, Sigma Chi, he probably gave his card and e-mail address to about a hundred people. As he checked his e-mail next morning, a message from a young member of the fraternity caught his eye, in which he thanked Ferrazzi for his speech, telling him what impression it made on him. He added that he hoped they would sit down for a cup of coffee one day. Over the next two weeks, Ferrazzi received hundreds of similar letters and phone calls, but he remembers best the follow-up he got first.

The most memorable gifts Ferrazzi ever received in his life cannot be measured in dollars and cents. Those are the heartfelt letters from people thanking him for his guidance and advice. And if you want to stand out from the crowd in the eyes of some person, the best way, according to Ferrazzi, is to follow up after a meeting. Unfortunately, not everyone is good at this, although this is one of the basic networking skills. "Good follow-up alone elevates you above 95 percent of your peers. In fact, follow-up is the key to success in any field."

Ferrazzi advises making it a rule to get in touch with a new acquaintance within 12-24 hours after meeting them. For example, if you meet someone on a plane, send them an e-mail that same day. If you met someone over a cocktail, contact them next morning. E-mail is an excellent tool for random encounters to tell them, "It was a pleasure meeting you. We must keep in touch." In these cases, you can also cite something you talked about, something you had in common, which will remind them of who you are.

An e-mail reminder can be supplemented with a request to add you to their contacts on LinkedIn, if your new acquaintance is registered on the site. After leaving the meeting, you can put the name and address of the new acquaintance in your database and set the program to remind you in a month's time to send the person one more e-mail. What's more, by a handwritten thank, you can capture the person's attention. We don't really get handwritten letters often these days. When you see that it's addressed to you and only to you, you will open and read it. The thank-you note always gives the relationship a sense of warmth and kindness. You can also specify in it some important point that wasn't mentioned during the conversation. In any case, the note should reflect your desire to meet with this person again, as well as your offer to help.

Here are a few more reminders of what to include in your follow-ups from Keith Ferrazzi:

Always express your gratitude.

Be sure to include an item of interest from your meeting or conversation – a joke or a shared moment of humor.

Reaffirm whatever commitments you both made – going both ways.

Be brief and to the point.

Always address the thank-you note to the person by name.

Use e-mail and snail mail. The combination adds a personalized touch.

Timeliness is key. Send them as soon as possible after the meeting or interview.

Many people wait until the holidays to say thank you or reach out. Why wait? Your follow-ups will be timelier, more appropriate, and certainly better remembered.

Don't forget to follow up with those who have acted as the go-between for you and someone else. Let the original referrer know how the conversation went, and express your appreciation for their help.

The wider your connections are, the more chances you have for their further expansion. In a way, they are like muscles. The more you work them, the stronger they get.

6. Pinging - all the time – As you form a circle of friends, always remember that you should never fade from the sight of your friends under any circumstances. Your calendar of meetings and events should always be filled to capacity. You must be visible and active all the time. You shouldn't let people forget about you. As Woody Allen once said, "Eighty percent of success is showing up." According to Ferrazzi, "eighty percent of building and maintaining relationships is just staying in touch," which he calls pinging. That's a quick, casual greeting by which you remind others of yourself, and there are a number of ways of doing it.

Once you develop your own style, you'll be able to maintain contact with lots of people without spending too much time, even though it requires some effort. "You have to feed the fire of your network or it will wither or die." Relationships are to be maintained 24 hours a day, seven days a week, 365 days a year. When reaching out to people that are of interest to you, you can add congratulations on promotion, celebrate the success of their company or their birth of their child. You can also send them relevant articles, offer small business advice, or show other signs of attention that convey that you think about them and are eager to help.

Ferrazzi's overall insight on what "pinging all the time" is about:

People you're contacting to create a new relationship need to see or hear your name in at least three modes of communication – by, say, an e-mail, a phone call, and a face-to-face encounter – before there is substantive recognition.

Once you have gained some early recognition, you need to nurture a developing relationship with a phone call or e-mail at least once a month.

If you want to transform a contact into a friend, you need a minimum of two face-to-face meetings out of the office.

Maintaining a secondary relationship requires two to three pings a year.

7. Be interesting. – Being interesting is a simple principle that marketers and networkers alike should adopt, according to Ferrazzi. Whatever you've read and learned means nothing if it doesn't make you into someone worth talking to or being talked about. So Ferrazzi advises paying attention to interesting tidbits you hear and keep them in mind to pass on to others. Subscribe to the *New York Times* or *Wall Street Journal* and read these papers every day. One thing is obvious – people do not hire someone they just like, but someone who can be useful for the company, that is, a person with an expanded view of the world. This means that you have to develop your intellectual property and understand how others can benefit from it.

That shows you are someone involved in the world. And when you don't have a platform of ideas you are ready to defend, you just lose in the election. Another interesting factor Ferrazzi touches upon is that you can be interesting and talk intelligently about politics, sports, travel, science etc., but another thing is having content. To have content means to have a more specialized form of knowledge. "It's knowing what you have that most others do not. It's your differentiation. It's your expertise. It's the message that will make your brand unique, attracting others to become a part of your network."

In 2012, I decided to start my blog with an aim to share marketing tools and techniques, as well as interesting stories on motivation and entrepreneurs. I read every day and shared interesting content, and there came a time when my audience reached 31,772 (at the moment), a quite big figure for our country, also given that I focused on a narrow segment. My daily updates and interesting content made me more and more known, and many were eager to communicate with me. As a result, I acquired a large number of acquaintances. I haven't neglected or left unanswered even one user's question. I have helped without demanding anything in advance. I love sharing and giving, and I enjoy being helpful. The blog changed my life. For instance, I met my wife through the blog, as well as my current business partner, the publishing house, and so on. Create interesting and useful content, and people will be interested and willing to communicate with you.

By posting messages, photos and updates, we leave an information trail of our lives on the web. The people who find the best way to manage their content, by choosing the correct channels and the right time, will create the most productive and diversified network of connections and can easily turn their careers in the right direction. Today, people live in their news feeds. Therefore, if you want to attract the attention of the customers, colleagues and even friends, share something meaningful that will make them laugh or cry. There are many ways to set you apart from the mass. There are many. Discover yours.

Be generous

Generosity on the Web – it's a desire to share and receive. It's also a generosity of the soul, a willingness to step forward, to pay heed to someone, to introduce your views. As it is in other cases, generosity is a good means to overcome the indifference of others and attract their interest.

Mix and shake

Most people use Facebook for friendly contacts and LinkedIn for professional contacts without mixing these two resources. Ferrazzi is not a fan of such a strict separation. He suggests combining them. Aren't your friends and family curious about what you're doing at work? You can write about it in a way that will interest them. The personal social circle may well become a source of business opportunities, expert advice, and, finally, support.

Talk about your failures

Be honest with your readers and tell them about the mistakes you happened to make. You will make them understand that you have nothing to hide. Besides, if we all ceased to be ashamed of failure, we would finally dispel the harmful illusion that nothing has ever gone wrong with the most successful people. This is not so: They failed and went on with more and more daring experiments until they reached real success. So tell about everything - about what worked and what didn't work. *In my posts, I often share not only our success but also failures, as both success and failure can be instructive topics for people to learn from. Only those who do nothing never make mistakes. So even sharing your wrong actions teaches something new to people. Share your failure.*

Become your own editor

Regular information update is a prerequisite to attract readers. You have to think like an editor when you carry the information to your online customers. Place the content according to a timetable of a certain type. You will see that a systematic approach to communicating through social networks can be effective. Try to create your own "brand" of content that is unique. *I usually try to post something interesting on Facebook and LinkedIn at least once a day, something instructive that will convey something new or interesting to the readers.*

For example, in our country political and everyday topics are routinely discussed, but my niche is within the sphere of marketing stories, tools, motivation, and the success of our business. I hope to arouse people's interest even more and become widely read. And I'm completely honest. There are no made-up cases and stories. Keep your readers informed of your successes and failures. And do it within the sight of those interested enough in your work to follow it and offer help when needed.

Secret 13. People spend most of their time in front of screens, meaning that you should create interesting content. Create content and you will have an army of followers.

Secret 14

Even the pharaohs promoted themselves through pyramids.

Ramón Gómez de la Serna

11 Interesting Stories

1. Hutchison Whampoa – Li Ka-shing, the founder of Hutchison Whampoa, is a responsible and conscientious man. During an interview, it became evident that Li follows a strict set of business ethics and personal morals. They include a belief in trust, hard work, frugality, understanding risk, and the power of knowledge. Li maintains his credibility with all business partners. Even when one partner cancelled an order the day before it was due to be delivered, Li told the partner "do not worry about compensating me for my loss, there are other buyers for this shipment," when in fact there were no takers for the shipment Li had ready to send. This inspired the partner to recommend Li to an international client, who ended up purchasing six months worth of supplies in one order. *Life is like a boomerang. These words should be kept in mind. Not always are the profits justified. Sometimes it's worth yielding for the sake of the partner. If you value long-term relationships, then yield, because it's business, and you may appear in a similar situation in another case.*

2. Inecobank – The next case is connected with Inecobank, which is, indeed, worthy of attention. Due to the specialists' skillful operation, the bank enrolled one more customer. Inecobank credit specialists had a meeting with the head of one of the fast food outlets in Yerevan city, and during the negotiations it turned out that the potential client needed $1,000,000 for the growth and expansion of his business.

155

The Inecobank employees had observed that on each customer's table in this fast food outlet there was placed a paper menu that at the same time served as a tablecloth and was changed after each customer's visit. Then, the credit specialists contacted the company printing the menus and discovered the client's monthly order of menus. Combining it with the market research results concerning the average amount of one customer's order, Inecobank estimated the potential client's average monthly profit, and this served as basis for loan approval and disbursement.

When the client's financial indicators became available to Inecobank through cooperation and cross-check, it was revealed that the client's monthly revenue figures differed from the bank's credit specialists' results only by a few percent. Bravo to the skilled professionals who managed to find a right way out of the situation.

3. Menu.am – Menu.am is a food delivery service based in Yerevan, Armenia. Customers order food online from the list of restaurants on the site, and the delivery is performed by the team of Menu.am.

Vahan Kerobyan tells,

"When we just started out, we got the phone numbers of all the food outlets. I called a friend of mine who worked at one of the mobile operators and asked him if he could give me all the phone numbers that had been used to call these food outlets. The idea was very simply – if someone has called a food outlet, it means that they are interested in food delivery."

The friend said it was impossible to provide the list of numbers, but it was possible to send text messages instead. And thus the proposal of Menu.am was sent to all those phone numbers. As a result, the company received quite good orders for the start and acquired its first customers.

4. A method to beat the competitors – In the 70s there was only one man selling liquid soap, an American called Robert Taylor. This product was Taylor's invention, and he was confident that a great future awaited this soap. But the problem was that the liquid soap was not a patentable invention. The idea of liquid soap already existed, and pumps had been created long ago. Taylor feared that some of the powerful soap manufacturers could steal the idea and sweep his business off the shelves.

At that time Taylor decided to start to accumulate all the plastic pumps being produced in the country. In those years only two companies produced plastic pumps in the USA, and Taylor spent around $12 million to order 100 million pumps. To produce such a number of pumps, the two companies would have to work incessantly for several years. By this move Taylor deprived his competitors of the access to pumps for quite a while, because none of them could order pumps. This gave Taylor time to calmly handle his sales, as he simply had no competitors. After two years Taylor sold his business to Colgate-Palmolive for $61 million.

5. Dow Chemical - Herbert Henry Dow, a Canadian by birth, was a remarkable man. A chemist and an entrepreneur, Dow was one of the first people to realize that brine, an abundant mixture of chemicals that often hampers oil drilling, could be broken down into more useful components. Of these, bromine - an essential ingredient for most medicines as well as a vital element to photography - was the most marketable. Unfortunately for Dow, the world supply of bromine was controlled by Bromkonvention, a German cartel backed by the German government. This powerful monopoly sold bromine at a fixed price of 49 cents per pound, but it would, if challenged, implement a predatory pricing strategy quickly.

Inventing a cheaper and more efficient process of splitting brine into usable bromine using electricity and air currents, Dow went into business. Dow Chemical, established in 1896, began to edge its way into the bromine monopoly. The increased efficiency and cheaper costs allowed Dow to sell its bromine in the U.S. for about 10 cents less per pound. When the profits rolled in, Dow expanded into world markets. The Germans responded by flooding the American market with artificially cheap bromine: 15 cents per pound to Dow's 36 cents.

Bromkonvention kept the world price of bromine fixed because many of the producers in the cartel simply would cease production if they were losing money. Quietly, Dow purchased large amounts of the cheap German bromine, repackaged it, and sold it back to the Germans as an export for 27 cents - 22 cents cheaper than the domestic bromine from the same company. The large purchases in the U.S. encouraged the Germans to think they were winning. Unbeknownst to them, the cheap bromine from Dow that flooded the German market was, in fact, their own. Thus, Dow's product had not been marketed for a loss. Instead, Dow made profits from his export and solidified the company's position in world markets. Bromkonvention was forced to admit defeat and raise its prices back to previous levels. As a result, its worldwide market share inevitably decreased in the face of Dow's superior extraction process[1].

6. Pillsbury – Pillsbury Company was selling baking soda. There came a time when its market had matured. In other words, the company had reached a point when the sales were not increasing – there was a box of baking soda in every American kitchen - that is, the number of customers was a constant. The director convened a meeting and told the marketers they had to add sales volumes. Find one more USA, and we shall no doubt add sales volumes, - reportedly was the answer of the marketers. But the director was not interested in the circumstances. He wanted to see the sales volumes increase by the end of the year.

What did the marketers do? Pillsbury announced a competition - Find all the possible uses of baking soda.

As a result, a large list of 100 uses of baking soda was compiled. It appeared, people used baking soda for different means; one made lemonade; another used it to clean some device; a third washed teeth with it; someone else put it in the fridge to get bad smells out of it, and so on. The 100 uses of baking soda were printed on a paper and placed in each box. After buying it, the customers started to use baking soda for different means, so they ran out of it sooner and had to buy a new one. Thus, in a mature market the sales grew by around 10%.

7. Tabasco – The sales of sauces by the Tabasco Company were also experiencing a decline. Throughout the hundred years of its history, the company had seen constantly growing sales. But there came a time when the sales were declining significantly. Up to that point, the company had never advertised, as the product sold itself. Anxiety disturbed the sleep of the head of the company. Finally, he appealed to everyone who could help to increase sales. Soon he scheduled a meeting during which the steps to be taken in the future would be discussed. Everybody presented suggestions to

1 http://www.investopedia.com/ask/answers/09/dow-chemical-bromine-monopoly.asp

the director. An advertising company suggested advertising, as the product had never been advertised and the customers had to be well informed, but it would take a lot of money.

The next one said that a good PR was needed and again demanded a large sum of money, and so on. Different marketing companies came presenting their offers all day long. After all this, a woman approached the director and humbly said she had an idea.

So she suggested enlarging the hole on the sauce cap with a nail, so that every time someone wants to pour sauce, much more sauce will come out of the bottle. What they needed was just a small nail that cost $5. The company's director decided it was worth trying given the low cost, and they did enlarge the holes.

That same year the company's sales grew by 4%, and the expense was only $5.

8. Monster- Red Bull was the first energy drink in the US market and the only one in its category. One of the most important reasons for Red Bull's success is the company's 250ml can. Very often it seems to people that they are holding a grenade, and this affects their subconscious minds: They feel strong and powerful. Naturally, this novelty attracted Americans, and a few companies decided to enter this market. Almost all of them were defeated, as they had the same 250ml cans that were practically indistinguishable from Red Bull's.

One of them survived though. That was Monster energy drink, which had a bigger can that resembled its name, "monster," and, to be honest, the name itself is energizing. Today Red Bull has 43% of the market, and Monster has 35%. Monster's success was not that the bigger can contained more drink but that it was different from Red Bull.

Until now I have observed with amazement how companies that do not understand that business is not about imitating but being different disappear one after another. It took Red Bull 10 years to reach to $100 million in sales. That's why Coca-Cola ignored the energy drinks market. However, when Coca-Cola did enter the market, Red Bull was already well ingrained in the subconscious of people, so Coca-Cola's KMX energy drink failed in the market.

9. Asus – There was a time when a modest Taiwanese company produced some spare parts for the Dell Company. Once, the small company suggested to Dell that it produce the entire computer and not just parts of it.

It was a profitable moment for Dell, which agreed. Then the Taiwanese company suggested to Michael Dell that it manage the supply itself. It was an excellent condition for Dell, an offer that ensured higher income at a lower cost. Dell realized the branding, while the Taiwanese realized the hard work - production and supply. This system justified itself, and the Taiwanese company arrived in the United States, though not as a Dell Company unit, but within the chain of Best Buy stores, where it wanted to sell its own computers. These computers were as good as Dell's but less expensive. Yes, the name of that company was ASUS.

10. Lipton - Legends circulated about Thomas Lipton's marketing stunts. One of them is that when Lipton was on his way to England, the ship he was on ran aground. The crew needed to throw cargo into the ocean to right the ship. Lipton ordered a crew member to create a stencil and have "Drink Liptons Tea" emblazoned onto each barrel or box that had to be thrown overboard. It was possible that the boxes would get to an island or be noticed from another ship, it was not so important. The important thing was that Lipton used any opportunity to advertise his brand.

11. Axe Effect – This theme answers a number of questions and can be illustrated by the marketing of personal hygiene products. According to Unilever executive David Cousino, men think of sex more than 32 times a day. In 2002, when Axe, a men's personal-care manufacturer, was introduced in the US market, it positioned itself as a brand that could transform a greasy, scrawny, acne-prone specimen into a confident, gorgeous, chiselled sex magnet.

Initially, Unilever conducted an extensive online survey of 12,000 boys and men aged 15 to 50 from all over the world - Japan, USA, Mexico, Great Britain, South Africa, etc. The survey was not ordinary; the questions in it were highly personal and intimate. The survey was anonymous and the answers were sincere and almost identical. The results were shocking. It turns out that the number one fantasy among men is to lounge in a hot tub with three or four naked women by their side and a have corked bottle of champagne nearby with its foam bubbling over into the hot tub.

Based on these responses, the Axe marketing team concluded that men dream to be irresistible not for one specific woman but for many women. Axe started building its commercial campaigns, which you see on TV today, based on this revelation. David Cousino explains,

"We realized – or rather, had it confirmed... that if the campaign was to be successful, it would have to emphasize the pheromone aspects of the brand."

Next, Cousino and his Unilever colleagues chose men aged 15 to 50 from different countries and accompanied them to pubs. The Unilever team was not drinking with them, but filming secretly. The goal was to see how these men would pick women out of the crowd and approach them.

After long studies, the marketers of Unilever came to the conclusion that men or the potential consumers of Axe can be broken down into six profiles:

The predator – He drives a brand-name car, adorns himself with high-end fashion brands, and is constantly on the prowl. He had little if any respect for women and is markedly deceptive.

Natural talent - He's intelligent, athletic, achieving, appealing, confident. This man usually gets the woman he's after, though never deceptively. What's more, most boys want to be the natural talent man.

The marriage material guy – the name speaks for itself: a gentle, respectful, and self-confident man.

Always the friend – Which words turn down the man who's in love? I think you guessed, "Sorry, but you're like a brother for me. Can we be just good friends?"

The insecure novice – This poor young man doesn't really know how to behave around women. He's weak, less bold, and uninteresting for women.

The enthusiastic novice – He doesn't have a clue what he's doing either; however, he's eager and tries valiantly.

And so, the Axe team now had to choose their target out of the six segments they had isolated. The marketers unanimously selected the insecure novice, followed by the enthusiastic novice as their main targets. Why? Because of their lack of self-esteem and experience, it would be easier to persuade them that Axe would become their key to success with women. The other men seemed to already know how to attract women. The natural talent could perhaps be convinced to use Axe a finishing touch before going out, while the predator would never feel he needed the product or anything else other than his own sexy self to attract women. So with the insecure novice as its main target, Axe released a number of commercials in which the man is in his fantasy - that is, irresistible to not only one but several sexy women.

These ads became an excellent marketing move with a message that suggested, "If you spray it, women will come." Imagine, just a few months later Axe became the number one male brand in the industry, bringing an income of about $71 million. In addition, the sales of Unilever's other products started increasing. Axe achieved global fame thanks to its ads, which contained banned scenes and funny behavior that offered people food for thought.

But such rapid success became a real headache for the company because the insecure novices and enthusiastic novices were buying boxes of Axe. You're going to ask why big purchases would cause problems for the company. First, Axe had so strongly instilled in young people the idea of its brand's advantage that they were washing with it, covering their bodies, hair and face with Axe. It was impossible to have classes in educational institutions because of the unbearable smells. The teachers' complaints increased so much that Axe was forbidden in Minnesota.

There was no growth in sales for some time. The reason was that many young people thought Axe was a brand for pathetic losers, and no one would buy it. In response to these problems, today Unilever tries to guide the consumers by viral videos as to how and where to use Axe. The example of Axe once again shows that people's deepest, most hidden fantasies can be an excellent weapon for marketers and provide a huge increase in sales.

Few people reading this book may have the huge resources needed to invest in marketing research, but by going to supermarkets for a week and watching people's behavior in relation to your product and asking them questions, you can understand what makes them satisfied or dissatisfied. I am sure they will open new paths for your marketing activities.

Secret 14. Always improve your product or service. Think of different uses of your product that will increase consumption volumes. The sooner it is consumed, the more sales you'll have.

Secret 15

If I am not a millionaire before I'm 30, I'll jump off the tallest building in Omaha.

Warren Buffett

Berkshire Hathaway (Warren Buffett)

In 1993, during the PBS show Money World, Warren Buffett was asked what investment advice he would give a novice money manager. "I'd tell him to do exactly what I did 40-odd years ago, which is to learn about every company in the United States that has publicly traded securities." Moderator Adam Smith protested, "But there's 27,000 public companies." "Well," said Buffett, "start with the A's."

Warren Buffett has created one of the most successful investment companies in the world, Berkshire Hathaway. According to Forbes, in 2016 his fortune was $60.8 billion. When acquiring stocks, he follows a simple rule "Be fearful when others are greedy and greedy when others are fearful." Warren Buffett is considered one of the planet's most successful investors. He determines what to invest in based on fundamental analysis, a process based on an assessment of a company's financial and productive indicators. He doesn't just buy a stock; he buys a successful business that stands behind security.

Moreover, Buffett chooses stocks that are, in his opinion, undervalued at the moment. Buffett is considered a long-term investor who owns stocks for 10 years on average. He says he's not worried what will happen after he acquires the stocks. He admits that he will hold onto the good stocks as long as they are able to bring profit. They say that Warren Buffett doesn't have an e-mail or a fax and that he devotes most of his time to reading. *Remember*

164

these words. He's continuously indulged in reading. Devote some part of your day to self-development.

His annual salary is $100,000 and hasn't changed for years. Buffett lives a frugal lifestyle. For instance, he still lives in the house he bought for $32,000 in the 1950s and drives a second hand car. Another interesting fact is that Buffett tries to avoid selling stocks. Yes, if he bought them, he'd love to hold onto them forever.

Warren Buffett was born on August 30, 1930, in Omaha, Nebraska. Since childhood he demonstrated a knack for adding large numbers in his head. He could at once memorize the number of residents living in different cities of the USA. Buffett's first transaction was performed at the age of 6. He bought 6 bottles of Coca-Cola for 25 cents and resold them to his family members for 30 cents. And already at 11 Warren developed interest in his father's job - stock exchange transactions.

Uniting with his elder sister, Doris, and borrowing money from his father, he bought three shares of Cities Service at $38 per share. Soon the stock dropped to only $27, and then reached $40. At this point Warren sold his shares, earning $6, but in just a few days Cities Service shot up to over $200 a share. He still remembers his mistake and says that life taught him the basic principle in investing - patience is rewarded.

At the age of 13 he made around $170 delivering Washington Post newspapers. After changing three universities, Buffett eventually enrolled in the Colombia Business School. Here he attended Benjamin Graham's seminars on the analysis of securities. Warren's grade was A+. In fact, it was the first such grade Graham awarded in his career. Graham preached the importance of a company's intrinsic value. If the shares were below it in price, the investors would profit by buying them.

At the age of 21, he received a master's degree and tried to get into Graham's investment firm, but Graham refused even though Buffett was ready to work for him for free. The reason for the refusal was quite unusual. He felt the big firms and large investment banks on Wall Street didn't take the Jews. So he saved the few spots he had for Jews. Warren went to Omaha; he started working for his father, got married and even taught at the University of Nebraska. Two years passed. In 1954 Graham changed his mind all of a sudden and invited Buffett to his firm. There Buffett worked as an analyst for two years. Under Graham's leadership, Buffett acquired enormous experience, as well as some serious money. *You don't achieve success alone.*

Thus, already in 1956, Buffett founded his own Buffett Partnership Ldt. with an initial capital of $105,000, made up of his family's and friends' investments, to which he had contributed $100. How was he able to accumulate such wealth? Berkshire Hathaway, founded in 1888, was going through hard times. Buffett took control of the company. In 1964 he acquired the American Express Company's shares, the value of which had dropped from $65 to $35 overnight.

He bought them bearing in mind one of Graham's most important tips – when the intrinsic value of the company exceeds the company's stock price, it's time to get down to business. *Great investment opportunities emerge when first-class companies get into unusual circumstances, because of which their shares become undervalued by the market.* Buffett took the risk in acquiring 40% shares in American Express. In the subsequent years, the company's stock price tripled, from which Buffett and his partners earned around $20 million.

In 1967 a new law in compulsory insurance was adopted in the United States, and Buffett immediately realized that a new lucrative field had opened up. He invested $8.6 million in two insurance companies, National Indemnity Company and National Fire & Marine Insurance Company. This became the foundation of his rapid success. For instance, the annual revenue of National Indemnity Company grew from $1.6 million to $2 million. Furthermore, Warren invested in three more insurance companies, including a transaction in 1976, when he started buying shares of GEICO Company after the price dropped from $61 to $2 per share. One year later, in 1977, the company began to make a profit again. If in 1976, Buffett bought the very first package of GEICO shares at a price of $2 per share. In 1996, each share was worth $70.

As the company gathered momentum, he purchased it entirely and made it a Berkshire Hathaway Holding. In 1987, Buffett purchased large numbers of Coca-Cola stocks and in 1989-2006 became a member of the company's board of directors. For him, Coca-Cola is the most respected brand in the world.

Currently, no company can be compared with Coca-Cola when it comes to the stability of its operating history. Its core business, the production of soft drinks, has practically remained unchanged. The only thing that makes today's Coca-Cola different from the previous company is the company's size and global reach. One hundred years ago, the company employed ten salesmen to serve the whole territory of the United States. At the time, the company was selling 111,492 gallons of syrup a year and had annual sales of about $148,000.

Fifty years later, in 1938, the company was selling 207 million cases soft drinks a year. An article in *Fortune Magazine* noted, "It would be hard to name any company comparable to Coca-Cola. There is no company like Coca-Cola that sells an unchanged product that can point to a ten-year record anything like Coca-Cola's." At present, almost 70 years after the publication of the article, Coca-Cola still sells the same beverage. The only difference is in the number of sales. For example, in 2003, the company sold 19 billion cases of its product in more than 200 countries around the world, generating $22 billion in sales.

Buffett also bought large quantities of Gillette stocks, because the company owned most of the shaving product market. "It's pleasant to go to bed every night knowing there are 2.5 billion males in the world who have to shave in the morning." Another of Buffett's achievements was *Nebraska Furniture Mart*. This huge furniture retailer started out in Omaha, when a Russian immigrant, Rose Blumkin, who used to sell furniture from the basement of her house, invested $500 to open a small furniture store. In 1983, Buffett paid $55million to Mrs. B for 80% of her business. The company that has managed to retain leadership status for 25-30 years will be interesting to Warren Buffett. A strong brand, high quality and a powerful distribution network allow an investor to own these companies' stocks in the long run. Such companies do not survive: They expand. This is the reason for Buffett's pick.

Currently, Nebraska Furniture Mart, which consists of three retail stores with a total area of 1.2 million square feet located on a large plot of land, sells more furniture than any other US furniture store. Buffett ties the success of this retail store to Mrs B., who did not retire from business but continued working until her death at the age of 104. A piece of wisdom Mrs. B preached was, "If you have the lowest price, customers will find you at the bottom of a river."

MiTek Inc. produces steel connector products and engineering software for the building components market. Berkshire acquired a 90 % equity interest in MiTek in 2011 for $400 million. The remaining 10% is owned by MiTek management, which loves its company and expressed a desire to remain co-owners. Such an entrepreneurial spirit is one of the qualities highly appreciated by Warren Buffett.

Ben Bridge Jeweler, owned and managed by the representatives of four generations of one family, is an American jewelry retailer located in various cities on the West Coast. A mandatory purchase condition by Berkshire Hathaway was the requirement that the members of the family continued to run the company. It was purchased in 2000 at a price that has not been disclosed.

Over the years, Warren Buffett has owned assets of companies in the most varied sectors: Wholesale and Manufacturing, Banking, Technology, Clothing, Retail, Insurance and Finance, Household Products, Materials and Construction, Oil and Gas, Food and Drink, Telecommunication and Media, and so on. In some he has complete control; in others he owns a partial stake. However, in all cases, he is deeply versed in the fundamental aspects of the businesses. In particular, such aspects include: the revenue and expenditure, flow of funds, labor relations, pricing, and capital allocation.

Buffett manages to maintain a high level of knowledge about the companies wholly or partly owned by Berkshire Hathaway because he consciously limits his choice to businesses he is able understand. He calls these limits the "circle of competence." Buffett's reasoning is quite logical and convincing: say, an investor owns the company (wholly or partly), and this company operates in a field he has no knowledge of. This means it's impossible to accurately assess the events taking place in the company and, thus, make the right decisions. Buffett recommends, "What an investor needs is the ability to correctly evaluate selected businesses. Note that word 'selected': You don't have to be an expert on every company, or even many. You only have to be able to evaluate companies within your circle of competence. The size of that circle is not very important; knowing its boundaries, however, is vital."

The critics argue that the restrictions Buffett imposes on himself prevent him from acting in the sectors that offer great opportunities for investors. Buffett's answer to such criticisms is, "What counts for most people in investing is not how much they know, but rather how realistically they define what they don't know."

When Buffett is considering new investments, he uses the stocks already held by his company as a criterion of buying new ones. Charlie Munger, the right hand of Warren Buffett, is of the same opinion that if the new target for investment you're considering is no better than the ones you already have, you'd better forget about it. As a result, 99 percent of all possible options for investments are eliminated.

One of the key principles adopted by Buffett is that he doesn't interfere with the operational management of the purchased companies. He just purchases the company he finds attractive, and the only operational decision he makes is the appointment of the CEO, as well as determining his salary and bonus. Buffett's requirements are simple. He expects these two approaches from his managers:

- He gives the manager the owner's right, that is - run the business the way you'd run your own.

- The manager cannot sell his business or merge it into another company in the next 100 years, so the only focus is to develop the business.

These two simple rules enable Buffett to think about long-term development, not short-term profits. Risk reduction is one of Buffett's cornerstones. He asserts that he would rather say no to an attractive acquisition than increase the company's debt burden by taking loans from banks.

Warren Buffett's business principles:

Investment is when you invest certain amount of money today and get more tomorrow. Warren Buffett has led a modest life, and instead of eating at luxury restaurants and buying expensive items, he's invested money in buying shares.

Buy stocks of the products you use and really enjoy. For instance, Warren Buffett loves to shave with Gillette and drink Coca-Cola.

Do not invest in a business you don't really understand. Investing in a business you are familiar with is more useful.

Invest in a company that is more global.

To make a clear decision, you have to gauge the company's historical performance, not only success years.

When Buffett buys stocks, he doesn't care what will happen with them tomorrow. The important thing is to know what will happen in the market in the long run.

"I can't be involved in 50 or 70 things. That's a Noah's ark way of investing – you end up with a zoo that way. I like to put meaningful amounts of money in a few things," says Warren Buffett.

Lessons from Warren Buffett:

When buying shares, Warren Buffett doesn't look at any employee's photo, study the product, or visit the factory. He's only interested in the annual and semi-annual reports. If the report is submitted by the accountant, he does not study this company. The report must be submitted by the director general, the person who will not hide anything. The idea is to know his opinions and goals, along with what results will be achieved in the near future. Buffett wants to understand how all of this information will be relevant to his expectations.

Suppose you meet a company's director general and he promises a 15% annual stock price growth. If you study the issue, you'll see that such growth is just not reasonable based on what the 200 largest companies have historically experienced. You'll see that from 1970 to 1980 none of them recorded such growth. Warren Buffett won't believe the company director, who'll try to assure him that the stocks will grow by such unbelievable numbers.

The bonus amount depends not on Berkshire indicators, but the given company's. For example, Ralph Schey, the chairman of Scott Fetzer, would be rewarded based on the indicators of Scott Fetzer, not those of Berkshire. Summing up the award scheme, I can say that each head of the companies under Berkshire receives his bonuses separately and does not depend on the indicators of others.

Warren Buffett appreciates the top managers who have the courage to openly acknowledge and discuss their failures. That's because the managers who admit their mistakes are more capable of correcting them. Over time, every company, both large and small, makes mistakes. Managers of many companies present their reports to the shareholders with excessive optimism instead of explaining the situation as it is. In doing so, the managers, perhaps, realize their own short-term interests, but they ignore the long-term interests of others.

On acquiring shares of a certain company, Buffett will promise the director that there won't be any surprises. Everything is decided on the spot, and they get down to work at once. Very often Buffett buys companies that have great potential but no significant success at the moment. Sometimes he will sell certain stocks at cost or below cost price to attract financial means to acquire stocks with good prospects.

Warren Buffett advises investing in industries and companies you know, companies whose management you are familiar with. It's better to make large investments in three companies than small investments in many companies. He sticks to this rule when investing.

As an investor, he'll recommend that you buy stocks of companies that have the potential to be profitable in the next 5, 10 or 20 years. "If you aren't willing to own a stock for ten years, don't even think about owning it for ten minutes," says Buffett. For example, he considers buying Berkshire stocks as one of his biggest mistakes. He knew that the industry was unpromising but was tempted by its availability.

Remember that if you buy cheap stocks, you're going to encounter big problems. Therefore, after the purchase of Berkshire, Buffett had to carry the whole burden on his shoulders. But he prefers the other way - to stay away from business and hand the management over to a professional manager. You will ask – what's the secret of Buffett's success. I'll answer: He simply avoids problems. It's better to be sure of a good result than hope for an ideal result.

Banking was the only sector Warren Buffett always avoided investing in. As to Wells Fargo, the best leaders he had ever met, Carl Reichardt and Paul Hazen, worked there. These partners trusted each other, paid the employees rather high salaries, and always fought expenses, even at the times when the bank had considerable revenues. Wells Fargo was Buffett's first exception, and he went into the banking sector.

Secret 15. If you're engaged in investment, remember Warren Buffett's principal and invest in a field where you have in-depth knowledge and a good understanding of the nuances.

Secret 16

Do you want the customers to leave your store in a happy mood? If yes, then offer "5% discount to all the good and kind people," and you will see their joy when coming out of the store.

Igor Mann

Sewell (Carl Sewell)

Today, companies are facing tough competition. Companies that keep imitating their competitors' steps fall into a difficult situation sooner or later, while others do not imitate but create their own face. This story is related to one such company, Sewell Automotive Companies and Carl Sewell, the chairman. He managed to expand his business from $10 million in 1968 to $850 million today. Let's observe the strategies behind the big growth of the company.

The company sells Cadillacs, Lexuses, Infinitis, Chevrolets, and other car brands and provides a car-service. Trying to figure out of ways to differentiate his company from others, Sewell started looking for solutions, and the first thing to do was to think about the company from the customers' point of view. "If you're good to your customers, they'll keep coming back because they like you," says Sewell. And if they come back, they will spend money in the place they liked. Therefore, it was necessary to treat the customers well. After you've been to a restaurant, you don't remember exactly what the hamburger cost. You only remember whether you liked it or not. They decided to ask customers – the people with whom they did business – about their complaints and received shocking results.

They would say that the service hours, 8:00 a.m. – 5:00 p.m. from Monday to Friday, were inconvenient, as many of them were at work during those hours. The others complained that the company didn't work on Saturdays.

They pointed out that some employees were rude: While the cars were under repair, the employees were not attentive enough and did not give any information as to when they would be ready.

The customers even complained that they often had to bring their cars back several times to get the repair done right. Some of them pointed out that the grounds were not clean enough and that the furniture was too old, leaving a bad impression on the visitor. They did not specify what the company should do to improve. They simply voiced what they would like to see. *From time to time, ask your customers how they would like to see your company. Here was an example of what precious advice they gave to Carl Sewell.*

These complaints allowed them to think seriously about the next steps. The first thing to do was to provide the customers with free loan cars, becoming the only company in the field with such an interesting approach. In other words, while the customer's car was being repaired, the company provided them with a free loan car. This move secured a huge army of clients.

At first they had 5 loaners. The number soon reached 257. In those years no dealers worked all day on Saturdays in the state, and it was one more incentive to stand out. So it was necessary to work on Saturdays. On the very first Saturday 25 people thanked the company for the initiative. The next decision had to do with working hours. They extended their service hours to 8 p.m. If Sewell was asked why he did so, he would immediately answer that it was what the customers wanted.

One question kept bothering Sewell: How could excellent customer service be provided? For the solution of this problem they visited the best car-dealers and studied their methods. They questioned them, took notes, and even took pictures to have a clear understanding of how the best dealers operated. But Sewell understood that by following their ideas, they would start imitating their competitors, while they needed an alternative. So they made a decision not to do what the competitors did. For example, there is a rule that customers must be greeted within 3 minutes, or that the phone should be answered by the second ring. Sewell decided to abandon such rules.

There is an accepted rule in the retail businesses that the customer does not like to be "attacked" as he walks inside the store. But, after analyzing all the letters sent to the company, it was obvious to Sewell that the customers never complained about aggressiveness. On the contrary, they complained far more about not receiving enough attention. *It follows that we should not necessarily imitate the competitors strategies but be different and listen to our customers.*

Every time the customers asked for something, they had the following answer, "Sure thing." If the customer had locked himself out of the car or got a flat tire, he could call, and the help would be there in no time. For example, a loyal client who lived half the year in Dallas and the other half in Paris called once from Paris and said that she wanted to go to New York and that she would like Sewell Automotive service to send a rental car to New York from Texas that would serve her. The reason was that she was not satisfied with the cleanliness of New York rental cars. Her request was fulfilled, because a loyal customer should not be refused.

Sewell believes that the customer must be taken care of so that he will become a customer for life. When the customers have some problems with the car, customer service does not charge them. But of course, if the battery has to be changed, then they pay only for the battery, while the service is free. If the customer asks, the answer is always YES.

Sewell explains that customer service is a 24-hour job. Sometimes the customers call after 18:00 or on Sundays, as they are not interested in what situation the company is. They want their problem to be solved. This is why the company works when a customer wants it to and not when it wants to. If a customer calls and says that he needs help at 21:30, it is no problem. He will be served without complaint in a manner convenient to him.

Naturally, it is difficult for the company, but the customer does not care about it. Cadillac service center works 24 hours a day. When the work is finished, only the security person stays in the center. He must answer every phone call, listen carefully to the customer's problem, and immediately contact the necessary employee. The staff regularly rotates. Each of the technicians is on duty for 24 hours and responsible for the customers' problems during that time. If the customer calls at 3:00 a.m., he receives instant help and an answer to his questions, and if necessary, a specialist visits him and solves the problem on the spot.

Provide all-day service – When the customer asks "Can you?" the answer at Sewell Automotive should always be "yes." *Do not say "No, we can't do it." If your customer needs help, then help him. If he has a problem with the car and needs to change the tire, do it together with him. Do not take extra money for a small service.* If the customer is not able to visit Sewell Automotive at 20:00, but at 22:00, then the staff will wait until he shows up. The strategy of the company is for people to call them and never pay attention to what hour of the day they are calling. The staff is ready to help the customers any hour of the day. Why?

The reason is that you cannot provide good service just between 8:00 a.m. and 5:00 p.m. Customer service has to be all day so that the customer can be certain he can apply without having to take a look at the clock. One call of the customer has to be sufficient. It's good when one number is always active. Keep a special employee who will answer all the calls.

Underpromise, overdeliver – There is an interesting rule at Sewell Automotive. They promise less and do more. Suppose a spare part has to be changed in 10 minutes. They say 20 minutes, then call the customer in 10 minutes. As a result, they have happy customers who really appreciate the fast service. If the spare part costs $90, they will price it at $100 and in the end return $10.

Do you know how happy you make the customer at that moment? The next most important condition is that they will do more for that amount of money. That is, they will fix any defect for free. Normally, such service costs $7, but they do it for free. Now the customer has two reasons to be happy – extra work has been done and he has paid less than expected. People love to interact with entrepreneurs who keep their promise.

When thinking about customer service, the first things that come to people's minds are words such as please; thank you; yes, ma'am; no, sir, etc. All this is part of providing a good service, but, according to Sewell, it's a small part. The bigger part is:

"Doing the job right the first time" and

"Having a plan in place to deal with things when they go wrong."

After all, no customer is interested in how kind you were if you haven't provided the service at once or have done it badly. Imagine that you have gone to a restaurant where the waiters always smile at you, change the dishes, and refresh the table, but, let's say, you find hair in the food. You sure you will not go there a second time. A system - how you should serve in different circumstances - is important in service. Nice treatment is 20% of good service.

Proper service is a complete system. Suppose a customer wants a spare part that you do not have in stock. Sewell believes that if you cannot provide it at that moment, no good treatment will help you. And what should you do in order to always have the product in stock? The answer is simple – just give the suppliers the opportunity to see the stock status, and they will immediately supply the absent products. For example, each Wal-Mart product has number. If it is sold, the information will reach both the head office and the supplier in the evening. Thus, the supplier already knows which product and in what amount must be supplied to the given Wal-Mart discounter. This very system constitutes 80% of service.

The aim of Sewell Automotive is to have satisfied customers; if the customer leaves the store dissatisfied, the employee serving him will not stay long in his position. All employees know that if they are not polite with the customer, they will be fired. During his career, Sewell has learned that there is nothing more important than the fulfilling a promise.

People love trust. If you gain their trust, they will come to you without thinking. *If you work in the service sector, my advice is to do what you have promised at once - without delay. Today you have many competitors. This means that if you do not do what you have promised at once, your competitor will do it. Believe me, it is preferable to fulfill your promise to the customer at once than offer thousands of smiles and chocolates.*

Sewell says that often the customers judge his company based on how well the company solves their problems. And so what does the company do when problems occur? At first, it immediately apologizes. If it's a tiny problem, the apology is verbal; if the item is pricey, the apology is by phone or mail;

if it's a serious problem involving female customers, the company sends a bouquet of roses. If the problem involves men, the company apologizes. As a rule, the person who is to blame for the problem has to apologize, but often the managers actually handle it.

After each such case Sewell reminds his staff that its job is to serve people and to eliminate additional problems. The basic strategy of Sewell Automotive is that to complete every task the first time. In other words, there is no need to do the same task for free a second time and make the customer wait and get stressed. They encourage the customers to express their complaints, because in that case they can apologize, solve the problem, give a present, and have a customer satisfied with the company's work.

There are certain characteristics to the company's service style. In particular, the company always keeps track of the product's shelf life. If the car does not sell in 45 days, then there is a reason for that. Maybe the color is no good; maybe it is dirty or stands in the corner, etc. Changes are made and everything is done to sell the cars. And most importantly, Sewell always has the car that the customer wants to have in stock. If it happens not to have the car, the company will buy it from the competitors or exchange it with them. In no case should the client be refused. In order to always have the products available in stock, it is necessary to have a clear agreement with the suppliers. To know how long the product has been around, the company attaches different colored papers to the cars (in places only the staff knows). Blue means January' red means February, etc. This helps them to stay informed as to how long the car has been in the showroom.

Beware of competitors, Sewell advises. There was a time when Sewell Automotive was the first dealer to work on Saturdays. In just a few years, competitors realized that working on Saturdays would give them a strong competitive edge too. Sewell replenished the warehouse to show the customers the variety; the competitors did the same thing.

They extended the working day to 20:00; this was also followed by the competitors' answer. Sewell Automotive offered the customers a service according to which the staff member would bring the car to the shop in case of a problem, fix it, and drive back to the customer's house. This technique was also copied. Sewell was well aware that if one of the competitors offered better comfort, price, service, the customers would go to it. Therefore, the company constantly developed new approaches to service to withstand the competition.

To improve service quality, the company has a set of questions that customers are asked to answer from time to time. For example,

- When you arrived at the service area, were you greeted promptly?

- Did your Service Adviser explain things to you clearly?

- Did we call to inform you that your automobile was ready?

By this method they could identify the staff's shortcomings and work more effectively. For example, the dealers at Sewell Automotive sold more than 16 cars a month. Not a bad indicator, but they realized that they could create a plan to sell more cars through it. A plan was developed according to which the employees who sold more than 20 cars would get more money and would travel more for free. The results were shocking. *Never stop improving performance and set higher goals.*

The customer isn't always right – If the customer is dissatisfied, the strategy of the company is to learn about the problem and solve it for free. If it comes to small amounts of money, then the customer is right. One of Sewell's friends tells an interesting story about a woman. The woman bought an item worth $5.98 from his store; the next week, when she saw the same item at a discounted price of $4.98, she demanded her one dollar back, which she could have saved had she bought it at this moment. The money was given back to the woman. Out of gratitude the woman would shop in his store for many years.

If you want to keep your business, you have to give the discontent customer what he wants. At Sewell Automotive, if it's about an amount below $500, the problem should be resolved in favor of the customer. If the customer bought a blue car and his wife disliked it, they will be change it. But sometimes really hard people appear. In these cases Sewell will send them to his competitors – let them also be tormented. Remember, the customer isn't always right. There is a limit after which he is not right anymore. Sewell also points out that one of the most important aspects of superior service is clean restrooms. They must always be clean, as many customers judge the essence of your business by this factor. Of course, no one buys a car because the restrooms are clean. Still, Sewell quotes Tom Peters:

"If that's how they take care of the restrooms, how'll they take care of me?"

Sewell holds and practices the belief that the customers should not see even a minor shortcoming, as they will begin doubting the quality of the service. He is attentive towards the managers because people are watching the ones who lead them. If they cheat the customers or mistreat them, the employees will do the same. Good employees will never work for an executive with a bad reputation. So the executives should show by their example how the customers should be served. If they do not behave well, regardless of their qualifications as a specialist, they ought to be fired.

Secret 16. Ask your customers about their complaints and how they would like to see your company.

Secret 17

*If I had asked people what they wanted,
they would have said faster horses.*

Henry Ford

Ford (Henry Ford)

Henry Ford was the king of automotive industry, the best businessman of the 20th century, a man for whom there was nothing impossible. Ford suffered numerous defeats, fell into desperate situations, and fought against his enemies, but he reached everything he dreamed of. Let me remind you that at the age of 39 he still had nothing, and he founded his company when he was around 40 years old. All his life he spent with one woman, who helped and believed in her husband most of all. And now from the beginning. Ford was born into a farmer's family on July 30, 1863, in Michigan. The family was not poor, but the father and children struggled to make ends meet.

Every day the children would cut trees, raise pigs, milk cows to help out. Ford did not go to university and finished school without being able to spell correctly.

Henry could not stand farm and avoided working there. This made his father discontent, because he wanted his son to become a farmer.

Perhaps life would have taken a different course had Ford not seen a steam traction engine at age 13. He was intrigued to think that the vehicle was self-propelled. While his father was busy with something, Henry went up to the engineer and asked questions about the steam engine, and the engineer described it to him with enthusiasm. Since that day, all of Henry's toys turned into tools for experiments.

In the same year his father gifted him a pocket watch. Unable to resist the temptation, Ford took it apart and then reassembled it; he was fascinated by the movements and work of the mechanisms. In 1879, when Henry was already 16 years old, he set out to Detroit on foot at night, where he began working as an apprentice machinist. Ford rented a room and paid $3.50 for food and bedding, at a time when his money did not suffice.

The circumstances made Ford work in the evenings as well. He rushed to the watchmaker from the machinist, and sometimes repaired watches at night. In order to convince Ford to return, his father provided a 40-acre area on the condition he never used the word "machine" in his life.

Ford built a house on the 40 acres of land and returned to farming, but, of course, he had other goals in mind. During one of rural gatherings he met his sister's friend, Clara Bryant. Clara's parents were farmers, and she had also grown up in a strict family environment. When Ford first invited Clara to dance, they could not have imagined that several decades later that area would become a tourist attraction. Ford was an excellent dancer. During gatherings he shocked everyone with his dancing and his self-made watch. Clara Bryant was a serious girl, and she knew that marriage was not fun, but an ordeal. "The man who has the patience to assemble a watch will definitely be a good husband," she thought, and accepted Ford's proposal.

"My wife believes in me more than I do. She had always been like this." Ford noted later.

Throughout her life Clara managed to keep balance and was aware of her husband's business affairs, but she never interfered. She could listen to her husband telling enthusiastically about this or that project for hours and never tell him, *it won't work out, do not do that* as many tend to say. For example, when Ford made his first car in the garage, it was so big that it was impossible to get it out of the doors.

Seeing that Ford did not know what to do, Clara took a hammer and started smashing the brick walls to bring the car out. *Never tell your husband that he won't succeed - never.* In 1893, Ford's first child, Edsel, was born, and it was necessary to support the family.

As time went by, one day Ford Sr. saw that the house his son had built was empty. With Clara's consent Henry had gone to Detroit to work as an engineer in an electrical factory. The aim was to get acquainted with electronics under the pretext of supporting the family. Here, Ford was working night shifts and receiving $45 a month, and it was difficult to undertake something else alongside, but when he switched to day shift, he was able to carve out time to create his gasoline engine. While Ford struggled to improve the idea of internal combustion engine, his associates would laugh when he said that future belonged to the gasoline - not the electric engine.

When Ford first met Thomas Edison, Ford told him about his ideas. Edison got interested and found out through questions what Ford actually wanted to do. Then he said to Ford,

"Yes, there is a big future for any lightweight engine that can develop a high horsepower and be self-contained. No one kind of motive power is ever going to do all the work of the country. We do not know what electricity can do, but I take for granted that it cannot do everything. Keep on with your engine. If you can get what you are after, I can see a great future."

Ford was elated. Besides his loyal wife, one more person favored him, the great Thomas Edison. In the same year, on Christmas Eve, Ford went into the kitchen where his wife was preparing turkey; he mounted the engine on the kitchen sink and instructed Clara to drip in the gasoline. As Henry spun the flywheel, exhaust and fumes filled the tiny kitchen. The Fords started laughing and crying with joy.

In 1896, Ford completed his first self-propelled vehicle, which he named the Ford Quadricycle. When assembling the vehicle, Ford would sleep 4 hours a night, as he had a goal to accomplish. When the vehicle was already ready, Ford hit the streets of Detroit with it. Every time he stopped the vehicle, numerous curious people would come and gather around Ford. There were people among them who would get into the car without permission, after which Ford had to fasten it with a chain. Since there were no road signs at the time, the police said nothing to him. He sold the vehicle for $200. It was the first sale, the proceeds of which Henry did not spend. He instead decided to invest in creating a lighter vehicle. He believed that heavy vehicles were no good for mass production, so he had to think of a lighter one. Ford's greatness was that he turned the car into a business.

In Detroit's electric factory people noticed that Ford was not busy with his responsibilities. In fact, he was obsessed with his ideas, so he spent most of his free time experimenting on his wheelchair machine. Such an approach to work could not last long, and Ford had to choose between his job and his dream.

On the one hand, he had to bring home the bacon; on the other hand, he desired to pursue vision. Seeing that Ford suffered because of this, Clara said she would favor any decision he made. Ford took the risk. Leaving the company, he decided to sell his idea, but no one came forth. He had no money, and the breath of each undertaking is money, so he had to find it.

To raise financial resources, Ford managed to convince a businessman to sit in his car and start driving it at high speed. The businessman was surprised that the car didn't fall apart after driving 100 km. Through him Ford raised funds and set up his first company. But he failed. He got on his feet and set up his own business again. But failed for the second time, too.

A solution was needed, and Ford kept thinking about days to attract public attention, for none of the rich wanted to hear about an automobile. At last, an interesting idea came to Ford's mind, and Ford decided that only by special auto races was it possible to attract public attention. And he set to work. Day and night husband and wife were making automobile engines in their small house. All night long Clara would stand with the kerosene lamp in her hand for her husband to make new engines.

To protect herself from the cold, she would wrap her hands with cloths and look at her husband with chattering teeth, Ford in his turn did all he could to have the automobiles ready for the race as soon as possible. *Success is not achieved alone.* He realized that something unusual should be organized for the public. In 1903, Ford made two automobiles, putting the emphasis on speed. After the race, everybody talked of the automobile as being the fastest means of transportation.

People were talking about his automobiles. The next step was to raise financial resources. Some investors believed in Ford. Among them was Alexander Malcomson, who invested $28,000. In 1908, one of global giants was born - the Ford Motor Company.

The automobile produced by Ford was named Model A, but it didn't sell well and only covered the expenses.

Then he created the Model B, which was $2,000. But again it didn't sell well. Ford's investigations were of no result, and he concluded that the reason was the price. He made up his mind to lower the price. Regarding this, Ford encountered serious problems. Some shareholders were not thinking of mass production but of large dividends. Thus, they were an obstacle. In response, Ford bought all the shares from them one by one, allowing him to make his own decisions. In 1906, Ford bought up all the shares of Malcomson for just $175 thousand. Henry was in a dilemma between producing sports cars or cars for the masses. But he decided that success could only be achieved by massive sales. So it was necessary to reduce the price.

In 1905, Ford attended a car race in Palm Beach, where a French racer crashed. All ran to his rescue at once. Ford also went close and picked up a piece of metal from the wrecked car. He thought to himself that the car was solid. He decided that it was necessary to study the opponent. He took the piece to the factory and, gathering his engineers, assigned them to study the composition of the piece. It turned out to be a mixture of vanadium and steel.

Without losing time, they decided to find US producers of vanadium but found only one factory in Ohio. By using this type of steel, Ford's cars became the strongest in the US, and this happened after he accidentally got to know a component of a European car. First, this steel was cheaper and lightweight. Ford's dream was coming true – the mass production of automobiles began.

Competitors must be constantly studied. For example, my partner allocates rather long hours only to study the competitors, and we greatly value this. Studying the competitors enables us to understand their actions and take appropriate steps.

In 1908, the Model T was created, and it had to be black. It is proper to recall Ford's famous quote, "People can have the Model T in any colour – so long as it's black." In fact, the cars were black because this colour paint was less expensive. Before the Model T was released, cars were expensive in the United States, costing between $1,100 and $1,700, and the luxury class cost

$2,500. In those years, the average wage of an American was from $48 to $100. Initially, the Model T cost between $825 and $850 and was available at a price within a worker's budget. Ford did not create demand so much as the conditions - through his low prices - for demand to grow. In the first year of this model's production 10,660 cars were sold, breaking all the records in the automotive industry.

The success of the Model T was in that the car could be used for all services: ambulance, cargo transportation, transportation of people, and so on. In other words, by building a multifunctional car, Ford managed to introduce its production in every sphere. The car was made of solid parts; the engine was quite powerful; the car could be driven in any conditions; it was light and safe to drive. For the initial period this model became so prevalent that Ford had to stop taking orders, because it could not manage to produce cars. How could production be organized to meet the existing demand?

At the time it was possible to assemble 25 units of Model T per day. Ford decided to build a factory that would produce around 1000 units per day, subsequently enabling him to cut costs. That is, large amounts of raw materials could naturally be acquired at a lower cost. When his competitors learned about Ford's intention, they predicted Ford would become bankrupt.

When Ford announced his intention, many people laughed at him because they found it impossible to create a cheaper car. Besides, there was one more problem here with the consumer psychology: if a product is low-cost, the quality has got to be poor. This stereotype had to be broken. It was important for him to have the customer's trust, so he started to provide potential buyers with all the necessary information concerning the car: how much fuel was needed, its power, what spare parts were needed, how to drive, and so on. This was the first caring attitude towards customers. The company impressed them so much that they would become loyal customers. Ford was the first entrepreneur who made sure that every car owner could obtain spare parts without difficulty.

Ford used to say,

"In the Ford Motor Company we emphasize service equally with sales. It has always been our belief that a sale does not complete the transaction between us and the buyer, but establishes a new obligation on us to see that his car gives service."

Thus, the first best-in-class warranty package was being offered in the automotive industry. Mass production was starting. Still, Henry Ford could never understand the look of a car based on sketches. So his engineers always made the new model of the car from wood to show to him.

At the time, there was no assembly line, and people took turns approaching the spare parts and doing their job. For instance, one car was built in 12.5 hours. After the implementation of the assembly line, it was reduced to 93 minutes. Imagine the level of efficiency. If before it was the worker going towards the car, after the implementation of the assembly line the car was moving towards the worker. In 1911-1912, Model T sold about 80,000 cars, two years later – almost 25,000, and in 1916-1917 – more than 700,000 cars. Thus, the production of this model of vehicle reached 2,000 per day. Already at that time, Ford released half of all cars sold in the United States. In the history of world's automotive industry only the famous German Volkswagen "beetles" have sold more cars. During the 19 years of the Model T production 15,007,033 cars were sold in the United States alone. Ford Motor Company became a huge industrial complex that took over the whole world. By the end of 1913, Ford Motor Company produced half of all cars in the United States.

Ford's plants in Detroit were expanding into new territories, and still they could not complete the orders for thousands of cars. It then crossed Ford's mind that it's easier and cheaper to build assembly plants in different parts of the United States rather than produce all the cars in Detroit alone and ship them to the customers. The idea paid off, and in just a few years Ford assembly plants appeared on the coast of the Atlantic and the Pacific and in the north and south of the United States.

In 1913, the accountants observed that the company was losing millions on employee turnover, as Ford spent around $100 on the training of each new worker. To solve the problem, the general manager of the company, James Couzens, suggested that the salary be $5 per day, that is, twice what it was. When this news was spread, people ran to Ford to find a job.

A salary of $5 was, indeed, a revolution, because it was the basis of the formation of the middle class, and people were able not only to survive thanks to their work but also enjoy other pleasures of life. Ford's success would be impossible without Couzens, as it was he who created the dealer network for Ford in 1915. Couzens had developed the after-sales service program for Ford. If there were problems with his cars, he repaired them, while the competitors with more expensive cars did not provide such service.

The car had been invented long before Ford, even better, more beautiful and of better quality than his. He just made cars affordable for all. Ford was the first in the world who created the entire production cycle - coal mining, metal processing, rail transportation up to production, and car sales. The most important key to Ford's success was constant improvement. At one point Henry noticed that there were two major disadvantages in the production, namely:

Workers were spending a lot of time moving the tools and spare parts.

The activities carried out by each worker were too physically demanding.

Ford solved these problems through the moving assembly line. This meant that the car itself moved past the workers. The workman installing a part didn't have to fasten it as well. This was done by the next workman. In such a case, the workmen's mental performance was minimized, and it was possible to quickly dismiss a bad worker and hire a new one.

But if the new worker did not assimilate the necessary knowledge in a defined period of time, he was also dismissed. In this regard, each worker started from the very beginning and could climb up only through his own efforts. That is to say, the so-called principle of justice was practiced – in the beginning all are equal, then everyone gets the work corresponding his abilities.

If a screw was used as a spare part, it had to be put into place after work so that time would not be wasted. This method helped to triple each worker's efficiency. Saving time allowed expenses to be cut as well. Due to the new mechanism, Ford reduced working time to 8 hours and divided the work week into six days at the factory and one day at home. In 1914, Ford used the 24-hour principle. He created three shifts, each 8 hours.

Ford's decision bound the workers to his factories, strengthened labor discipline, and reduced staff outflow. All the workers tried to do their best work, and it was to Ford's advantage.

At one of Henry Ford's factories, there was a crew of workers that was paid for resting. This was the service crew responsible for the smooth uninterrupted working of the assembly line. Simply put, they were the maintenance staff. They were paid only for the time they spent in the recreation room. Once the red light lit up signaling a breakdown in the assembly, the device that counted the money they earned stopped. This working method motivated them, first, to repair the assembly line quickly and efficiently in order to return to the recreation room as fast as possible and, second, to perform the repair work with great care in order not to leave the room because of the same problems with the assembly line. *Frankly, I am stunned by this method.*

Ford wouldn't let any engineer modify even a part of the car and kept repeating,

"The perfect is the enemy of the good."

Ford preferred to sell many cars at a small profit than to sell few cars at a large profit. In other words, he was in favor of large-scale production. Almost everything was being automated in Ford's factories, as it saved the most expensive thing – time.

Each worker was given a responsibility. Ford was not interested in profit but in the car and its quality. This caused the dissatisfaction of shareholders. In particular, there was a year when Ford Motor Company generated so much profit that it desired to return $50 to each buyer, saying that it made no sense to take more money from its buyers.

This was a surprising marketing move that left its mark in the hearts of Americans.

According to Ford, only a man with a healthy lifestyle could be employed at his company – one who didn't drink, gamble, smoke, and spent evenings with family. He had created a special social section that dealt with these issues. The employees in this section visited the workers' houses and asked the workers' wives questions about their husbands. If an employee was leading a healthy lifestyle, his name was registered in a special register. This employee was later rewarded with money. Ford rarely hired women, saying that their place was in the home and family.

Ford could not bear cigarettes, and no one would smoke at the factory. The employees were prohibited to talk about topics unrelated to work. Unsurprisingly, the bulk of the plant's workers were immigrants grouped in a way they wouldn't talk to each other. For example, a German was working with a Russian; a Frenchman was working with a Spaniard, and so on. Not understanding each other, they worked without talking. Ford did not encourage close and friendly relations among employees, as it could lead to concealing each other's mistakes, and many shortcomings would appear in the production.

Ford also did not like fat people, and they had no place in the company, either. He dismissed one of the managers but said he could be rehired if he lost weight. He did not call another employee and fire him, but the employee entered the factory and noticed all the items in his room scattered and his papers torn, meaning it was time to leave. Every employee could submit a suggestion if it came to production improvement. Every new employee would have to start from the beginning. Ford believed that any employee could rise if he wanted to. He never asked the new employee about the past; the desire to work was all that mattered.

The entire factory was responsible for each defect, so everybody strictly monitored the quality. It was forbidden to eat, drink, talk about other topics, refresh a little, smoke, etc. Someone who got fired from Ford's factory couldn't find a job in the community anymore. Ford could unexpectedly gather all the company managers and - regardless of their arrangements, plans, or schedule - send them on a two-week vacation. Afterwards, he would check out how different sections operated. If they went well without the manager, he'd reward them all. If not, he'd fire the manager. As for wages:

- Wages ought to cover the worker's all possible expenses and allow his family to be carefree.

- Workers also had stakes in company's total profits, but not all of them. The first condition was that the worker must have worked in Ford factory at least half a year. Second, he ought to be married. Besides, men and women under 22 could have stakes if they were the sole guardians of their families.

No job candidate was ever rejected because of physical problems. Disabled people worked equally with everyone else, 8 hours a day for $5. Interestingly, people with disabilities did certain tasks better than others did. For instance, blind people calculated and remembered small details best of all.

Ford estimated that a total of 7,882 operations went on at the factory, 3,595 of which did not require hard work and could be carried out by slim, weak men or women and children. Of these operations 670 could be performed by people without legs; 2637 operations - by people with one leg; 2 operations - by people without hands; 715 operations - by people with one hand; and 10 operations - by blind people. Thanks to Ford, people with such problems also had the opportunity to work.

To ensure security, Ford took every necessary step, examined all the devices and machines, and when he found potentially harmful parts, he neutralized them. As a result of these examinations, all the ropes of the machines were covered with special metals. The employees were forced to wear safety glasses in hazardous places. All the cars were covered with nets, a warning not to go too close. There were special inspectors to make sure the employees wore proper clothes for their job. Because of such attention, almost no accidents happened.

Ford did not like doing charity, but instead he created infrastructures. He built a special school and hospital for the children of his workers, so that they wouldn't worry about their children's education. Everyone was busy at school, studying the structure of cars and making auto parts. The peculiarity of the school was that the students were making auto parts, and Ford factory bought those parts from the school. All the students received a scholarship in accordance with their abilities.

By 1920, the US car market had seriously changed. The enriched Americans began to demand more beautiful and more comfortable cars. Ford's competitors were not slow to take advantage of this. The Dodge brothers, who had enriched themselves by supplying engines to the Ford enterprise (before Ford began to make them at the plant at River Rouge), produced a more modern car that was slightly more expensive than the Model T, but it was a great success with the customers. Dodge started an advertising campaign with the slogan "It speaks for itself," implying that it was superior to the Model T. Even more intense was the competition with General Motors. It entered the market with the car brand Chevrolet, which looked much more beautiful than the Model T. This car was designed by William Knudsen, a former employee of Ford. After a conflict with Ford, Knudsen left him and became his competitor. Henry Ford tried to resist the Dodge brothers and Knudsen by reducing prices on the Model T, but for the first time in many years his agents began to accumulate unsold cars.

In the times of the post-war depression, people preferred to buy even inexpensive cars like the Model T on credit and not pay cash. But Henry Ford would not even hear about trade on credit. His son, Edsel, tried to persuade his father to meet the demands of the market, but Ford was categorically against it. And even though the Model T was still in demand in the early 20s, the competition was getting more fierce, with Alfred Sloan heading General Motors, and later by a new automotive company founded by Walter Chrysler. Ford finally admitted his mistake and became more attentive to the financing policies of the competitors.

Meanwhile, General Motors, in contrast to the Ford Motor Company, didn't miss out the change in the buyer's demands and began to offer buyers more comfortable and larger cars in a variety of colors. They cost a bit more than Ford's Model T, but the buyer considered it worthwhile to pay a little more for such a vehicle. What's more, General Motors offered several brands: Chevrolet, Pontiac, Oldsmobile, Buick, Cadillac. And Ford had just the low-cost Model T and expensive Lincoln. If the person achieved certain success in life, but still could not afford Lincoln, he looked for something in between the Model T and Lincoln and found it at General Motors. Ford's flair for business and the market betrayed him.

You should also follow the market and listen to the customers. The market is changing – staying in the same place means to go backwards. Follow the market.

In January 1928 the Ford Model A appeared on the market. It had safety glass in the windshield, an innovation that has since become a mandatory in vehicles. Although the new model was liked by the buyers and dealers, Ford's former position as the undisputed leader of the automotive industry was never recaptured. By 1940, Ford already had less than 20% of the US automotive market.

Finally, on September 24, 1945, Ford Sr. passed company affairs on to his eldest grandson, Henry Ford II, and continued to live quietly with his wife Clara in their Fair Lane estate in Dearborn until his death. Henry Ford died on April 7, 1947, at the age of 83.

Secret 17. Staying in the same place means to regress. Follow the market.

Secret 18

If I see in a resume that the person was self-employed – that's the best employee for me.

Oleg Tinkov

Tinkoff Credit Systems (Oleg Tinkov)

Oleg Tinkov is among those Russian businessmen who must really be presented in 100 Business Secrets, because not every businessman is able to achieve such success in different spheres in such a short period. Besides, we can learn a lot from him given that he did business during the Soviet period and after its collapse. Whatever is going on in former Soviet countries is sometimes unusual for the West and East, since there's a different business environment and different approaches. It's that environment I want to share through Oleg Tinkov's example. So, let's start.

In the summer of 2005, Oleg Tinkov was on holiday in Tuscany. He was riding a bicycle and relaxing. He felt pretty good, as he had just sold his Tinkoff beer business to a Belgian company, InBev. At age 37, Tinkov had become a true multimillionaire. When he sold his Technoshock chain of stores in 1998 and his Daria business in 2002, everybody pitied him. For if he sold his businesses, it meant he was a loser. He lost his businesses. Now, when he concluded his Tinkoff deal, he was praised. This testified to a rapid change in the business environment; people had understood that selling your business can be cool. For Tinkov, there is nothing like selling: It's the only thing that quantifies your business, your investments, and your talents in monetary terms. It gives you the opportunity to start a new project, and then you have not only money but time for it.

Tinkov was thinking a lot about a new business, and he faced the dilemma of choosing an innovative product for the new project or trying to improve the already existing one. If you are smart enough, have good education, believe in your product, and have really found the niche, then creating a new product is the best option. You will gain a lot more money. You will get your million faster if you create a new product. But with all this said, Tinkov considers that creating a new product is something brilliant, talented people are capable of, not people of moderate abilities like him. All his life he would take existing products and improve them. Both models are good. There are great, brilliant people like Sergey Brin or Larry Page who invented a new product and became billionaires. Tinkov thinks that improving a product is enough for him. Therefore, he suggests that we choose: If you want to make billions, invent. If you want to make millions, improve. After selling his beer business, he was again thinking about starting a new business, one that was not going to be something new to the world either. But let's start from the beginning.

Tinkov's life radically changed thanks to sports. He was 14 when a friend of his told him he had joined the school's cycling team, and Tinkov decided to join the team, too. He trained less compared to the others, yet still he won the first place in one of the tournaments in 1983. This was followed by victories - one after another - first at the municipal and then at regional level. After this, he was travelling and taking part in races in a number of cities, in Tashkent, Novorossiysk, Kaliningrad, etc. Overall, Tinkov won 30 out of the 100 bike races he was in. That's quite a good result for this sport. *Anyway, always be active in sports. It keeps you healthy and instills a competitive and winning mentality in a person.* Tinkov's first business was connected to cycling. Before leaving for Leninabad, one of his friends told him to bring money with him, as they had a lot of good products out there. *The moment has to be used.* Tinkov followed his advice. As they went into the store in Leninabad, they saw mohair scarves and Montana jeans on the counter. They bought jeans for 50 rubles and sold them in Russia for 200 rubles, four times more. This became a habit. Every time they came back from competitions with goods and resold them at higher prices.

In 1988, Tinkov entered the Mining Institute of Leningrad, where he met a lot of smart people. The environment there was completely different. The students earned as they could. He did not lag behind either. He would buy vodka at the store for 10 rubles during the day and then sell it in the dormitory for 20 rubles at night. You have to pay for everything, including the sudden urge to drink. His fellow students would get mad about it, but they would buy the vodka. Tinkov engaged in trade. He also imported different goods from abroad. He then quit education and started working with the Pakhomov brothers, who were better known as Ilyiches. The business they did had to do with car sales.

They would fly to Novosibirsk, buy the cars for 50,000 rubles, and sell them for 80,000 rubles in St. Petersburg. The cars were delivered by military aircraft. They paid 5,000 rubles cash for each car. The profits were rather huge for those times. When the USSR collapsed in 1991, people were in panic, while Tinkov was not worried. He kept his savings in dollars and had savings of $10,000 in January 1992. He took it with him to Singapore, where he made his first really big money. From there, his Technoshock retail chain put down its roots. It was Igor Sukhanov who let him in on that Singapore idea. He would travel to Singapore frequently and import computers and fax machines. The importation of computer equipment to Russia had thus started.

Soon Tinkov switched suppliers from Future Systems Electronics to Cut Rate Electronics, headed by an Indian named Ashok Vasmani. Everyone called him Andy though. The goods he sold were perhaps of slightly lower quality, but they were less expensive. Once when Tinkov was buying yet another consignment of Record televisions, Andy asked, "Why don't get a container, it can hold 320 TVs." Tinkov couldn't allow himself to buy so many TVs. It cost $16,000. Plus, he had to pay $5,000 for the container and wait 40 days. And he couldn't take that much money out of circulation. But Andy showed him it was more advantageous. He said that when shipped in a container, it would cost him not five dollars a kilo as usual, but half as much. Tinkov decided to take advantage of the moment. *Seize the appropriate moment.* Andy trusted him, and so Tinkov could pay only half of the money, and Andy loaned him the rest. *Trust is the most important factor in business. Do not deceive, and you will be trusted.*

About forty days later, they were already emptying the TVs, and as soon as they hung up the "Cheap Televisions" banner, the flow of people would not stop. They made a considerable amount of money from the television sales. When the sales started going slowly in St. Petersburg and it was getting harder to sell them even at a price of $350, they decided to expand into other regions. In Siberia, for instance, a TV set cost $500. Andy was the person who believed in Tinkov and helped him to build his career. Tinkov considers him a gift that fate bestowed upon his life. He says that everyone needs to meet someone on his way who will believe in him. Otherwise, you can't become a businessman. *And I would add that you can't achieve any results alone. As I mentioned in Secret 1, you always need a person who will support you, who will believe in you, and who will help and trust you.*

In early 1994, Tinkov bought a store that had belonged to a friend of his, and, in parallel, he opened a Sony store. The Sony store sold products worth twenty thousand dollars a day, and the profit was phenomenal. Tinkov's business was growing and bringing good profit. After these purchases, Tinkov decided to create his own retail chain. The name of the chain was discussed with the whole staff, and in the end they settled upon Technoshock. On September 1, 1995, it all started; they hung up banners, advertised on as many billboards as possible, filmed a commercial, and called all the radio stations. As a result, they were running out of products all the time. The store had a turnover of $20,000 to $50,000 a day. As the business grew, Tinkov started opening new stores in different cities. In 1996, they already had 10 stores, and their prices were the highest of all. The reason was that they provided excellent service. The staff wore white shirts and had gone through special training. Besides, Technoshock had maximum brand awareness.

Tinkov has always preached that the profit margin must be large. Money is formed from a large profit margin. But first you are going to have a small sales volume. You have to survive the first one to three years. For this you need a good profit. Gradually, with the growth of your market share, with the increase in sales, the margin will decrease and adapt to market conditions. The market itself will force you to reduce the margin. But you should start with large profit margins. No business or startup can survive with a sales margin of 10%. This is a road to nowhere.

Tinkov underwent a metamorphosis. From a black-market speculator flying here and there, he turned into a serious retail businessman. He stopped flying to Singapore. The containers filled with electronics made their own way to his company, which became an official dealer for Indesit, Panasonic, Aiwa, JVC, Bosch and other leading brands. They received their products directly in Russia. This was already a serious business with more than 50 employees. "Our initial business philosophy was to work for profit. I am not so much impressed by how much was sold, but how much the company earned. For me the measure of business is pure profit." In addition, the most important factor in Tinkov's businesses is super profitability. All of the products were sold at a 200% to 400% markup.

But the chain *Eldorado* soon invaded St. Petersburg, and the price reductions began. In all the cities where Technoshock had stores, Eldorado would open a store and sell its products at much lower prices. Price setting is important in the retail business. It happens that competitors like price dumping. Yet, according to Tinkov, the last thing an entrepreneur should do is to get involved in a dumping competition. If the competitors are dumping, he says, keep your margin, sell less, look for new products, and find new niches. Bring and offer the consumer a new different product your competitor doesn't have. You can also go into another business. Never get involved in the dumping battle.

In 1997, Tinkov felt a slowdown - the electronics market was already saturated – and he started looking for new opportunities to sell his chain. The company's annual revenue had reached $60 million; the number of employees had increased. At the end of the year, Tinkov threw a corporate party at the Olympia Club, and he didn't know half the people there – it even scared him. Now, when Tinkov has his fifth business, he can say with certainty that when he sees a bunch of people at the office whom he doesn't know, it means it's time to sell the business. Besides, he had made a firm decision to leave the electronics retail business and start a pelmeni (*a type of Russian meat-filled dumpling, similar to Italian ravioli*) and restaurant business, which required money. *Here is some advice to startups.* Manufacturing will require both basic and working capital from you. It's better to start with trade.

Having foreseen that more than 100% of the investment would be covered by profits, Tinkov sold his share of Technoshock and went into the pelmeni business. For the first time he understood that manufacturing was cool, though he hadn't thought so in the past and would criticize it. But visiting a vodka plant owned by his friend Alexander Sabadash and learning how much he was making, Tinkov realized – it's time!

But before that, Tinkov had a phenomenal meeting with a Greek named Athanasius late in the autumn of 1997. Athanasius said he was importing equipment for food production to Russia and was going to import ravioli machines. *Each new contact opens up new opportunities.* After a long conversation, they traded contact information. When Tinkov came home, he asked his wife, "Rina, do you ever buy pelmeni?" The answer surprised him. It turned out she bought 2 packets of pelmeni a week. By the way, at the time pelmeni was made by hand or on semi-automated equipment, meaning that they could make it on automated equipment, build a more efficient production system, and produce quality pelmeni. *If you see a niche on the market, it's time for you to act.*

Then he called Ravioli, a St. Petersburg company, said he traded in food products, and asked if he could buy 1 ton of pelmeni. They answered that the distributors were given 20 tons and that it was useless to talk about 1 ton. Tinkov was astounded: There was really a big market. Calculating expenses for raw materials, labor, equipment, etc., he decided to buy the machines from Athanasius and found the factory. The business was in full swing. Tinkov was so immersed in it that when they returned from the USA, he immediately went to the factory and worked with everyone all night long, all the while examining how the machines worked and whether anything needed improvement.

According to Tinkov, at the start of your business you should think first of all about the work and about how to make money. All the thoughts should be concentrated on making the first ruble. You should go to bed and wake up with the thought of having the first coveted ruble on your account. It's an emotional, exciting moment. You need a full commitment. Tinkov gives the example of a professional athlete. He says that a professional athlete and a businessman are basically the same and that the methods and approaches used by each are similar. When a professional athlete is preparing for an important competition such as the World Cup or Olympics, he is in absolute self-denial. Many athletes live in the mountains at training camps; they think only about victory. If you're not concentrated, if you're distracted by trivial, insignificant things, you will never achieve success. Therefore, Tinkov's advice to startups during their first, hardest weeks is to forget about wife, family, friends, and even mom and dad. You should give yourselves over to the project. Live with it day and night. When the project gets ahead and you get the first ruble, you can relax and go back to normal life.

After the construction of the plant, they produced 300 kg of pelmeni an hour. And all that thanks to the modern equipment that distinguished them from their competitors, because it was impossible to have such results by making pelmeni by hand. Second, they used shock-freezing, which gave the pelmeni long shelf life, even at zero degrees. *Be different.* Tinkov's production was among the first in Russia that fully met Western hygiene standards. The inspectors were shocked: stainless steel, white coats, gloves, and even masks for workers in the meat department.

In those years, pelmeni producers on the market had no brand name. They sold them simply under the name "Pelmeni." At that time, Andrei Makarevich had a show named "Smak" during which they made food. It was a popular show in CIS countries. It happened so Tinkov accidently met Makarevich at the première of a film and decided to seize the opportunity. He talked to him and then with their director and bought the "Smak" trademark for their pelmeni line. And so Smak pelmeni appeared on the market. This was memorable because it was the name of the favorite show; it was familiar to people and had a good reputation. Later, they made an advertising campaign in which the hero explained why he preferred these pelmeni in particular. In parallel, they organized tastings in the stores. Everything was perfect; the sales were increasing day by day.

The sales were a breakthrough. Tinkov had to open a second production facility. Everything went well until he appeared in the trap he had been thinking about a lot. They were selling the product under the name of another brand, and with time that other brand started licensing the brand name to other producers as well. Low-quality Smak sausages, chips and even pelmeni were popping up in the market. The relationships were getting worse and worse. To deal with this situation, Tinkov decided to create his own brand and chose his daughter's name "Daria." Always choose a name that can be protected by patent rights. In the case of Smak pelmeni, they changed the trademark into "Pitersky Smak."

Thus, they segmented the market. "Pitersky Smak" was inexpensive pelmeni and "Daria" was expensive. By market segmentation you divide consumers into several target groups, making it easier to reach out to them through different products. The main principle of segmentation is price. There are people who love to pay more for better quality. They need to be provided with such a product, whereas the majority of people like to save: They take the simplest and plainest product. Thus, the manufacturer's task is to reduce the costs as much as possible and operate in a way that guarantees at least some minimum level of profitability. Many work this way, but not Tinkov. He has always gravitated towards premium brands so the consumers will understand that they pay more, but for a better product, be it non-sticking pelmeni or freshly brewed beer.

When it came to the Daria brand, they needed something noisy. Tinkov had a brilliant idea: Why not make use sex to advertise? Nothing sells like sex, he thought, and he was right. They came up with the slogan "Your favorite pelmeni" and decided to take a picture of a woman's buttocks covered with flour. People remember this ad with a bare bum up to this day, and the expression "Your favorite pelmeni" became a catchphrase. Even in a crisis, Tinkov's huge factory worked at full capacity. The company grew quickly.

They put up several posters in St. Petersburg and a few in Moscow. The posters remained hung for about 10 days, and although they were ordered to be taken down, the whole city talked about Daria. In Moscow, there is more bureaucracy, and the posters hung there for a month. This way, Moscow and St. Petersburg - the two largest markets of Russia - talked about the product. The brand was remembered. *Create noise around your brand. Share and spread it. Think of ways to make people talk about it. Surprise.* In 1999, Tinkov's team sold three thousand tons of products a month. A monthly net profit amounted to approximately $300,000. The cost price of pelmeni was $1 per kilo, and it was sold for $3 per kilo. They continued to sell at a higher price than their competitors.

In the manufacturing business it's crucial to determine the price and control your costs, loans, and interest rates in the right way. And, accordingly, set a price for the goods in accordance with the competition in the market. The company's director was trying to be rational in inventing some schemes for price setting. He would calculate everything, "Cost price plus a certain percentage, cost price plus taxes and something else, full cost plus 20 percent, plus 30 percent." Tinkov did it easier. He had a small office within the factory. He would go there and look out of the window. He saw the queues of the customers. When the trucks were especially numerous, he would call the sales department and say, "Let's raise the price by 10 percent." They would answer him, "But, Oleg, our prices are already too high. Daria is twice more expensive than the competitors' products." Yet still, Oleg insisted, and they raised the price.

When Oleg saw that the queue was not diminishing, he would call a month later and tell the sales department to raise the price by 10 percent again and so on. After all, they did a lot of advertising to promote the product. They could boast of an efficient, successful marketing and PR strategy. They had the most effective distribution. All the four Ps of marketing were met. The product was in demand. They were represented in all the regions, from Vladivostok to Kaliningrad. The distributors around Russia required their product. And once Oleg said, "double the price!" At first, the number of trucks decreased , but then they lined up again! The business was growing.

In 2009, Roman Abramovich's assistant called Tinkov because the billionaire was interested in buying Daria. Tinkov, in his turn, wanted to sell his pelmeni business. When they met, Tinkov offered his price, and, to his surprise, Abramovich agreed to the price without bargaining. The deal was great for Tinkov: The company was sold for $21 million, seven million of which went to pay back debts. He had 14 million in his hands. So why did Tinkov go out of pelmeni business? He doesn't regret having sold it, believing that it was a right move. Unfortunately, the market is relatively small. At the time of the sale, it was estimated to be probably $300 million on an annualized basis. Now, it's maybe $500 million. That is, it has had weak growth over the years. You need to look at the size of the market in general terms and assess what the sale volumes of a given product can be in it. In rubles, dollars, euros or shekels – it's all the same.

Tinkov had long dreamed of building a brewery, but let's start from the beginning. Before the creation of Daria, he had discussed the idea with businessman Alexander Sabadash. Since Sabadash owned the brand Our Vodka, he suggested that they name the beer brand Our Beer. Tinkov liked the idea and wrote a business plan where Sabadash was to be the main investor. He wanted to invest, too, but he didn't have the necessary funds. What was he to do? He started with banks. The bankers would give him surprised looks and say, "Listen, kid. Have you lost your mind? You're an electronics salesman. Go sell them. TVs and beer are like apples and oranges." All the banks refused to help him. In those years Baltica dominated the Russian market. Had the banks financed Tinkov, he would have been at least second in the market by now with billions of turnover, but he was late. In 2003, he did enter the beer market, and despite the late entry, he succeeded. But an incident completely changed the situation.

In October 1997, Tinkov flew to the Drinktec exhibition, which was held in Munich. There he met the owner of Wachsmann company, Joost Wachsmann, and told him about his dream of building a beer factory. He added that he did not have enough money. As Tinkov points out, Wachsmann put him on the right path, "Listen Oleg, don't get frustrated if you don't have enough money now. Build a restaurant with a brewery in it, create a brand, and then start on a big factory."

Oleg knew that there was demand for good restaurants in St Petersburg. He would often go out for beers with his colleagues to an Irish Pub, and sometimes there were lines there. One night, Andrei Mezgiryov, who would later work as director of the *Tinkoff* brewery, asked him, "Oleg, what if we opened a similar bar?" They needed to take action. They had settled upon the name "Our Beer" at first, but when one of the German suppliers learned about it, he said,

"Oleg, what do you mean 'Our Beer'? What nonsense! You are the owner! In Germany the owner names the beer after his name. Aren't you responsible for the quality of your brand?"

When Tinkov was buying equipment for his brewery, he had named the brand "Our Beer." When the equipment arrived from Germany, it was written "Tinkov" on the packaging. He asked the vendor,

"Why is my name on it?"

"Isn't it your beer?"

"It is."

"That's why it's your name on it. What does "Our Beer" have to do with it?""

It was 1997, gangster Petersburg. Tinkov was worried about attracting attention. Everyone would know him. On the other hand, he wanted to stand out and show that he was responsible for his work. So he made up his mind to name the brand Tinkov at his own risk, and yet, out of certain precautions, he changed "v" into double "ff." And this how the Tinkoff brand came into existence. It wasn't an easy decision, but it was breakthrough. Tinkov perhaps became one of the first in Russia who used his name in a business after the collapse of the Soviet Union. He already has his third brand under the brand Tinkoff: first, restaurants; then breweries; and now Tinkoff Credit Systems. Tinkov states that he has no regrets at all and advises against being shy. If you think your product is great, then you can bravely give it your name, he says.

After choosing a name, the next challenge was to find people who could brew beer. A brewer is someone who works ten hours a day with water and heavy metal objects. He must be strong and sturdy. For a long time he was thinking about whom to hire, and suddenly it dawned on him: Miners worked eight hours a day under much worse conditions and at the same humidity levels. Eureka! He thought of Oleg Sandakov, foreman at Yaroslavsky Mine in Leninsk-Kuznetsky. They recommended him to Tinkov because he wasn't a drinker. Tinkov had him and his family moved to St. Petersburg and then sent him to Germany for training. He participated in the installation work of the restaurant, as he knew all the instruments and mechanisms from the mine. The difference is that he had to work at the surface, rather than at a depth of two hundred meters under the ground, and this was for three times more money. Tinkov still thinks it was a superb decision, and he wasn't mistaken in his choice.

The menu was formed based on gut feelings about food they had tried in Germany and America. Prior to the opening of the restaurant, Tinkov sent the chef to the Bavaian city of Ulm for a two-week internship. As a result, Nuremberg sausages with potato salad and stewed cabbage, Bavarian sausages, pork shank, and similar foods were included in the menu.

The restaurant's signature dish, "meter of sausages," was the creation of Igor Sukhanov, who had encountered something similar in Germany. Up to now it's a mainstay at Tinkoff restaurants. He also offered to pour beer into bizarre, one-liter flasks, but this idea didn't work.

In addition to beer breweries at restaurants, Tinkov introduced many things that were unprecedented in Russia at the time. One such step in 1997 was the open kitchen at the restaurant. Everyone could see how people worked in it. The beer brewing equipment was also visible; it added to the charm of the restaurant.

The employees were well dressed and properly equipped; the waiters were trained. The restaurant had an advanced computer system for those years. Tinkov bought the best of everything. He imported stainless steel equipment and furniture from America. The sellers, says Tinkov, are perhaps still amazed that some Russian bought four containers of furniture, packaged them, and left. It seems inefficient from a modern point of view, but where could he find something similar in Russia in 1997? They bought necessary goods for some $200,000. All this made their restaurant stand out from others. *Create a unique environment that will be new for people. Uniqueness always attracts people.*

Of course, they made certain mistakes. They bought all the dishes, including glasses, from America. They even had "Tinkoff" written on them. But the paradox was that the unit for volume in America is in pints not in liters. So, instead of the usual 500 ml, these glasses contained 600 ml, and instead of 330 ml they contained 400 ml. The staff used them somehow but people complained. The glasses were thrown away. That was a mistake.

Tinkov bought everything from the USA because he wanted to have an American-style restaurant. But not always did it work. The difference in standards sometimes failed them. The spoons and forks at least were not different. And, most importantly, when Tinkov had just started as a restaurateur, he did not understand the obvious: Things break down. You can't replace half of the service set with another. They could not buy the same dishes in Russia. No one sold them. Buying small batches of 10 plates or 20 cups for the replacement of broken ones was too unprofitable and almost impossible to do in San Francisco. Tinkov had no one there who would do that job. The lack of uniformity in dishes was one more mistake.

Because it's such a detailed business that needs to be carefully thought out, Tinkov advises spending at least 2-3 months before opening a restaurant. You should think over all details, go to other restaurants, spend some time there, and even take pictures. You can go to your favorite restaurant with a camera, take pictures of the interior details, and understand how people work.

When the restaurant is ready to be launched, Tinkov advises having a well-publicized opening and feeding the journalists, as it always helps. Journalists love to write when they are well fed. Do not spare money on them. After all, marketing and PR are the most important factors about restaurants. People should know about your restaurant. They should come to you. So throw a loud party on the opening of your restaurant and treat your guests - from governors to journalists - to good, expensive alcohol, Tinkov says. Yes, it will cost money, but you can include it in the investment budget. Say you've put $200,000 in the restaurant. Spend $20,000 more – they will come back to you.

Some more of Tinkov's experience: When you've made money and the business is going well and there's demand, expand it into other territories, other cities, and other areas of the city. Create a chain. It is necessary to grow geographically. It is foolish to open a similar restaurant nearby or on the next street. It can kill the business of one of them, or both will suffer. To create an atmosphere, there must be people sitting in your restaurant. People stop visiting the restaurant when it's empty. People go where there are people. No people – no one goes there.

The opening of Tinkov's restaurant was held on August 1, 1998. The staff treated all of the guests to food and drinks for an entire day and night – it was perceived as something wild in St. Petersburg at the time. A large number of the city's restaurateurs came to the opening and were surprised to hear Tinkov's plans to have $10,000-$20,000 in sales a day. They believed that this was UNREALISTIC, because their more serious restaurants only managed to pull in $3000-$4000 a day. Supposedly, the record of $8,000 was set by Senate-Bar on Galernaya Street, where groups of foreigners were taken, and in 1996 US President Bill Clinton himself dined there.

Despite the skepticism, Tinkov's plans were realized. People just poured into the restaurant. From October to December the restaurant was full, with sales amounting to $15,000 – $20,000 dollars a day. One million dollars of the investments were covered within exactly one year. And all this in times of crisis. This is why Tinkov points out that in times of crisis you can and you should find a niche and start a business. If consumers need something, they will pay for it.

Tinkov encourages everyone to find a niche. After all, an entrepreneur is someone who sees opportunities, someone who can see what others do not see, someone who can find the positive in something that seems negative. An entrepreneur is an optimist by nature! Of course, luck plays a significant role, and he considers himself happy, because he's been lucky. But to make your luck work for you, you must do something. Remember, it's not enough to find a niche, he says, you must also find the right people and motivate them materially and morally. Tinkov has been lucky with good people. He often comes across them in life. Thanks to them, he grew as a person and as a businessman.

The equipment in the St Petersburg restaurant was so powerful that it was impossible to sell all the beer that they had on tap. So Tinkov, together with Igor Sukhanov, decided to buy a beer bottling line. He left for Italy and ordered one. It cost a few hundred thousand dollars. Later, Tinkov bought out the twenty-five percent held by Igor and became the sole owner of the restaurant. After an advertisement shot by Oleg Gusev, the demand for the bottled beer exceeded the supply. A bottle of beer cost them 30 cents to produce, and they sold it at wholesale for one dollar. The price reflected a stock factor: If the beer is out of stock, the price goes up. If it's in stock, the price remains the same. That's about marketing. The next step would be to build a factory. Building a factory on borrowed money was a risk, of course. The journalists were asking mean questions such as,
"The new plant is going to increase the company's production power by nine times. Aren't you afraid that the market will not be able to absorb so much beer from Tinkoff?"
To which Tinkov would answer,
"I'm always afraid, but I still act. Such is the fate of an entrepreneur and

a businessman. Only fools never fear."

So, now he had a plant capable of producing 37 million bottles a year. But what to do with them? A breakthrough was needed. Tinkov realized that you can't just launch the product. At the beginning there would need to be a sudden shortage. To create it, you need a unique product, unique price, and the right distribution. The bottle was designed by the company Koruna. It was original, with a woman's waist. No wonder it was so much liked by women. The bottle was non-returnable. Once you had finished the beer, it could only be thrown away. Twist-off caps and six packs also became Tinkoff's hallmarks. The recipe was German and required high-quality, Bavarian hops. What should the price be? Tinkov realized that it was possible to set any price. And so they did.

He started with the selling price of 30 cents per bottle, eventually reaching a price point of $1, given that the cost price was 18 cents. That is, they started with a 60% markup and ended up at 230%. Why? The product was in demand. There was not enough beer. Tinkov's principle is that if you keep running out of the product, safely raise the price. Do not be afraid. Many people, after reading these lines, would dispute this. His judgment may seem controversial. And yet, he's of the opinion that as long as you have the product in the warehouse and it's sold, the price must be raised. Instead of racking your brains to come up with all sorts of formulas, use one formula. If the product is being sold, raise the price. If it's not, leave it the way it is. If it's not being sold at all, reduce the price. Make sales. In a nutshell, Tinkov's formula is that you need to intuitively feel the market. That's being a businessman.

In fact, Tinkov spent $10 million dollars on advertising Tinkoff beer. These are just peanuts, though, when compared to the expenses of the competitors. For instance, this would constitute just a small part of Baltica's marketing budget. All in all, Tinkov and his team built up a huge brand. Even though years have passed since the sale of his brewery business, people keep thinking that Tinkov is a brewer, the one and only. He's proud of the results. The competitors were in a state of shock. But he cared the least about their shock. The distributors began to scoop up Tinkoff beer. They would take out product loans, which were provided by Baltica, and would buy Tinkoff beer instead. Tinkov accepted cash only. Then the company became so self-confident that it would sell beer only on a prepaid basis. And then it doubled the prices, and the factory could hardly keep up with the orders. This is what advertising does. This is what impact marketing has!

In 2005, Tinkov was on holiday in Dubai, when he got a call. It was the director of Sun Interbrew. He wanted to buy Tinkov's company. As a result, he sold it for $260 million and decided to have a rest, but …

While living in the United States, every day Tinkov would constantly receive credit card offers by mail. He got a couple and at the same time started to think that this was a good idea for Russia, a massive country like the USA. The roads and airports in Russia may be subpar, but mail can be sent anywhere. Sending offers to customers through the mail! It was not a bad idea. *Oleg again noticed the niche.* Of course, he realized that he needed a huge sum of money to open a bank, and he didn't even picture himself as a banker. But because his own experience had left him discontent with the way Russian banks gave loans, he very much wanted to be the one lending money, not the other way around.

In early autumn, 2005, Tinkov asked Stephan Dertnig, chief at the Moscow office of Boston Consulting Group, to do a feasibility study examining how realistic it was to turn his idea into a business. He asked Stephan to prepare a concept and determine whether it was possible to market credit cards directly in Russia. Soon Stephan presented the study and answered that it was worth engaging in that business. Tinkov set to work and met representatives from Mastercard and Visa. They agreed to work with him.

Now certain that this business was a real possibility, Tinkov flew to Necker island and took some of the key staff members from his beer business with him. They were all Tinkoff people who were working in Tinkov's restaurant chain, temporarily, after the sale of his beer business. Unfortunately, he had not been able to sell the chain to the Belgians. In fact, he had been paying salary to his staff for half a year to keep them as a team in order not to lose valuable human resources. But for some of them there were no appropriate jobs in the bank, and Tinkov provided them a bridge to go on working in their respective fields. The trip was an additional bonus for their excellent work in the beer business. They had fun the whole week, and on the last day Tinkov asked for a projector. Then he set it up on the table, directed the ray on the wall, and went through the report of Boston Consulting Group. He then asked, "Do you believe in this idea?" Everyone exclaimed "Yes." In the end they all shook hands at the table, drank rum, and decided that Tinkov's next business would be in credit cards. They chose the name "T-Bank." It was symbolic for Tinkov that the decision was made on Necker island. Thus, on November 18, 2005, Tinkoff Credit Systems was launched. *This is how the team should be treated, by listening to their views, celebrating victories together, and helping them if you have sold your business and they have difficulty finding another job. This was an admirable step by Tinkov.*

Tinkov believes that celebrating the holidays and small successes is necessary. Before an important event in Tinkoff Credit Systems – the release of the millionth card – he made a gift to the top managers of the bank, and they flew to the world's most expensive island, Necker, and took a rest there with Richard Branson. In this way, the employees fix the end of a certain phase in their minds. Since the days of Daria, Tinkov has tried to encourage his employees with interesting trips to places like Jamaica, Sicily, Hawaii, Verbier, Necker.

He advises celebrating any events – the first customer, the first ruble, the first million clients, the first ten million clients. It's important to fix the stages of success in the brain. It's metaphysics. Success is then transmitted to the further growth and development of the organization. If you are not successful, your business is also not successful. If you don't think positively, nothing good will come out, Tinkov says. *Celebrate the significant occasions. We also celebrate any noticeable progress, events, and big orders with our team.*

Tinkov discussed his bank business a lot with Rustam Tariko. The latter told him,

"Are you sure? Oleg, you are being involved into a serious fight. It's a complicated technology business." A bit later he said, "When I started working on the bank, I met Mikhail Freedman, head of Alfa-Group, and he told me that it was a bad idea, that it was a big business, and that there was no place for me in it. And now my share of the customer loan market is several times bigger than that of Alpha Group, and when it comes to credit cards, my business is ten times larger than his."

"Listen, Rustam, you just tried to talk me out of it, and now you told about Freedman. If it worked for you, why do you think it won't work for me?"

"It's your decision, Oleg. Give it a shot! But you should know it will not be easy."

Perhaps Rustam did not quite believe that Tinkov would actually start the project. Perhaps he still does not believe in what Tinkov is doing. A note – in 2009 Rustam's bank suffered a loss, while Tinkov's bank had profit of more than $18 million. The funny thing is that before the launch of the bank, Tinkov also had a conversation with Mikhail Freedman, who did not believe in his idea, either. But the good thing is he is already used to skepticism. "What are you doing? You are already late. The market is saturated with professionals. You're being ridiculous." He'd hear these words every time he was to start a business. He heard it when opening Technoshock, Daria, Tinkoff restaurants, Tinkoff breweries, and Tinkoff Credit Systems. But these conversations only made Oleg even more excited because he loves achieving what others think impossible, even though he does not consider himself more gifted than others.

According to Tinkov, you can discuss it with everyone you can, with friends and foes, with your wife, girlfriend or lover, but do not take it all at face value. Try to analyze and think it over yourself. A true entrepreneur has the right to decide for himself. The entrepreneur should not be stopped by other people's lack of faith. The main thing is to believe.

At first, they had decided to name the bank "T-Bank," but one of the branding companies said that though Tinkov's bank was going to do direct mail marketing and did not need advertising, it still needed initial recognition. No one could understand what T meant, while everyone knew Tinkoff. So they proposed him to call the bank "Tinkoff Credit Systems." That name first surprised Tinkov, but he realized later that "Tinkoff" was a recognizable name, and "Credit Systems" sounded solid and gave the opportunity to offer not only credit cards, but other services as well. In September 2006, they closed a deal on the purchase of Khimmashbank. In fact, they bought an empty bank with a clean license and renamed it Tinkoff Credit Systems. It was then when Tinkov left the United States for good and started gathering a team.

At the initial stage of a company's development, the entrepreneur often has to combine different positions. He's the owner, the general manager, sales manager, and HR manager in one person. If the entrepreneur does everything himself at the start, gradually, as the company grows, he should start to delegate authority. He will have to hire the first, the second, the twentieth employee. And if development is successful, there may come the moment when the number of employees reaches ten thousand. Here, the entrepreneur should give one of his important functions, hiring people, to the personnel department, says Tinkov.

His success has always been based on tight control of costs. He has never tried to hire too many people, especially now in Tinkoff Credit Systems. The payroll in the 1990s sometimes comprised 2-3% of the expenses, and today it's over 30%, and sometimes 50%, depending on the business. Of course, each new hire is a matter of cost, it's a serious decision. Tinkov finds that one should hire new employees only if there is a great need.

How can it be determined when it is time to hire a new employee? In all Tinkov's businesses it was usually like this. If a person works till midnight because he's inefficient and unable to accomplish the required amount of work before 7 p.m., there is no need to hire a new employee. If a person works till midnight and passes out from exhaustion, it looks as though it's time to help him by hiring one more employee. You are going to come across the fact that managers always complain that they have loads of work and that they want someone to help them. This is perfectly normal. But Tinkov wouldn't pay attention to that. He hires when it comes to fainting from fatigue.

Tinkov suggests that initially it is better to pick people through your friends. If you have just started a business, look for employees through friends. Tinkov very much liked the response of Gary Cohn, the president of the American banking firm Goldman Sachs, who is the second person after the CEO and Chairman Lloyd Blankfein. To Tinkov's question how Goldman Sachs managed to build its recruitment policy so perfectly and achieve good results, he answered, "You know, we don't have an HR department." This came as a shock to Tinkov.

He further explained that when their employees meet with contractors, partners, or potential clients – and they have dozens, hundreds of meetings – they act as their human resources agents. They return to the office and share information with their colleagues. They say they met such a person at the meeting. They talk about who is talented, smart, and interesting. So they take him into account, and if there's vacancy, they try to invite the person they spotted to an interview or offer him a job. So, as it turns out, even such advanced companies as Goldman Sachs are not keen on using agencies. This was an example of the richest bank in the world. Meet, talk, watch people. Try to make them interested. Encourage and attract them. Persuade them to work for you. This is a difficult, non-trivial task, Tinkov says, but it's worthy of a great entrepreneur-psychologist.

By the way, after this conversation with Gary Cohn, Tinkov tried to get the top management of Tinkoff Credit Systems to look out for "stars" during the meetings. Especially now, when there's shortage of people who understand online processes and the technology of internet business. But this method hasn't worked yet. Tinkov explains this by the Russian mentality – people are not yet ready to nurture competitors for themselves. Say there's a top manager with an annual salary of $300,000, plus bonuses. What if he hired someone smarter and more talented? It is a threat to his salary.

Half of the bank's employees are mathematicians and analysts from Phystech and Mechmath. In fact, their business is about science, processing of massive information, comparing it, analysis, and tests. The motto of the bank is, "Test. Test. Test." They never say it may be this or it may be that. They test everything. Tinkov says he has even turned off his famous intuition. They make all the decisions on the basis of carefully constructed mathematical models. Intuition is good. They use it to make strategic decisions. But all their tactics and concrete steps are based on tests, studies, mathematical models, and accumulated data. Now, they have, perhaps, one of the best databases in the market.

The more investments there are in the business, the more difficult it is to cover them. But in the long run, it will only bring profit. After all, you already have the technology and equipment. You need to hire fewer people. The processes have been debugged. For example, Tinkoff Credit Systems spent $20 million – that's a lot of money – on the IT infrastructure. For the first couple of years no profit was expected. They lost $20 million in the first year, and $40 million in the second year. This is natural for the start-up stage. Those are the accumulated investments, costs. In the third and fourth years these investments started to perform well and bring profit. Tinkov understands well that it's impossible to survive today without an IT platform. He recommends that startups use new technologies, as it makes it possible for them to beat the players using the old infrastructure. After all, you have the opportunity to buy new and efficient equipment and use the most advanced sales channels, while competitors are hostages to their old business model.

In early 2007, Oleg began to realize that he needed someone to deal with the overall management. In March, he sat in the office thinking about who it would be. And he suddenly remembered an Englishman from Visa. He was a serious man, the head of Visa. Would he agree to work at a bank that was still taking losses? Tinkov thought. What's more, they had had a heated argument once. Would he go to work for someone so "high-handed"? Tinkov supposed that he wouldn't, but here's a piece of advice from him: Never be shy, if you want something, be sure to try. He picked up the phone, called Oliver and asked him to meet. Before that, he had called a few people with such qualifications, and they had declined. He was ready to receive a similar answer. Oliver asked,

"Oleg, why do you want to meet?"

"I want to offer you a job."

"Well, that sounds interesting, let's meet."

Oleg almost fell off the chair. He thought Oliver was joking. Another thought flashed through his mind: Perhaps, this Oliver Hughes will demand a salary of $10 million per year. But they met and came to an agreement. This news caused a storm in the market; everyone was shocked; a man who had worked as the head of Visa for eight years shifted jobs to work in a small bank under the leadership of some crazy man. In fact, like the other top managers at their bank, Oliver is Tinkov's partner. Tinkov believes that one of the conditions of the company's growth is having the top management as partners because such individuals will be interested in the growth of capitalization and profits. The top ten people are all shareholders of their company. This makes their model more sustainable and is their strong point.

When you reach the desired result, hand over the tasks to more professional people who are more skilled in their fields. By doing so, you will have quite a lot of time to deal with strategic issues. Oliver Hughes was criticized by everyone. They thought he was mad to leave a company like Visa for an unknown bank. But if Oliver had put his reputation at risk, Tinkov had put his entire fortune at risk.

So, according to Tinkov, what kind of work should the entrepreneur do himself and what should be delegated? Initially, the entrepreneur should do everything himself. For example, technology works best when the businessman himself goes through all the stages and gets a grasp of what is going on in it. It's even helpful to unload the car with goods because you will understand what the work of a porter is like. And then, when you pay him for that work, you can understand where he can cheat or trick you. Tinkov is of the opinion that the entrepreneur must himself do the maximum amount of work for the first weeks or months. Even if he's not quite familiar with it or doesn't quite like it, it will still give him a certain knowledge base, which will help him in the future.

Little by little, Tinkoff Credit Systems began to attract more clients. But it became clear that the money would not last long. The business of a bank consists of buying money cheaply and then selling it for more. Tinkov had invested the money he had obtained from the sale of his brewery business in starting the business. Now, he had to borrow money to further develop his business. But where could he borrow more? The bank had no offices, so it couldn't serve the customers as a full-service bank. There remained the capital market. It was necessary to issue bonds. But it became clear in autumn that those who had money preferred to keep it to themselves, while the Western markets had completely closed their doors to Russian borrowers. The last months of 2007 became a real nightmare for Tinkov and his team.

The situation in the market was poor and the bank had little success selling, and, though no other firm would have done any better, the company's reputation took a hard blow. It was as if the investors did not believe in Tinkov. They decided to complete the circulation later. Tinkov called all of his financer acquaintances and tried to convince them to take part in the circulation, but this achieved little. In total, they managed to place 400 million rubles worth of bonds and bought out the remaining 600 million rubles. The investors had just scattered. This was a serious blow for Tinkov. Crushed, he sat in his office at his round table and he cried. Of course, he's a strong Siberian man, but he had tears running down his face. He couldn't understand why those people were willing to buy garbage. And a year later they saw all those "shit retail and shit construction companies," which had been built on debt defaults.

An acquaintance of Tinkov bought $100 million in bonds from Tinkoff Credit Systems and nine more companies. Out of the billion he had invested, 900 million ended up in default. Only Tinkov's company returned it in a year. Why were they buying from others and not from his company? What was with this attitude towards him? Why did everybody hate him? Why did they think Tinkov was worthless? Tinkov could not understand; he just sat there and cried. Oliver Hughes walked into the room; Oleg could see the tears in his eyes. They just hugged each other and Tinkov said, "We shall win this war!" *Never give up, I repeat, never give up.* And from that moment on Tinkov has always felt Oliver's support, and he hopes Oliver feels his as well. They were going to prove everyone that they were not in that business for nothing. *You don't achieve success alone.*

Tinkov had little money left in the bank. There was no money for the ongoing costs, for expanding the portfolio. The management did not receive a salary for a while. They constantly met with investors, hoping to get debt financing. In the end they managed to agree on a syndicated loan of $60 million - $20 million from their shareholder Goldman Sachs, $30 million from the Swedish Vostok Nafta fund, and $10 million from the American hedge fund Blue Crest. In the meantime, they began negotiations with the latter two investors on the sale of stakes in the bank.

Of course, not only the Swedes but also Oliver deserves the credit in all this. All the transactions of capital-attracting came about by way of a road show. Oleg and Oliver toured America together, and then Oliver did it on his own in Europe. You had to tell the same thing for two weeks for five or six times every day. Tinkov didn't speak much. Oliver gave the presentations in English. But Tinkov admits that by the third day even he felt sick listening to it. It was such exhausting and serious work.

In late December, Julian Salisbury of Goldman Sachs sent the famous letter, which is still kept in Tinkov's office. It read, "We're giving you more money. Use it as you have the other money we've given you. We believe in you, but it's quite possible that this is the last money the bank will be able to attract. A serious crisis is coming." This was the essence of the letter. Many ask Tinkov, "What made TCS be ready for the crisis?" He explains that it's due to partners such as Goldman Sachs that send letters like this one and that they never lived only for today but also for tomorrow. They saved money. They saved every penny. In the middle of 2011, Tinkov had 68%, Goldman Sachs had 15%, and Vostok Nafta had 17%.

Despite the crisis, the bank already operated at a profit in 2009, generating $18 million net profit. In 2010, the profit was twice as less, but the reason was that they invested huge sums for the future growth. In 2011, it generated a record profit. The bank turned out to be very effective: It has no departments for customer service and no chain of ATMs. It pays other banks to have their customers use their ATMs, as it's still more beneficial than buying, installing, and maintaining the ATMs themselves throughout Russia. Tinkov insisted that loan repayments be free for the customer. That's in line with his principle: Make the process of parting with the money as easy as possible for the client.

If traditional bank customers are used to going to a branch, then this shift to a model with no branches will cause them a shock. Banks with branch locations have to continue to keep expensive infrastructure in the form of offices and make sure the ATMs always have cash, even though half of the clients are ready to stop going to them, Tinkov says. The clients of TCS knew from the start that they were going to be serviced remotely. Many people are not mentally prepared yet to work with a bank with no physical locations. But such banks save a lot of money on rent, repairs, and maintenance. That's TCS's competitive edge. Tinkov treats the matter a bit philosophically. After all, TCS is not so large and is not ready to serve all either. Their target audience is the people who are ready to accept remote banking. Thanks to a small focus, TCS managed to become one of the market leaders in credit cards competing with much larger players, such as the Russian Standard, Sberbank, VTB 24, Citibank, OTP Bank, Alpha Bank, Home Credit and Finance Bank.

For the banks with remote service to survive in a competitive market, the quality of their services should be higher. 24/7 service is a necessity for the bank. The customers appreciate speed and attention. In a bank like TCS lines are even theoretically impossible, as there are no departments. The bank solves all the questions with the clients by means of the call center, online banking, and e-mail. If you do not have offices, two things are essentially important: your call center and your website.

Tinkov explains that they started referring to call centers as "contact centers" because they serve the customers not only through the phone but other channels as well. TCS receives several thousand letters on its email address, *service@tcsbank.ru,* on a daily basis. None of them is left unattended. Responses are made in the shortest possible time. The team is also developing a public communication with customers on the Internet – on blogs, forums, social networks. As Tinkov puts it, the contact center is the face of the bank. The friendlier it is, the more loyal its clients are, and the higher the profit is.

Tinkov says the website is the second face of the bank. The website sells services. The road to the purchase should be as short and intuitively understandable as possible. There should be as few steps as possible. Increase the conversion rate. That's your task. Even most offline businesses should now have their own websites. It's a must. Whoever neglects the Internet will simply leave the market soon. Of course, Tinkov is pleased that he is in the credit card market. The penetration of credit cards in the Russian market is only 10%. If each American on average has four credit cards, this figure in Russia is 0.1. The growth potential is huge!

This was a brief account of the path Oleg Tinkov has travelled in his creation and sale of a number of businesses. His daughter Daria loved pelmeni. He then decided to make a product "people deserved," so as he ate it with pleasure, too. His pelmeni were more expensive for people with average income, but they were of high quality. Next, he couldn't find a place to drink good beer; there were lines everywhere, and he opened his brewery restaurant. He liked unfiltered and unpasteurized beer, and he made it himself. He was fond of credit cards, but he couldn't find a bank in Russia that would allow him to use the speed of modern technology, and so he opened his bank of credit cards.

Some more advice from Oleg Tinkov: "The entrepreneur reaches everything by blood, sweat and tears. On the one hand, it is better to improve the business you are already in. On the other hand, if you see a different category, even if it's unfamiliar to you, but you feel you are an entrepreneur, visionary, and successful person, just go into it. That's what I did. I knew nothing about video trade, nor about pelmeni. Beer was just a dark forest to me. I thought beer was made like vodka: They take alcohol and mix it with something. By investing money in my bank project, I didn't know any of the terms, I didn't understand what the requirements of the Central Bank were. But there's nothing wrong about it. If you have the will, desire, and imagination, then go into the business that you find profitable and interesting. You don't have to know it in all details."

Secret 18. Find a niche and fill it with an original approach to the best of your ability.

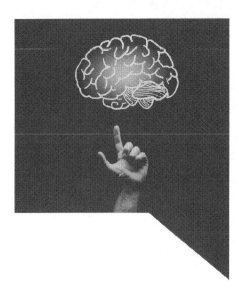

Secret 19

The Wal-Mart discounter in the USA spread the smell of mandarin throughout the store during the Christmas season; the sales increased by 22 %.

How to Influence the Purchase Decisions

The goal of marketing is to influence purchase decisions. To do this, marketers need to know how consumers actually decide what to purchase. The psychology of choice helps to answer it, revealing mechanisms, principles and rules of decision-making process. Over the past few years, many interesting discoveries have been spreading quickly. Yet, the true reasons why people act one way or another still remain a mystery. For example, none of the focus group members liked Baileys liquor, but after the product made it to the market, it was successfully sold. Red Bull also had the same fate. Thee test results were as follows: "Disgusting," "Tastes like a pill," and "I will never drink it." But the reality is different. Red Bull was also a great success.

In the following five sections, I'll present the tools and techniques pertaining to purchasing. They have been studied and applied in the United States and Europe. We make 40-70% of our purchasing decisions without planning, meaning that everything takes place on the spot. Even if the buyers know what they want, all the same, certain factors affect the decisions. Here are the tools that make people shop:

1. The habit factor – 70% of smartphone owners look at the phone within 15 minutes of waking up. Per day, people check their phones 34 times on average, and sometimes up to 150 times. And now let's face the reality – we are trapped. This means being a prisoner of habit: The companies know well how to increase profits through people's habits. Now you know that if you need information, you should visit Google.com, or if you want to communicate or post pictures, you go to Facebook.com, etc. These very companies make money on your habits.

Warren Buffett and his partner, Charlie Munger, understand that if the customers like the product, the price does not bother them that much. For example, you're sitting in front of the computer and playing a free game. You pass several levels and become skilled at it. Your interest increases and the desire to win is intense, but there comes a point when you are required to pay for the next level.

You already need to play. You want to win and are ready to pay for that. In this virtual reality you also pay for more "lives," weapons, and products that you need to reach the next levels. *In this way, by working on the force of habit, the marketers realize an increase in their income. The force of habit makes people faithful.*

2. Be like stars – To better understand how the stars can be used, let's observe Vitaminwater's steps. The marketers had made a shrewd decision: Why not offer the celebrities shares of the company and require in return constant free advertising? Through this shrewd plan they realized two goals – Vitaminwater had a star-filled team, and the stars became more motivated to use the product and promote it on the screen. For example, Ellen DeGeneres would show up on her shows with Vitaminwater Zero, drink it, and keep the conversation going.

Marketers know well that - though not in all cases - if celebrities advertise a certain product in daily life, and not in front of the camera, the sales increase. For example, in 2007, Victoria Beckham was accidentally photographed buying the book Skinny Bitch. Though the book was a bestseller in Great Britain, it was not quite widespread in the USA. The moment when the photograph appeared in magazines and on the Internet, the sales of the book increased by 37,000%, and the book appeared in the New York Times Bestseller list and stayed in it for 84 weeks.

Taking all this into account, marketers try to photograph the celebrities using their products in daily life and make it work for the increase of the sales. Vitaminwater followed a sensible policy in this regard, as celebrities such as Sarah Jessica Parker, Tyra Banks, Heidi Klum and others would be spotted with the Vitaminwater bottle in their hands in different environments. *Making us feel like celebrities is one of the marketers' weapons and is successfully applied up to this day.*

3. Expert advice – Emory University studies have shown that people stop thinking when the advice is coming from an expert in the field. The marketers use this fact a lot; you must have seen many times specialists in white robes proclaiming the high quality of a product in advertisements.

4. Decisions based on database – A Canadian chain store found out that coconuts were best sold alongside with calling cards. This fact gave the marketers food for thought, and finding a solution was a real headache. What did the coconut fruit have to do with a calling card? Shortly after, they observed that coconut is mostly bought by the Asians, as it was part of their diet. Besides, they called home a lot to communicate with their relatives. The next step is predictable; these products were placed side by side. When the Asian buys a coconut, he notices the calling card, and it reminds him that he must call his parents, and so the sales increase.

5. Intuitive decision – Let's also not forget that the customers often make intuitive decisions. Let's take Daniel Kahneman's query as an example: "A bat and a ball cost $1.10 in total. The bat costs $1 more than the ball. How much does the ball cost?" Many of you answered at once, and I am certain that most of you were wrong. So did the majority of students at Harvard and Princeton Universities, who answered - 10 cents. In fact, the ball costs $0.05, and the bat costs $1.05, that is $1 more. What happened with the brains of people that gave a wrong answer to the simple problem? They are just not accustomed to thinking hard and answered intuitively.

By this example Kahneman examined the buyer decision process. If one thinks for hours before buying a product, he will die of hunger and thirst, and to discuss every product will overload the brain, so he thinks intuitively.

We know that brands influence people's decisions, adding to the value of the product in the eyes of people. For example, Volkswagen Sharan and Ford Galaxy are similar cars, both are assembled in the same factory, but people are ready to pay $1000 more for VW, because of the reliability of the brand. In Great Britain, for example, it was believed that Virgin Mobile was of higher quality than T-Mobile even though both used the same network. If an American is asked what Honda is, he replies that it's a car, and a Japanese says it's a motorcycle. It all depends on perceptions.

But the most important question remains open – how people make decisions and what factors affect the decision-making. In 2007, Stanford University professors performed an experiment to deduce how certain centers of the human brain function. At first, they showed chocolate boxes to people, and then their prices; by pressing the button the participants indicated whether they agreed to make a purchase or not. The brain scans revealed that at the sight of the chocolate box the pleasure centers of the brain were activated; the brain seemed to be saying that it wants it.

We all know that the consumer's strength of desire depends on the value. If the value is high, that center of the brain activity increases, and the opposite is true. And what happens when the price comes into sight? When the price comes into sight, the part of the brain responsible for pain is activated. Paying, being deprived of money, makes one feel pain and suffering. And now imagine how overloaded the brain is when considering a purchase amidst the various products in the supermarket, and all this leads to an intuitive result.

Thus, it becomes clear that the purchasing decision is made due to the correlation between pleasure and pain. So, the marketers have to do everything to increase pleasure and decrease pain. *Now you will ask me how to achieve such result. The answer is as follows: In an advertisement the product's value needs to as visible as possible, and, at the same time, the "pain" must be reduced through certain discounts or special offers. Companies are generally guided by this very policy in their advertising campaigns.*

I think many of you have heard phrases like "Superior stain removal or stronger than dirt" often accompanied by words like "Until 4 March 20% off the entire range." Together, these phrases reflect the value and reveal the savings. Do you want to relieve the pain? Increase the product's value in the eyes of the consumer and apply methods of reducing the price.

The experiment convinced us that the price affects the part of the brain that experiences pain, but the high price, in its turn, reflects the value. It confirms that the product is really good and that you need to pay for the quality. The solution to this problem was given by a German specialist in neuromarketing, Hilke Plassmann, whose research studied the influence of price on the perception of the product.

The participants were to taste wine. They were informed of the prices of the wines, but they didn't know that each wine they tasted was, in fact, the same. The price tags were simply different. The prices ranged from $10 to $80. The research results showed that the participants thought the wine that cost $80 was better than the less expensive ones and that when tasting it, their brain centers of pleasure were activated. Let's not forget that the wines were the same except for the fake price tags.

6. Adding spice – A researcher from Cornell University emphasizes that it's better to spice the product name with attractive words than use the ordinary name. For example, in one study people were shown menus in which the same dish had different names: "Smoked and unique fish made in Italian style" and "smoked fish." The researchers wanted to understand how the alluring adjectives affected people in decision-making. And, indeed, the dishes with enticing names were ordered more than the ordinary ones.

The dishes with such adjectives were even called "tasty" by people, meaning that the additional words had added to their value in the eyes of people. The description had an impact on the taste perception, as expectations grow when reading sentences with colorful words. On the packaging of a number of products in the supermarket you can only see next to the name of the product a word such as "snack," which doesn't say anything to the buyer, while "subtle and delicious snacks" adds to its value in the eyes of the consumer.

Spicing up the texts with such enticing words adds to the product's value in the customer's eyes. For example, a study was carried out in a supermarket. Two different sentences were written on two meat packages, "75% lean meat" and "25% fat meat." The first variant was better perceived by people, and after trying the meats, they said that the second one was fatty. But, in fact, both meats were the same, and both writings expressed the same idea. In practice, this means that when indicating the product's benefits for the customers, one must be governed by the factors they give importance to. *Spice up advertising texts with alluring words.*

7. Value through the price tag – Look at Picture 1 in which Phil Barden presents price tags and you'll see that the price tag at the top of it seems to be a higher number than the one at the bottom. In all the price tags, the price is the same, but because of the design, they are perceived differently by the subconscious mind. Thus, by the form of the price tag it is possible to raise or lower the product value in the eyes of people; the design simply needs to be carefully considered. *If the product price is high, display it with a corresponding price tag.*

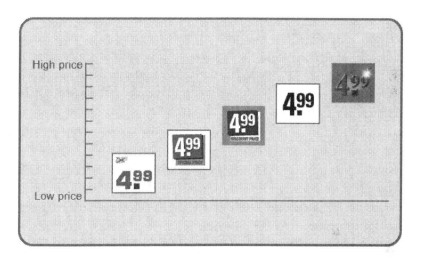

picture 1

8. Anchoring effect – What is this? For example, during an iPad presentation Steve Jobs asked the audience:

"What should we price it at? Well, if you listen to the pundits, we're going to price it at under a $1000, which means $999."

At that moment $999 appeared on the screen. Jobs paused for a few minutes and added:

225

"Just like we were able to meet or exceed our technical goals, we have met our cost goals, and I am thrilled to announce to you that the iPad pricing starts not at $999, but at just $499."

As a result, this price really became more attractive in the eyes of people, because they had subconsciously adjusted to $999. Actually, Jobs did not compare it with the laptop computer, but with the iPad's pre-invented price. The anchor is considered to be $999. The mechanism of anchoring, which presupposes the comparison of one product's price with another, is quite effective. Let's take negotiations as an example. The study shows that during negotiations the final price is always different from the initial one.

This golden rule known as anchoring was discovered by Daniel Kahneman and Amos Tversky in the 1970s.[1] Anchoring happens not only when the starting point is given to the subject but also when the subject bases his estimate on the result of some incomplete computation. To understand how it works, let's take a look at this study. Two groups of high school students were to estimate a numerical expression written on the blackboard in a descending and ascending sequence, giving them 5 seconds - (8 x 7 x 6 x 5 x 4 x 3 x 2 x 1) and (1 x 2 x 3 x 4 x 5 x 6 x 7 x 8). It's clear that in such a short time no one in the group could perform multiplication, so they would have to give an approximate answer. Interestingly, the median estimate for the ascending sequence was 512, while the median estimate for the descending sequence was 2,250. The correct answer is 40,320.

Why do the answers vary so much? Since people are given just a few seconds, they have no other choice but to guess the answer. Because the result of the first few steps of multiplication that they manage to do is higher in the descending sequence than in the ascending sequence, it is judged to be larger than the second one (for instance, 1 x 2 x 3 = 6), while (8 x 7 x 6 = 336). Retail companies use the rule of anchoring as a method of instilling a sort of confidence in the buyer that he made the right choice and thus offer a good correlation between the price and quality of their goods.

Key value items (KVI) can also serve as a means of anchoring. KVI are those most indispensable items such as milk, bread, beans and bananas.

1 Judgment under Uncertainty: Heuristics and Biases Amos Tversky; Daniel Kahneman Science, New Series, Vol. 185, No. 4157. (Sep. 27, 1974), pp. 1124-1131.

Supermarkets call them traffic generators, as people buy them most of all, and they are more sensitive to price changes. Although the average consumer is not well versed in prices, most people know the prices of the items they buy most frequently and can therefore compare the competing stores. By ensuring that the prices of basic KVI are maintained at an artificially low level, sometimes even below cost, the supermarkets can use anchoring to convince the buyers that it's just as beneficial to buy all the other goods from them.

In this way the customers are persuaded that the store is on their side in the fight for the reduction of the cost of living. One of the best illustrations of this promise is the slogan of Tesco supermarkets "Every little helps." Retailers, as well as advertising specialists, believe that these three words turned the store offering goods at low prices into a retail network trusted by the British people for many years. *Use the anchoring effect in your business.*

Secret 19. In advertising we should present the value of the brand as much as possible and, at the same time, reduce the "pain" through certain discounts and special offers.

Secret 20

Since the emergence of modern marketing, professional communicators have relied on the "inadequacy approach." Tell your audience that the world is dangerous, that they lack what they need, that they don't quite fit in. Then offer the magic cure – your product.

Jonah Sachs (Co-founder and CEO of Free Range Studios)

How to influence the purchase decisions

Let's proceed with the other factors that influence the decision to make a purchase.

9. Create a sense of inadequacy– *Almost every day we are overwhelmed by various commercials, most of which try to convince us that we are imperfect. We are told that we are overweight or skinny, have pimples on the face or bad breath. We are told that our body odor is unpleasant, our hairstyle is not good, and our clothes are out of fashion. We hear that "our personal relationships may be ruined because of body odor, dandruff, skin that is too dry or too oily, indigestion, heartburn, or stained teeth."*

We see all this in advertisements every day; one gets the impression that if we don't buy the advertised goods or service, we are far from ideal. All this has one purpose – to show that we are imperfect and that only after buying this product will we become ideal, perfect, or desirable. Pay attention to the current commercials that make people into heroes. See how in the Axe commercials some lean, scrawny specimen transforms into a confident man, attractive to all. Anyway, remember that people are ready to pay to be ideal, and the marketers make use of this factor. They offer a shortcoming - and then a solution through a product - and in the end there's the happy hero.

10. Leave a good impression, one that exceeds expectations – There is a policy in Disney that is worth attention. Each attraction has a wait time showing how much time is needed for a ride. But it shows more than the actual time. For example, if the wait time is 15 minutes, in 10 minutes the doors are opened. People have agreed to wait for 15 minutes, but the doors are opened in 10 minutes, exceeding their expectations. *From a psychological perspective, people are happier. Exceed expectations.*

11. Threshold price and odd pricing – It would be incomplete to talk about price psychology without mentioning the threshold price and the 9 pricing practice. The threshold price is the price the increase of which causes significant changes in sales. The effect of the threshold price is usually observed at such price points as $1, $5, $10, or $100. That is why many prices are set below these thresholds, often ending up at nine. Eckhard Kucher, one of the founders of Simon-Kucher & Partners, analyzed 18,096 prices of consumer goods and found that 43.5 % of them end in the digit 9.[1]

None of the prices ended in zero. Another study showed that 25.9% of the prices ended in 9[2]. Almost all prices end in 9 at a filling station, but there's one more peculiarity: They are expressed in tenths of a cent, not in whole numbers, that is, 0.1 cents instead of 1 cent. If you need to fill the tank with 20 gallons at $3.599 per gallon, you will pay $71.98. If it cost $3.60 a gallon, you would have to pay $72.00. That is a tiny difference of 2 cents. The most compelling argument for such "strange" prices is in that the buyers perceive the digits of price in a descending order, from left to right. The first digit affects our perception most of all. That is, $9.99 is perceived as 9 plus something less than $10. Neuropsychologists confirm that the rightmost digit has the least influence on our perception. According to this hypothesis, buyers discount prices that are slightly smaller than the integers.

Let's take as an example a survey conducted by Nicola Lacetera on this issue. Analyzing 22 million used-car transactions, Lacetera came to the conclusion that sales prices dropped every time the car crossed the threshold of the next 10 thousand miles. That is, the cars with 28,999 miles on them are significantly more attractive for people than the ones with 30,000 miles.[3]

1 Eckhard Kucher. Scannerdaten und Preissensitivität bei Konsumgütern.Wiesbaden: Gabler-Verlag, 1985.
2 Hermann Diller and G. Brambach. "Die Entwicklung der Preise und Preisfiguren nach der Euro-Ein-führung im Konsumgüter-Einzelhandel", in: Handel im Fokus: Mitteilungen des Instituts für Handels-forschung an der Universität zu Köln, 54. Jg., Nr. 2, s. 228–238.
3 [46 - N.Lacetera, et al, Inattention in the used car market, Working paper, october (2009).]:

The leftmost digit 3, being bigger than 2, "added" the mileage by 10,000, but in reality it wasn't so. This phenomenon hasn't been deeply studied yet, but the fact is that people focus first on the number's leftmost digit, and the rest doesn't get much attention. For example, eBay studies have shown that people wouldn't notice additional information such as shipping costs and taxes.[4]

Imagine that you walk into your favorite coffee shop around the corner and you see that the price for the cup of coffee with milk you always get has increased from $3.20 to $3.52. Would you still buy it? In another scenario, the price of your drink has increased from $2.60 to $2.86. Would you buy that same cup of coffee or would you find a cheaper coffee shop? And now, imagine that the price of your favorite cup of coffee has increased from $2.90 to $3.19. Would you still buy it? According to Lydia Ashton from the University of California at Berkeley, while the proportional increase in price in each scenario is always the same, 10 percent, some people would answer "yes" to the first two questions and "no" to the last. [5] In the first and second scenarios, the leftmost digit doesn't change, and in the third scenario it changes from 2 to 3. This means the left digit is what really matters to the consumer and not the increase in price.

The left-digit bias, which affects consumer's willingness to pay, has been known for more than 75 years. It was revealed by Eli Ginzberg of Columbia University in 1936.[6] However, it's been thoroughly analyzed recently. Any goods at a price of 9.99 will be perceived by the majority of consumers to be less expensive. Another hypothesis says that consumers tend to associate prices ending in nine with a sale, discounts, and special offers.

If you reduce the price from $1.00 to 99 cents, sometimes it leads to a spike in sales. Can this be explained by the fact that the price resembles a discount rather than price reduction of 1%? The question regarding the cause and effect remains open. The fact or rather the belief in the existence of threshold prices led to the widespread practice of odd pricing, prices that do

4 [47 - T.Hossain, J.Morgan, Plus shipping and handling: Revenue (non) equivalence in field experiments on eBay, Advances in Economic Analysis and Policy, 6(3) (2006).]

5 L.Ashton, Left-digit bias and inattention in retail purchases: Evidence from a field experiment, Unpublished paper, march (2009).

6 E.Ginzberg, Customary prices, American Economic Review, 26(2) (1936).

not end in zero. Hermann Simon's (Simon-Kucher & Partners) own research shows that there's no point in setting the price at $9.90 or $9.95. If you want to remain below the threshold price, set it as close to the threshold as possible, in this case at $9.99.

12. Magic numbers – One of the specialists of Massachusetts Institute of Technology conducted an interesting study on a company that sold clothes via catalogue. Like other companies, this company also used "the magic numbers ending with 9" in the catalogue. It priced one of the goods at $39, after which it printed additional catalogues and priced the same product at $34 in one case and $44 in another.

All the three catalogs were sent to customers with same characteristics selected from the database. So what happened? The product priced at $39 sold best of all. Surprisingly, sales of it were 23% higher than sales of the same product priced at $34. And there was no big quantitative difference in sales between the products sold at $44 and $34. Hence, it becomes clear that it's desirable that the figures indicating the price end with 9, because psychologically people notice the initial digit only. That is, 39 is perceived as 30.

A company selling products via catalogue often organized campaigns during which it stated the "Regular price, X dollars" and the "Discounted price, Y dollars." The company decided to perform an experiment and not mention that the prices are discounted. As a result, the sales didn't register any growth.

The customers did not know that the prices were discounted. That is, the concept of anchor did not work. Then the customers were informed about the discounts and campaigns. What do you think the result was? Of course, the sales increased. If the price was indicated as "Regular price, $48" and "Discounted price, $40," people would buy more of the product than when it was simply indicated $39. *Hence, it follows that relative pricing affects decision-making.*

13. Repetition – *Repetition is one of the most important elements of advertising; it annoys you to see washing powder, shampoo, lotteries, soap and other commercials constantly repeated. Commercial repetition is one of the factors that pesters people most of all. But the marketers know that no matter how great and effective a message is, it's impossible to achieve results without repetition. To be more precise, it's the repetition that achieves success – the more the better.*

Frequency makes people focus on the message; the more you say the same thing to a four-year-old child, the sooner he will get your message. You can achieve significant results if you repeat the same skill several times. Or if are you are explaining a topic, repeat it several times. Repetition is aimed at being heard by the consumers.

Many marketing experts are faced with a choice: Either present the commercial to a larger audience less frequently or to a smaller audience more frequently. Many tend to a larger audience, forgetting that frequency is more efficient. They think that it's better to broadcast it to 1,000 people once a day than to 250 people 4 times a day.

On the contrary, I believe it is better to focus on frequency than the number of people. Even though repetition is not the most creative form of persuasion, it is one of the most effective ones. In the 1930s, Joseph Goebbels, Reich Minister of propaganda of Nazi Germany, based his entire campaign on a simple premise that the most familiar information will become accepted as truth. He wrote, "Propaganda must therefore always be essentially simple and repetitive. In the long run basic results in influencing public opinion will be achieved only by the man who is able to reduce problems to the simplest terms and who has the courage to keep forever repeating them in this simplified form, despite the objections of the intellectuals[7]."

Working at the University of Michigan in 1961s, a social psychologist Robert Zajonc offered a hypothesis according to which mere repeated exposure of the individual to a stimulus object enhances his attitude toward it.[8] By "mere exposure" he meant a condition which just makes the given stimulus accessible to the individual's perception. His interest was triggered by the fact that the words with positive connotation are used more often in the ordinary speech than their negative counterparts. In a random selection of one million English words, the word "good" occurred 5,122 times, "bad"

---

7 R.Herzstein, The War That Hitler Won (1987).
8 R.Zajonc, Attitudinal effects of mere exposures, Journal of Personality and Social Psychology, 9(2) (1968).

occurred only 1,001 times; "right" (3,874) was used more frequently than "wrong" (890), "on" (30,224) more than "off" (3,644), and "love" (5,129) more than "hate" (756), etc.

In one study, Zajonc exposed Chinese characters to two groups of participants. He explained to them that the symbols represented adjectives and asked them to say whether they had positive or negative connotations. The group to whom the symbols had been shown before the experiment rated them more positively than the group of individuals that hadn't seen them previously. In a similar experiment, individuals were asked to rate their moods. Those with repeated exposure said they felt more optimistic and positive than the ones for whom the objects were unfamiliar. Zajonc's consumer study showed that we prefer goods or styles we have already seen, no matter whether we have had previous experience with these goods.

A marketing guru, Jay Levinson, says that you need to send your message 27 times to people so that it has any effect. Why? People on average pay attention to one of ten commercials; they have to see it at least three times for the marketing message to penetrate into their minds.

Frequency leads to trust. Why do you always go to the same place for lunch or shopping? Why do you prefer products of the same brand? The reason is trust, and trust comes from repetitious advertising and trying the product. For years you see the commercials for the same brand. You come across it in restaurants and supermarkets, or you see might it on the table when you are a guest at a friend's. Frequent advertising leads to recognition, and recognition leads to familiarity; familiarity leads to trust, and trust leads to income.

Now it's important for you to draw the consumers' attention, and to do it, you must enter into dialogue with them within 30 minutes to solve their problem. If they allow you, then you win. If people trust you, they will definitely be interested in you. They will subscribe to receive new information about your offers. The biggest benefit of the Internet is that it's a marketing tool to influence people. People connect with everything that they trust, and trust comes from how often people receive the message.

14.The impact of the word "free" – And now consider the impact of the word "free" through the example of Amazon.com. The website made an interesting move: if the site visitor bought a book for $16.95, he would have to pay $3.95 for delivery. And if the visitor ordered one more book, and the total sum exceeded $31.9, the delivery was free. Perhaps many people did not need the second book, but the free delivery tempted them to order it.

Amazon staff was in a wonderful mood, as the idea had worked, but there was a country where no sales growth was recorded. That country was France. It was surprising. Does it mean that French consumers think differently? But in reality something else happened. Instead of organizing free delivery, the French branch of Amazon had made the delivery payable, and that was only 1 franc, or 20 cents. It seems that it's a trifle, almost free. But the 1 franc became crucial. Later, when France announced free delivery too, the sales increased. This is what the word "Free" can do. *In any case, this word must be treated carefully. You can offer free delivery, a certain service, equipment installation or some gift.*

Another experiment: The authors decided to set up a large booth in a building in a busy area and sell two types of chocolate truffles, Lindt and Hershey's Kisses. The experiment was simple: Which would you take (only one piece per person)? The price tags were placed so that only the person who approached could see them. For those who are not familiar with Lindt, let me point out that it is Swiss chocolate, produced for more than 170 years. It is quite a high-end premium and expensive candy. As to Hershey's Kisses, it is an ordinary candy, not really exceptional, with a production of 80 million pieces per day.

The price of Lindt was discounted to 15 cents, and Hershey's was discounted to 1 cent. The people passing buy would get interested, approach, and buy the candies. 73% of them bought Lindt, and 27% bought Hershey's. Then the researchers decided to bring down the prices: Both products got equally discounted by one cent - Lindt Truffles became 14 cents and Hershey's became free. The experiment results were surprising: 69% of people had preferred Hershey's, and the rest – Lindt. By discounting the price by 1 cent and with an available free candy by its side, the Lindt sales went down from 73% to 31%. This great is the impact of the word "Free."

Thus, if a person is faced with a choice, remember that he is going to choose a free product, because he has no fear of loss. Money is not paid. So if the choice turns out to be undesirable, it will not trouble him that much. If you are offered a loyalty card, but you have to pay for it, many of you refuse it, and if you are offered it for free, you take it. It's more attractive when you can buy goods on credit without advance than when you cannot.

Suppose two car salespeople offer the same features, almost the same prices. What can be decisive for you? Of course, the offer of a free oil change for a year. Summing up, you have two options: Either keep selling by your former method or offer something for free and attract more customers. Think about the power of this idea. It is neither a campaign nor a discount. While the difference between 1 and 2 cents is negligible, the difference between 1 and 0 cents is huge. Do you want to attract a large number of customers? - Provide something for free.

Secret 20. Remember, a free offer affects the customer's decision.

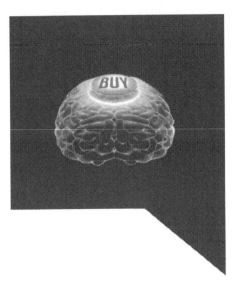

Secret 21

Build a better mousetrap and the world will beat a path to your door.

Ralph Waldo Emerson

How to Influence the Purchase Decisions

Let's continue.

15. Comparison effect– The New York Times placed an article authored by Gregg Rapp, a menu engineer and consultant. Rapp asserted that the expensive dishes on the menu increase the average check, even if no one orders those expensive dishes. Why? If people do not buy the most expensive dish, they still tend to order the second most expensive dish. Thus, by placing a more expensive dish on the menu, the restaurant owner can entice people to select the second most expensive dish, which is quite profitable for him.

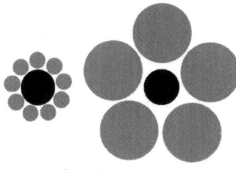

Picture 2

And now I will prove this by a test by Dan Ariely. See Picture 2, and you will notice that in the first case the black circle looks larger than the second one. When the black circle is within the range of smaller circles, it looks large to us, and if it is among large circles, it looks small to us.

Yet still in both cases the circles are the same. The same applies to price when it changes in accordance with its environment. This is how our minds are structured; we look at things by taking into account the environment and by comparing. That is our essence. We are constantly comparing, one job to another, a wine to another, friends, items, etc.

We have a tendency to compare not only different items but also similar items to each other. For example, suppose you have made up your mind to spend your holidays in Europe this year. The travel agency has offered two tours – Rome and Paris – that include the ticket, hotel, free food and sightseeing. Which one would you choose? For many it is really hard to make a decision. The Colosseum in Rome and the Louvre in Paris may seem equally attractive. Now let's imagine a different scenario. Suppose the travel agency offers an alternative tour to Rome, but there is no free food, in other words, Rome with a minus (-).

In this case, we have three offers – Paris, Rome and Rome (-). It follows that Paris and Rome are more attractive to us than Rome (-). The Rome (-) option makes the Rome option so attractive that people start to choose Rome, despite the fact that in the previous scenario it was hard to decide. So it becomes clear that an alternative makes people compare it with a similar option and choose the more attractive one.

The next interesting survey was conducted by The Economist. The following post appeared on the magazine's website.

You can get access to all our web content for $59, a subscription to the print edition for $125, a combined print and web subscription, *also* for $125.

People had to make a choice so that the staff would know in what form to send the magazine. It was difficult for people to decide whether to pay $59 for the web content or $125 for the print edition. Apparently, it is more desirable to pay $125 for both options combined. As a result, only 16% opted for the web subscription, and 84% opted for the combination deal. No one chose the print subscription alone, and this unpopular alternative was eliminated. After which, the offer looked like this:

You can get access to all our web content for $59, a subscription to the print edition for $125.

And what changed in the people's behavior? After the change, of course, 68% chose the first option, and only 32% preferred to go for the second option. It is obvious that the editorial should offer three options; the second offer resulted in decline in the income. So what happened in reality? The option of print edition only seemed meaningless, but it was because of it that, by comparing, the subscribers chose the option of $125, web content and print edition combined. *This example allows us to understand an important fact – our brains perceive values when comparing. They compare the existing options and choose the most valuable one.*

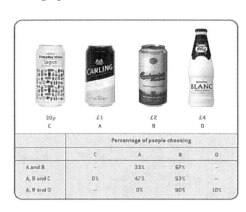

Picture 3*

Besides comparing the value of the goods, the buyers compare the prices with those of competitors, too. In Picture 3, you can see the results of the survey of Mountainview concerning the impact of relative prices on the sales of Carling and Budweiser beers. Look carefully at the picture. When offered "A" and "B" products, 67% bought 2-pound Budweiser, and 33% bought Carling. Then products "A", "B" and "C" were offered. 30-pence Tesco was added to the two beers. Nobody bought Tesco; 47% preferred Carling, and 53% bought Budweiser.

In the next scenario, 4-pound Kronenbourg, a French premium beer, marked as "D" was added to the list of "A" and "B" beers. At this point, 10% preferred Kronenbourg, and 90% went for Budweiser, but nobody bought Carling. Can you imagine now how much the purchases depend on comparisons? Always consider the importance of the relative price effect.

In another example, Williams-Sonoma Inc. introduced to the market a home bread maker priced at $275. It was mainly ignored by the customers and didn't sell well. Who would bake bread at home? Nobody seemed to be interested in the product. Williams-Sonoma applied to a market research company, which recommended that they create a similar bread maker, but

---

* Phil Barden, Decoded, 2013

one twice as large and as expensive as the first model. As a result, sales mainly of the first model started to grow.

Let's move on to the next survey conducted by Amos Tversky and Daniel Kahneman. Suppose you are faced with a dilemma. In one scenario you have entered a store and found a fine pen for $25. You were about to buy it, and suddenly you remember that you have seen the same pen that cost $18 in another store. What would you do? Would you spend 15 minutes to save $7? Most people facing this dilemma would prefer to spend the 15 minutes and buy the pen for $18.

Let's move on to the second example. You are buying a suit that costs $455. A customer tells you the same suit can be found in another store at a discounted price of $448. It will again take you 15 minutes to reach that store. Would you take the trip? Most people said they wouldn't. What happened in reality? The only question at this point is whether it is worthwhile to walk 15 minutes for $7.

If we compare the prices of pens, then $7 seems like a big amount to save, and is worth the 15-minute walk. But in the case of $455 and $448, $7 does not seem to make a big difference. That is why many people refuse to take the trip. *All these examples prompted one important rule: People tend to compare when making decisions.*

Willingness to pay is also determined, among other things, by the way consumers perceive the relative value of alternative goods. The consumers who have no idea of substitute goods are less sensitive to price. But if they are aware of alternatives, they use them as a reference. Memories of previous purchases give an indication of an acceptable level of prices. When buyers see several goods on the shelves, they tend to purchase the less expensive goods. The Financial Times (January 31, 2005) published a report on the activity of Seiyu, the Japanese branch of Wal-Mart. Seiyu experts admitted that the sales volumes had decreased due to a narrow range of goods. "For example, we made the mistake of featuring only Y197 packs of toilet paper, when we should have also featured packs for Y450, so consumers can choose." *Create the opportunity for your customers to be able to compare prices.*

16. Contrast effect – Contrast has a big impact on people's perceptions, how two different items affect each other, in other words. If the second item is different from the first one, we have a tendency to enhance the difference. For example, if we initially lift a light item and then a heavy one, the second item will seem heavier to us than if we had lifted only it. Many sales experts practice this method. At first they present a rather an expensive product, and then a slightly less costly option, and the second option seems better than if it had been presented from the start.

A student at the University of Chicago tells of his experience at O'Hare Airport. He was waiting for his flight when it was announced that the flight was delayed, and if the passengers agreed to take the next flight, they would receive a refund of $10,000. Naturally, this number was a joke, and people had a good laugh. Shortly after, the real sum of refund was announced, $200, and nobody agreed to take the money and wait for the next flight. The management had to raise the price first to $300 and then to $500, after which a few agreed.

Of course, the perception of contrast was broken here because at the beginning they showed the $10,000, which made the $200 look insignificant. The lack of knowledge of this rule cost the airline an additional $300 for each passenger. And what would you do? They could just have announced a $5 compensation and then declared that it was a joke and that they are ready to provide $200. The joke would be perceived and the money would be saved.

Another case from the field of real estate. Sometimes certain real estate agents apply this trick. At the beginning they bring forward several unsightly and unattractive houses for rather high prices. These houses are there to provide the contrast effect. Then the agent shows the buyer a well furnished and renovated apartment at an affordable price. And, of course, it looks more attractive in the eyes of the buyer. *Keep the contrast effect in mind, and, likewise, promise a lower refund at the beginning, but give more, and you will feel the customer's positive attitude.*

17. Environment – People's decisions are also affected by the environment. World renowned violinist Joshua Bell decided to give a free concert at the metro station. This musician regularly gathers an audience that is ready to pay more than $100 for a ticket. Yet, when Bell was playing in the subway, nobody listened to him. Almost nobody came close to one of the most talented musicians in the world. We can conclude that the environment affects people's decisions, and by making an intuitive decision, the brain signals that if someone plays in the subway, he is not a famous musician and has no other place to perform. So, the famous musician was neglected.

18. Perception – Perception is the way through which the marketers influence people's subconscious. Promo campaigns, products, packaging, websites or TV advertisements constitute the middle link between the human subconscious and the brand and affect perception. Now see Picture 4. A

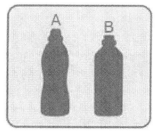

Picture 4*

survey has revealed that many people pick up Variant "A," thinking that such a bottle contains more liquid than Variant "B". However, both bottles actually have the same capacity. But what makes us perceive it differently?

Professor of Marketing at New York University, Priya Raghubir, has studied the effect of package shape on perception. The researcher has revealed that the first thing people pay attention to is the height of the package. The taller the container is, the more desirable and preferable it

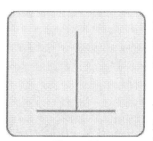

Picture 5*

becomes for the buyer. Therefore, if you are trying to minimize the product's packaging, consider this fact. And why is the height perceived as more important than the volume by people?

Look carefully at Picture 5: It seems to all of us that the vertical one is longer, doesn't it? But in reality they are of the same length. The reason is that the brain perceives tall objects as larger and more capacious than the others. *Knowing this law of human perception, the marketers manage to get more elongated and capacious containers, increasing the likelihood that products in such containers will be sold.*

19. Price Distance – Have you ever thought that the distance between regular and sale prices can affect the sales? In Picture 6, there are images of two pizza cutters. And now the question: Does the distance between the

---

** Phil Barden, Decoded, 2013

*Picture 6**

prices affect people's perceptions? An article concerning this issue was submitted to the Journal of Consumer Psychology. The author of the article, Keith Coulter, revealed that the greater the horizontal separation of prices is on the price tag, the more attractive the discount looks. And this discount will result in increased sales.

We better perceive the horizontal price tags than the vertical ones, so it is more effective to present the prices in a horizontally. Based on his study, Coulter came to the conclusion that the greater the distance between the regular and sale prices is, the more attractive the discount is in the consumer's eyes. *So always try to use the second option – prices apart from each other.*

20. Social pressure – There's a phenomenon called social pressure, which is about the influence on people. In other words, if others are doing something, then it is worth following. For instance, researchers ran a test in a hotel room. One card read "Please help save nature's valuable resources by reusing your bed linens during your stay." 35% of visitors participated. The other card read "Most of our guests reuse their bed linens at least once during their stay." The level of participation increased to 44%. And when it was mentioned that "Most of our guests of this room have reused bed linens during their stay," the participation rate reached 49%.

21. The fear of loss – An American company offered one of its customers a power save mode that allowed people to save money. They said that it would help them to save $200. In other words, at the end of the year they would have an extra $200. But few people got interested in the offer. So the

* Phil Barden, Decoded, 2013

company changed its approach and offered the following: if the customers didn't use that mode, they would lose $200 per year. As a result, people took it more seriously, and more people responded than in the first case. *Indeed, the money lost seems greater than the money gained.*

22. Tangibility factor – There is an interesting mechanism in the Lego Group. When you bring the toy box close to that device, you can see the ready assembled toy on a special screen, increasing its appeal in the eyes of children and parents. This strategy pursues one more goal – the more one touches the product, the more likely he is to purchase it. To see the final look of the toy, children will take more toys and bring them close to the screen. By showing the final look of the toy on the screen, the marketers made the toy more appealing in the eyes of people, thus its value and sales volumes increased as well. *Create an environment that will encourage people to put the product into their hands, touch it, and have a closer look at it.*

Secret 21. Create the opportunity for your customers to be able to compare prices.

Secret 22

Even if you buy a cow, make sure whether the tail is included in the price or not.

Janina Ipokhorska

How to Influence the Purchase Decisions

23. It is better to get it today than tomorrow – Indeed, the idea of falling ill in 20 years is not as scary as falling ill tomorrow. Having $100 today is more attractive than $120 in the next year. It follows that people look at the future more lightly than at the present. And now to be more specific: How can this principle be applied in marketing? Automakers sometimes make specific proposals based on this principle. In 2012 Fiat Company offered to pay half the car's price, and the other half would be paid after 2 years. In the TV commercials they only mentioned the first half of the payment, € 5900, thus breaking the stereotype of the high price. The buyers would perceive the second half of the payment as "price drop" because it can be paid in the future.

24. Scarcity effect – Creating scarcity is one of the trickiest methods of increasing sales. If the customers get the impression that the given product is

---

The Fighter (2010)
Christian Bale (Actor), Mark Wahlberg (Actor), David O. Russell (Director) | Rated: R | Format: DVD
★★★★☆ ☑ (282 customer reviews)

List Price: $14.98
Price: $8.99 √Prime
You Save: $5.99 (40%)

Only 14 left in stock.
Sold by newbury comics and Fulfilled by Amazon. Gift-wrap available.

Picture 7

244

available only in limited quantities, they will want to buy it. People tend to think that if there's little of something and that it's already sold out, then it has got to be good. For example, Amazon.com has an interesting practice. If you want to buy a certain product, the image in Picture 7 appears. It shows that only 14 copies of the product are left in stock. Are there only 14 copies of DVD left in stock in the largest online store in the world? In fact, the rule of deficit is applied here because when one sees that there's few quantity left, he can't wait to acquire the product, as it was acquired by others as well.

We all know that January and February are months of decline for certain types of business, and the marketers of many companies face the challenge of boosting sales during these months. Let's take the toy business as an example. It is a well-known fact that the Christmas season is marked by a toy sales boom. In January and February, people have already spent their money, and there are no sales. Thus, toy manufacturers face a dilemma: how to have effective sales during the Christmas holidays and in January-February simultaneously.

The biggest difficulty is that some mechanism is needed by which children will force their parents to buy toys after the Christmas holidays. Imagine that during the Christmas holidays children have received lots of presents and that their parents have spent lots of money. What can be done in this case?

A familiar phenomenon occurs when parents promise their children to buy an expensive and trendy toy much advertised before Christmas, but when they visit the store, it is not there. Naturally, if parents are not able to buy the toy during Christmas, they will buy it after Christmas. Yes, many parents visit the store, ask for the much advertised and trendy toy and hear the following answer, "Sorry, the toy is sold out, but we shall have it soon. We have ordered it."

I think the idea is simple: The popular toys are advertised before Christmas; children want to have them, and parents promise to buy them. Manufacturers deliver a small number of the advertised toys and a large number of the non-advertised toys. Most parents walk around the store and do not find the advertised toy. What can they do? They have no other option but to buy another toy for the child. In January and February, the advertising starts again, and suddenly the much advertised and trendy toy appears in the stores again.

And do you think children are not going to remind their parents of their promise? Of course, they will. Parents fulfill the promise and once again fall into the trap of marketers. *Anyway, apply this strategy, which also affects the decision-making, because if the product is scarce, no one wants to miss the opportunity.*

I will still expand on the creation, marketing, and sales of "100 Business Secrets," but before that, I want to point out that after the amazing reception of the book, we did not put it on the market and did not supply any bookstores with it. People knew that there was a scarcity of the book and asked us to let them know as soon as it appeared in the bookstores, as it was being sold from our office in high speed. There had been no such enthusiasm in connection with books in our country for years. People stood in line for the book (I will talk more about this). So by creating scarcity, we achieved a significant increase in demand.

25. The Endowed Progress Effect – Retail shopping centers often provide their customers with loyalty cards and stimulate new purchases. Thanks to these cards, customers sometimes get free products. In general, the customers are handed blank cards, and they need to accumulate some money, bonus, or points and then use them. And now get acquainted with research results that will change your attitude towards the blank cards.

A special study was carried out on the effectiveness of the cards; the participants were divided into two groups and were given loyalty cards. They were told that each time they washed their cars in the same car wash they would be given a stamp on their card. When the card was filled, they would have the opportunity to get one free car wash. One group was given a card with 8 blank stamps, while the other was given a card with 10 blank stamps but 2 were pre-stamped which meant they had the same 8 blank stamps. For a free car wash, the participants of both groups would have to pay 8 times.

The study showed that 19% of the members of the first group returned to the car wash to complete their loyalty card, and 34% of the other group came back to finish their loyalty card, almost twice as many. *Hence, if you want* *your loyalty cards to be more effective, do not give them to people empty. Include some stimulating factor to make them interested in using the card - it can be $2 or 100 points. It is difficult to start something from scratch.*

26. Increase, do not decrease – There were two shops of pick and mix sweets close to one school. Everything was the same about them – the sweets, their prices, the distance from the school - and the sellers were equally nice. But apparently children loved one of these stores more than the other. Why? Everything was ingeniously simple. In the first shop the seller would put a few sweets on the scales and then add them to the desired weight. In the second shop they'd put more on the scales and then take away the extra sweets. Which approach do you think children would like more? Naturally, when the sweets are added. The sellers in the first shop had indeed a deep understanding of the children's inner world. This made the basis of their work, and they achieved excellent results. That's what it means – an approach based on the customer's point of view.

27. Determining the value of the goods – When the pharmaceutical company Glaxo launched its remedy against ulcers, Zantac, in 1983, it had to set its price against the dominant brand in the field sold by SmithKline. Its medication was called Tagamet, which then enjoyed the highest demand in the world. The obvious strategies were either to set a price equal to or lower than that of the competitor. But these strategies were wrong. If the new medication was sold at the same or at a lower price, the market would consider Zantac as a simple analogue of the existing means and wouldn't see any special reasons for shifting to it.

Zantac should be taken only twice a day, while Tagamet four times. In addition, the new drug offered fewer side effects. While Glaxo experts knew about the price sensitivity of the market, they, oddly enough, priced Zantac 50 percent higher than Tagamet. The higher price attracted attention and challenged the stakeholders to think about Zantac's benefits. The doctors decided that the new drug must be more effective. Shortly after, Zantac's sales exceeded Tagamet's. Glaxo profits increased from £90 million to more than £600 million in five years.

The restaurant industry was particularly hard hit by the crisis of 2008-2012. After all, it is less expensive to dine at home. However, Panera

Bread chain, which had 1,300 restaurants in the United States, responded differently to the crisis than the competitors. Instead of cutting prices and promotions, Panera reworked the menu and increased prices. A lobster sandwich appeared on the menu for $16.99. Panera Chief Executive Ron Shaich explained these developments as follows, "Most of the world seems to be focused on the Americans who are unemployed. We're focused on the 90% that are still employed."[1] Contrary to industry trends, Panera had a 4% increase in revenue in a year, and its profits rose by 28%. As it turned out, the target audience of the restaurant was ready to pay a high price for a high value.

28. Influencing the customer's behavior – Here's an interesting pricing strategy that can influence people's behavior. It's about paying the dentist when the patient misses an appointment. This type of bad behavior by patients results in extra administrative time for rebooking, and treatments for other patients are delayed. A dentist in Monmouth charges £70 for the first appointment and £85 for the missed ones. This pricing method can influence people to change their behavior for the better.

29. The ultimate price promise – Often people hold back making purchases until prices come down. Carphone Warehouse, one of the leading retailers of mobile phones in Great Britain, tried to break the practice of "buying later and cheaper."

When you buy a mobile phone from Carphone Warehouse, the computer compares the price paid and the price 90 days later. If the later price is lower than the paid price, the customer automatically receives a voucher for the difference in price that he can use to acquire some other goods from the store. As the CEO of Carphone Warehouse, Charles Dunstone says, "In the last 14 months we've given away £10 million to customers, but they are astounded when they get the voucher. They can't believe that any company would do that." *Eliminate the barrier to purchase because the customers can also buy what they need from the competitors. That's why it's pointless to keep them from buying from you.*

30. $10 cash is better than $100 on a credit card – Research carried out by John Gourville and Dilip Soman in 2002 showed the connection between

1 Julie Jargon. "Slicing the Bread but not the Prices". The Wall Street Journal. August 18, 2009.

the actual cost and perceived cost. The authors noted that a cash transaction is about counting currency, receiving change. The more there are of these stages, the more impressed the buyer is by the magnitude of the transaction, while with a credit card it's just about signing a slip of paper.

That's why paying with cash seems more costly than paying with credit cards. Hence, the desire to consume the goods purchased with cash is greater than with credit cards. A study in a theater company revealed that the ticket holders who paid with credit cards did not show up at the theater 10 times more than those who had paid with cash. It then follows that cash payment increases the pressure of consumption; On the other hand, payment with credit cards weakens the perception of price and the cost fear.

Find methods to encourage purchases with credit cards: In 2002, Lufthansa Cargo introduced processing charge of €5 for traditional method of booking, while electronic bookings with the slogan "e for free" would be free of this processing charge. These measures significantly increased the percentage of electronic bookings. Once the customers got accustomed to electronic booking, Lufthansa Cargo canceled the entire processing fees for the traditional method of booking.

31. Prices containing message – A smart pricing policy played a big role in the success of London 2012 Olympic Games. Paul Williamson, the head of ticketing, used the prices not only as an effective tool for profit, but also as a powerful tool of communication. The prices carried a specific message without further commentary. With minimum price of £20,12 and maximum price of £2012 for the tickets, they reminded people over and over again of the Olympic Games.

They also provided tickets under a "pay your age" promotion for young and old spectators. Anyone who was 16 or under would pay their age in pounds. Anyone over 60 would pay a flat £16.The pricing policy caused a surprisingly positive response. The media talked about it a hundred times. Even the Queen and the Prime Minister publicly praised the "pay your age" pricing plan. These prices not only became an effective method of communication but also reflected the principle of fairness.

Another important characteristic of the ticketing strategy was that there were absolutely no discounts. The London Olympics committee firmly adhered to this policy, even when the tickets sold poorly. It explicitly spoke about the value: The tickets and the event were worth the money. In addition, no bundling, a common practice in sports when tickets to more popular sports are bundled to less popular sports, was offered. The experience with bundling in the past showed that people typically skip the secondary event. The committee did, however, bundle public transportation into the ticket price.

The organizers conducted almost all communication and sales via the Internet. Approximately 99% of the tickets were sold online. The London Olympic Games aimed at £376 million of profit ($625 million). Thanks to its ingenious pricing strategy and communication campaign, Williamson and his team surpassed this figure, profiting £660 million ($1,1 billion). That's 75% more than expected and much more than the previous three Olympics (in Beijing, Athens and Sydney) combined.

32. The golden middle – Neither the cheapest, nor the most expensive wine – Looking at the wine list, most people order wine at an average price. Only a few opt for the most expensive or the cheapest wine. The middle has a magical attraction. The same applies to a food menu. If a restaurant offers appetizers priced from $10 to $20, 20% of the demand goes to the dish priced $18. If the restaurant adds a meal for $25 to the menu, the share of the dish for $18 will most likely increase. Similarly, if the restaurant adds an entrée that is less expensive than the least expensive entrée of the old menu, the sales of the latter will increase even if hardly anyone ordered it before. The reason is simple. The cost of the cheapest meal on the old menu has now moved closer to the average price category.

The less the buyer knows about the objective quality of the goods and the price range of the products, the more he tends to choose those priced in the middle. One could even argue that this behavior is rational, since the buyer is committed to take the optimal decision based on limited information. By choosing items from the middle of the price range, the buyers are less likely to buy a product of poor quality or spend too much money. But the sellers must not go to extremes. *It's good to be careful when setting an excessively low or excessively high anchor price. An excessively high a price can scare off the customers who are not ready to spend so much , and an overly low a price will cause them to question the quality of the product.*

33. Sticker label – Stickers are generally pasted directly on the product, or on its packaging, or elsewhere (e.g. in points of sale) for informational purposes. The information on the stickers can also be decisive for buyers and can be used for online and offline sales. There are several types of stickers, here are the examples,

Picture 8

You can write sales-boosting words on the stickers such as,

1   Product launch date – Soon, New Product, Free Sample, New Arrival, New Collection

2   Balance – X PCs Left, The Last Example

3. Sales Pace – Blockbuster, Topseller, Bestseller

4. Price - Reduced Price, Discount, Excellent Offer, Promotion, Half Price

5. Recommendation - Recommended, Staff Picks, Customer Choice, Expert Choice

251

6. Savings – Save Money, Free, Gift

7. Emotion – It's necessary to take it. I bought it myself

Secret 22. Remember, do not introduce blank loyalty cards. Include some small amount of money in them

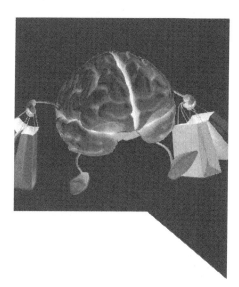

Secret 23

"Understand price. Think about price. Don't ignore price."

Steve Ballmer

How to Influence the Purchase Decisions

34. Smaller quantity and the same price – Today, companies are actively using the strategy of selling smaller quantities of a product for the same price. This enables them to maintain or increase their profits without additional expenses. Such price manipulations work well as, once acquainted with the product, the consumers believe that the quantity remains unchanged. To squeeze as much money from each sale as possible, maintaining the impression that the buyer gets the best for his money, retail companies hire highly trained professionals known as pricing consultants. One of the tips these experts offer is to shrink the packaging while keeping the same price. As Harvard Business School Professor John Gourville says, "Consumers are generally more sensitive to changes in prices than to changes in quantity, and companies try to do it in such a way that you don't notice, maybe keeping the height and width the same, but changing the depth so the silhouette of the package on the shelf looks the same. Or sometimes they add more air to the chips bag or a scoop in the bottom of the peanut butter jar so it looks the same size.[1]"

This is what Kellogg's did. It started to use a slightly tinier packaging for its Apple Jacks, Honey Snacks, Cocoa Krispies and Corn Pops breakfast cereals. The difference was so small that the buyers didn't notice it. However, given the huge quantities of breakfast cereals the company sells, the impact

---

1 S.Clifford, C.Rampell, Food inflation kept hidden in tinier bags (2011).

on profits was significant. A similar tactic was used by the American producer of lavatory paper Quilted Northern, which reduced the width of its Ultra Plush paper by half an inch. Another example: Skippy peanut butter is now sold in a new plastic jar. The old one had a smooth base and the new one has a dimple in it. The consumers don't spot these changes or don't pay attention to them, while the increase in profits is usually significant: The old jar contained 18 ounces of peanut butter, and the new one contains 16.3 ounces. Donald MacGregor from the American company MacGregor-Bates, which studies consumer decision making, comments on this,

"If a company reduces the price of something by 5% but gives you 10% less, you look at the price and think you are getting a bargain. But they have increased their profit margin by 5%. It looks good to you, but you're really paying more to get less." *In any case, be careful with such strategy because if the customers detect the trick, your brand trust can be broken.* Nevertheless, the brain study shows that we subconsciously do detect it. It might not have an immediate effect on the shopping habits and product preferences, but over time it can arouse distrust and suspicion in the regular buyers. As William Poundstone comments in *Priceless: Psychology of Hidden Value,* "Though price is just a number, it can evoke a complex set of emotions... Depending on context, the same price may be perceived as a bargain or a rip-off; or it may not matter at all."

35. Penetration strategy – Price penetration is about setting the product at a relatively low price to win the market quickly and have the product positively talked about, ensuring larger customer base. Toyota used a classic strategy of price penetration when it released its Lexus brand in the United States. Although Lexus was completely new and was advertised separately from Toyota, it became widely known as Toyota's brand. More than a million of these cars are sold in the US market annually.

Toyota introduced Lexus LS400 in 1989 at $35,000 and sold 16,000 cars in the first year. Within 6 months the price increased by 48%. In the second year the sales rose to 63,000 units thanks to "word of mouth" and positive reviews of the first buyers. Model LS400 became an example of a successful price-quality relationship in this segment and regularly topped the list of customer satisfaction. The initial doubts whether Toyota would be able to create a truly luxury car disappeared. Toyota continued to raise the prices of Lexus models.

The low initial prices allowed Lexus to enter the market easily and quickly, helped to attract attention, and built an enviable reputation. This is a classic example of a price penetration strategy. The price of $35,000 when entering the market was too low to bring high, short-term profits but rather an example of a clever strategy. In contrast to its success in the US, Lexus was unable to establish itself in Germany. One reason is that the prices of luxury cars in Germany are associated with quality and status to a much greater degree much greater than they are in the US. In this situation price penetration won't work. The risk of this strategy is the excessively low launch price. This mistake is easy to make when launching a new product. In early 2006, Audi priced its new model Q7 SUV too low. The company received 80,000 orders for the initial price of €55,000 ($71,500). The annual production was limited to 70,000 units. It can be argued that the longer you wait for the car, the more valuable it is, but some impatient customers probably went over to the competitors.

Hewlett Packard introduced its innovative fourth-generation printer in the early 1990s at a price significantly below the prevailing prices of competitors. Within a month, the company completed the yearly sales target. HP withdrew the printer from the market and later introduced a similar model at a much higher price. Another example of unsuccessful skimming:

The Taiwanese manufacturer of Asus computers released its Eee netbook computers in January 2008 for €299 ($388). The product was sold out in a few days. As the netbook was launched into the market, the company was able to meet customer demand by only 10%. Price penetration is recommended only for those goods whose quality is difficult to estimate in advance, that is, when consumers can assess the value of the goods only at the time of use. Low prices during the product launch motivate many consumers to try it and can cause the multiplier effect if the customers like the product and start promoting it to others.

36. Pricing based on skimming – Apple used the strategy of skimming when it launched its revolutionary iPhone in June 2007. The original price was $599. A few months later Apple dropped the price to $399. What is the reason for the high original price? The price of $599 testifies to high technical characteristics and quality, as well as prestige. And, despite the high price, people stood in long lines at Apple stores. And another reason was probably that Apple wanted to limit the demand for the iPhone at the initial stage because production capacity was limited. Nor can it be ruled out that Apple simply made a mistake.

The significant price reduction to $399 led to a dramatic rise in demand. There's a big difference between offering the iPhone for $599 initially and then cutting $200 off the price in a few months. Prospect theory says that the discount gives the buyer an additional positive utility. The downside of this strategy is that some consumers who had purchased the phone for $599 were upset when the price suddenly dropped. They protested, and, in response, Apple offered $100 credit at Apple stores to all iPhone users who paid the original price. The price of the iPhone continued to drop over the coming years.

Skimming - which probes customer willingness to pay at a given period of time - was justified not only in terms of demand. Costs also decreased because of skyrocketing sales. Apple sold 125 million iPhones during the 2011/2012 financial year, grossing $80.5 billion in revenue, or about half of the company's annual revenue. If we divide the revenue by sales volume, the average price for an iPhone will be $640.

Apple supplemented the skimming strategy by constant innovation and the expansion of its product line. Each new version offers a higher level of quality compared to the previous generation, allowing Apple to keep the prices of its devices relatively stable. It's a familiar strategy for personal computers. Prices for PCs practically don't change over time, but each new generation brings a new level of quality. From the point of view of price-quality relationship, this is also a case of skimming, as the consumers pay less and less over time.

37. That's not all technique – That's-Not-All is an interesting technique. The seller makes the product more attractive to the buyer by reducing the price. For instance, a jar of coffee sold for $5 is offered for $3.80. For experimental verification of the effectiveness of lower prices, Carrie Pollock and her colleagues from the University of Arkansas used a gourmet chocolate sale on campus.[2] A table was set up selling large and small boxes of chocolates. Students who were interested in the price were randomly assigned to one of two groups. In one group, the control condition, the salesperson – in fact, one of the researchers - said that the little box cost $1 and that the big box cost $5. In the second condition, the salesperson said the original price for the small box was $1.25 and $6.25 for the big one. At that point, a colleague corrected her, saying that the boxes actually cost $1 and $5. When it turned out that the price was lower, even by 25 cents, sales increased from 45% to 76% of visitors.

38. Deceptive pricing – In everyday life, we are regularly faced with list prices that no one really pays, the so-called moon prices. Which is more beneficial for the seller, to offer a product for $100 with a discount of 25%, or just for $75? Classical economics is not in a position to answer the question because it is only interested in the end result – the buyer pays $75 in the end. However, prospect theory offers an answer: The total utility is higher when the consumer sees the price of $100 and receives a discount of 25% than when he simply pays $75. A *discount gives the buyer an additional positive utility.*

39. Pay-per-use – According to the traditional pricing model, a person buys a product, pays for it, after which he owns it and can use it. An airline buys jet engines for its aircraft; a logistics company buys tires for its trucks, and a car care center buys paint and painting equipment and paints cars. But if you focus on the needs of customers, the price is set according to a different principle. Not always do the customers want to own the item. They need benefits, usage, and the satisfaction of needs that the product can provide. Instead of setting the price of the product, the manufacturer or the supplier can suggest a price for what this product gives to the customer.

---

2 C.Pollock, et al, Mindfulness limits compliance with the «that's-not-all» technique, Personality and Social Psychology Bulletin, 24 (1998).

This is the basic principle of an innovative pricing model, when payment is charged for the use of goods. This explains why General Electric and Rolls Royce sell power and not engines to their clients - the airlines. According to this pricing model, they charge a fee for hourly use. For the manufacturer this means a completely different business model, as it marks the transition from a commodity business to the service sector. Now, the company does not sell products but services, offering a system that can significantly increase revenue in comparison with the trade business. At GE, the hourly fee includes the work of a jet engine, its service, and other services. Customers of the airline get several advantages thanks to this pricing model: process simplification, reduction of investments, and disposal of fixed costs and excess personnel.

40. Construction of emotions through the power of images and words – Eyes can be dazzled; ears can be deafened; nostrils can be filled with scents. And all this can be done with the help of a wide variety of visual, audible and olfactory technologies. Yet, when it comes to the construction of emotions only through brand, the marketers are usually limited to pictures, words, and, with some products – tactile, gustatory, and olfactory sensations. It is often said it's better to see once than hear a hundred times. Indeed, an image instantly conveys much more information and emotions than words do, even if they are uttered quickly. This occurs because although the words are important to most people – except for mathematicians and artists – when they think and convey their thoughts, their brains work more quickly, fluently, and effortlessly when processing images. *Even the activity pictures cause in social networks shows how important the visual image is.*

Mindlab experts conducted a number of studies that clearly demonstrate the superiority of images over words in a retail environment and in the virtual space. In one such study Mindlab compared speed and ease with which people are able to comprehend complex data presented to them in the form of words or images. The difference was shocking. When tasks were presented by images, it required almost 20% less mental effort. The subjects not only performed more efficiently but also better remembered the information. Neuroscientist Lynda Shaw explains it this way, "The visual brain is this incredibly flexible and adaptable design to help us see and remember and make sense of everything around us. If we can stop feeling overwhelmed… we can actually start enjoying this information, and by enjoying it we might be able to increase our brain capacity because we're using it better."

All of this will seem less strange if we remember that people have been processing visual images since long before than the invention of writing, which, according to generally accepted belief, took place not earlier than 3200 B.C.

The way the words can evoke emotions is well known to copywriters in direct marketing who write sentimental letters "on behalf of the good causes." But words can have a powerful effect, even if they are not so blatantly aimed to pull at consumers' heartstrings. Dan Jones, a leading hypnotist and expert on the hypnotic power of words, explains:

"Many brands manipulate your decision making with emotive words and other linguistic tricks. Emotional states are trance states and memories are state dependent, so if advertisers can trigger an emotion linked with their brand and with some real world event, that will subconsciously remind you of the brand each time you experience the same emotion. It's a form of autosuggestion. The effectiveness of auto suggestion when used repeatedly and frequently has been known since Emile Coue promoted the use of autosuggestion for self help with phrases like 'Each day in every way I am getting better and better.'"

Take McDonald's slogan "i'm lovin' it." This phrase was coined by Paul Tilly for DDB advertising agency in 2003, and it has been translated into more than 20 languages. But why is it "i'm lovin' it" and not "you're lovin' it"? By instructing people to behave in a certain way, you risk running into a strong negative reaction. You create a psychological resistance, even if not on a conscious level, and it makes the person do the opposite. And so the viewers will ascribe the words "i'm lovin' it" to the actors who utter them; the message will penetrate their minds and become a brainworm. Afterwards, hearing that phrase over and over again, they will begin to repeat it in their minds themselves. Linking the emotion of love with the McDonald's brand and saying "I" instead of "you," the consumers will inspire themselves to love McDonald's.

Another widely used technique both in writing and in speech is about turning products into advantages. It operates as follows, "X has Y, which means Z." For instance, the seller is trying to sell you a camera, he says, "Its lens is f1.4 and the maximum shutter speed is 1/10000 seconds." But the buyer will have to use a lot of mental energy to understand the meaning of what was said, if such information means anything to them at all. Instead, you can turn these specifications into benefits. For example, the seller will tell the young mother who wants to buy a camera,

"Imagine that you're taking pictures of your child's birthday and want to accurately convey the atmosphere. This lens opening of f1.4 allows excellent shots without a flash."

Or you can ask the father, "Does your son play on the school football team? If you want to take photos of all the important moments of the game, this camera with a maximum shutter speed of 1/10000 seconds allows you to capture even the most rapid shots and goals. And if you use the telephoto lens, you will feel almost as if you are part of the game!"

We are accustomed to narratives. We love being told stories. By transferring the customer from the store to her son's birthday or to the football field, the seller not only switches the customer's automatic thought processes but also builds positive emotions.

Even if the customer brings an opposing fact, you can simply convince them by words. Apple's Genius Training Manual reveals the 5-pong sales strategy, summed up with five cute letters: (A)pproach, (P)robe, (P)resent, (L)isten, (E)nd. So the genius needs to approach the customers (approach), then probe them about why they are at the store (probe), present buying and servicing options (present), listen to their problems and concerns (listen). The next technique with the three Fs "Feel, Felt, and Found" helps to deal with concerns the customers have. The following dialog shows how it works:

Customer: "This iPad's too expensive."*Genius*: "I can understand how you'd **feel** this way. I **felt** it was a little pricey too, but I **found** that there's actually real value there, thanks to all the built-in software and features."

At this point the deal can be considered concluded, and the process ends (end). Each Apple customer should feel empowered, when it's really the genius pulling strings.

This much about the research and their results that showed what factors people focus on in making purchase decisions. I hope you will apply at least one of these methods to your business or working style.

Of course, there are many approaches, but I tried to briefly present 40 exciting marketing techniques and experiments through which customers' decisions can be influenced. Naturally, it's not possible to apply all 40 of them, because each business is unique, but they will help to make even more effective marketing decisions.

Secret 23. An image instantly conveys much more information and emotions than words do, even if they are uttered quickly.

Secret 24

Oilmen are like cats; you can never tell from the sound of them whether they are fighting or making love.

Calouste Gulbenkian

Calouste Gulbenkian

Today Gulbenkian's name is mentioned alongside such oil magnates as John Rockefeller, Armand Hammer, and Jean Paul Getty. Due to his skillful actions he managed to accumulate billions.

Calouste was talented and hardworking. He was fluent in 7 languages. Despite this, he was a modest man, and family was the most important thing for him. He was a great patriot and philanthropist and had his own foundation founded in Lisbon. The purpose of the foundation was to contribute to the development of science, education, healthcare, and the arts. And how did his career start?

Gulbenkian's family is said to be descended from the Rshtunis, a noble Armenian family centered around Lake Van in the 4th century AD. Centuries later the family established themselves in the town of Talas where they had become rich through trade. Ultimately, they moved to Constantinople, where Calouste Gulbenkian was born on March 21, 1869. Calouste did his first transaction at age 7 when his father gave him a silver coin and sent him to the bazaar. He exchanged the coin for an antique Armenian coin, as he loved antiquities. The father scolded the son for such a financial deal, "If that's the way you're going to use your money, you'll end up in the gutter."

The entrepreneur sent his son to King's College London when he was in early teens to study petroleum engineering. In 1887, he graduated with a first class degree in engineering and applied sciences. In 1891, Gulbenkian was invited to the oil fields in Baku, where the prominent Armenian oil magnate and philanthropist Alexander Mantashev became his mentor in oil industry. *Success is not achieved alone.* The young man thoroughly studied the oil production process in the region and published an article about it in a French magazine. He was then entrusted by the Ottoman Empire leadership to survey the oil of Mesopotamia. Calouste's explorations of the oil reserves of the Middle East countries were so profound that they attracted the attention of Europe and the West. Yes, why not. It is also thanks to him that the world was able to discover the greatest wealth of the Arab world – black gold.

A brilliant scientific career awaited the young researcher, but eventually Calouste started his own oil operation business with the £30,000 he got from his father as start-up capital. In 1892, he moved to England, and the same year he married Nevarte Yesayan. The period of intensive activity had begun.

In the mid-1890s, as a result of fierce persecution and massacres of Armenians in the Ottoman Empire, Gulbenkian's family fled to Egypt. There he met the famous diplomat and politician of Armenian descent, Nubar Pasha. Under his patronage, all the doors of the influential people in the Middle East were open for Gulbenkian. These connections enabled Calouste to arrange deals in the oil business. With the assistance of Nubar Pasha, Gulbenkian became the sales representative for Baku oil in London, and in 1898, he was appointed Economic Advisor to the Ottoman embassies in France and the United Kingdom. He initiated negotiations with politicians and officials, with oil tycoons and large corporations of his time telling them about the fabulous Middle East oil reserves. He knew by heart the geological data and geographical features of different regions of the world, and particularly, the map of oil reserves.

He had oil bearing lands in Venezuela, Iran, Iraq, Saudi Arabia, the UAE, and he had close connections with Ottoman and Persian courts. The superpowers often solved their problems with Gulbenkian's support. During the San Remo conference the oil companies had disputes over the boundaries of the "self-denying clause." Gulbenkian himself took a red pencil and drew a line around what he meant by "Ottoman Empire." Thus, the San Remo Agreement came to be known as the Red Line Agreement.

What was the genius of Gulbenkian? First, his position as the Economic Advisor to the Ottoman embassies in Paris and London and the fact that he had become a naturalized British citizen in 1902 provided the oilman political influence in the Middle East and Europe. He was the first to notice that the Middle East was a sea of oil and first to set to work. In the early 20th century Gulbenkian was, indeed, a citizen of the world – dual citizenship, activity all over Europe, residence in Paris, and a perfect connecting link between the East and Europe.

In Egypt, Gulbenkian met the Samuel brothers, the owners of Shell, and Henri Deterding, the chairman of Royal Dutch. Realizing that the oil market should be competitive, Gulbenkian was able to convince them to unite in order to be able to withstand the monopoly of Standard Oil in the Caucasus. In 1907, he persuaded them to open an office in Constantinople under his charge.

He became the head of this branch; his ability to persuade people left everyone amazed. Each negotiation would take place the way Gulbenkian had predicted. In 1912, the Turkish Petroleum Company was created through Gulbenkian's efforts: the National Bank of Turkey held 35% stake in the company; Royal Dutch Shell owned 25%; another 25% belonged to the Deutsche Bank; the remaining 15% belonged to Calouste Gulbenkian.

Yet, England would not put up with this idea and made them redistribute the shares. As a result, the Turkish Petroleum Company was reorganized and redistributed among the Anglo-Persian Oil Company with Deutsche Bank receiving 50% and Royal Dutch Shell with 25% each. In addition, the Anglo-Persian Oil Company and the Royal Dutch Shell each provided a 2.5% share to Calouste Gulbenkian. This was fixed forever. Gulbenkian's shares didn't give him the right to vote, but he had 5% of the revenues. Hence, Calouste Gulbenkian earned his famous "Mr. Five Percent" nickname.

It sufficed both the Armenian businessman and the great powers that had to reckon with this individual. The secret of his success was the business connections that he made with ease. Guided by this practice, at age 30 Gulbenkian was a millionaire. In 1918, after World War I, new players appeared on the world stage. Germany was left out of the game, and the USA, as one of the victors, was trying to establish itself in the Middle East.

Thanks to Gulbenkian, a new agreement was signed, and the Iraq Petroleum Company was created: The United States, England, France, Iran and Gulbenkian had shares, of which 5% belonged to him. In almost all big oil fields Gulbenkian secured a 5% stake. As he had famously said once, "Better a small piece of a big pie, than a big piece of a small one."

As mentioned, Calouste was an art lover. When Soviet Russia urgently needed foreign currency for its industrialization, it started to sell many valuable works of art. It was broadly interpreted as "Russia is selling its culture." Naturally, an art lover like Gulbenkian could not miss the opportunity and immediately purchased many Hermitage paintings. Gulbenkian was described as an eccentric personality by the man performing the transaction with him; he had, in fact, gained the reputation of a strange and solitary figure. He kept everyone guessing.

"I have never known anybody so suspicious," said Sir Kenneth Clerk, the director of the National Gallery in London. "I've never met anybody who went to such extremes. He always had people spying for him." He had different experts who would have to appraise a piece of art before he bought it.

In 1942, he was looking for a country where he could find peace – a neutral country away from Nazi Germany. And he found Portugal, where he moved all his belongings and collection. After his death, they were all left to this country where he spent the last years of his life.

Secret 24. Make business connections.

Secret 25

Give me snuff, whiskey, and Swedes, and I will build a railroad to hell.

James. J. Hill

IKEA (Ingvar Kamprad)

Ingvar Kamprad is a man who created the world's most famous furniture empire, IKEA, and whose career path is studied in many business schools. He drives a cheap car, flies economy class, always turns off the lights when leaving, uses both sides of a piece of paper, buys clothes at car boot sales, and has his house furnished solely with IKEA furniture. Kamprad does not have a personal chauffeur, doorkeeper, or bodyguard. He simply walks the streets alone. In his office he has a table, chair, bookcase and certain office supplies. Kamprad believes that only in this way he can instill frugality in his employees.

Kamprad hugs those whom he loves. Every meeting with employees ends with hugs. Ingvar always prefers budget hotels. If he has to stay at a hotel with an employee, they will choose to share a room together and even fit into a single bed. That's who he is - one of the richest men in Europe, whose word is not subject to discussion. And how did Ingvar Kamprad manage to create this giant empire?

Kamprad was born on March 30, 1926, in Sweden. His grandmother would help him sell products when he was still 5 years old; he would sell this or that product to his grandmother and get money for it. The grandmother's attitude instilled courage in little Ingvar: At the age of 10 he would already bring various types of pens and sell them. His mother was against it, saying that no one would buy them, but Ingvar was too stubborn.

266

If the children of his age had toys or cars in their rooms, he had only boxes of pens, newspapers, belts, and watches for sale. When he turned 17, he decided to create his own company. To do it, he had to obtain permission from his uncle Ernest. One day, Ingvar left their village, Elmtaryd, and set off for his uncle's village, Agunnaryd. When his uncle heard about Ingvar's business plans, he asked him:

"Well, everything is clear to me, and how do you want to name the company?" It was followed by a short answer – IKEA – Ingvar Kamprad Elmtaryd Agunnaryd.

From that day on Ingvar's first steps in the retail business began. It was based on distribution – purchasing furniture parts from manufacturers and organizing sales. It's worth mentioning the words of a friend who used to say:

"If you are unemployed, get involved in distribution."

To be successful in the competitive struggle, several problems had to be solved, including how to deliver the product from the manufacturer to the consumer at lower prices. This was the basis of Kamprad's business model.

Kamprad has been in sales since childhood. By 1948, he had become the sole supplier of pens to a British company. He had a good relationship with one of his competitors, Gunnar Jansson. He got acquainted with Jansson's company in an interesting way - when selling watches. At the time restrictions were placed on imports, so Kamprad bought watches from Gunnar Jansson, who sold them for 55 kronor or $7. Kamprad did not have enough money for the watches, but his passion for business had appealed to Gunnar, so he suggested:

"Well, you look like a lively young man, I think I'll sell the watches for 52 kronor."

Kamprad was so happy that he agreed at once.

Taking his fat cigar out of his mouth, Gunnar then said,

"Young man, you'll never become a businessman. If you say... that you can pay 50 when I say 55, then you can't accept 52 without first having tried offering 50 kronor 50 oere. One thing you have to learn in business is that 10 oere on a price can mean everything."

"I promise I'll never forget that," Kamprad said politely, and he has kept that promise ever since.

Even now, if you ask Kamprad what the secret of his success is, he'll answer – purchase at the lowest price possible. While he sold pens, pencils, belts and watches, a few companies sold furniture with success. This couldn't escape his attention, and he decided to engage in furniture selling. The idea was the following: He ordered furniture from manufacturers and sold it. But he didn't have quick success selling furniture, so he decided to use the most famous weapon of sales increase – advertising. He started with an advertisement for the chairs, and the result was shocking.

Through advertising Kamprad sold a huge number of chairs. He was so excited about this opportunity that he started printing and sending IKEA news booklets to everyone. He was so excited he couldn't sleep; at nights they would pack the chairs to deliver the orders in the mornings. All of his family members helped him, and still they were not enough, so he had to quickly recruit new employees. And all this thanks to an advertisement. It was the first practical lesson Kamprad learned.

Thus, furniture production completely changed Kamprad's life. The principle of Kamprad's business was to sell at the lowest prices possible. This continued until he received the first complaints. That very day he learned his second lesson: Quality is the most important thing. In 1952, Kamprad hired a man whose endeavors made IKEA first in the world. We're talking about Sven Hansen, who encouraged Kamprad to start with catalogs in order to have good sales.

They did so, and it surpassed all the expectations. The sudden growth of sales made Kamprad wonder how it was possible to achieve such success through catalogs. That was the main reason why up to this day a part of IKEA's sales is realized through catalogs. *Sometimes I ask myself - If there is such a person as Hansen, why is only Ingvar Kamprad well-known? The same can be said about Bonaparte: His powerful marshals, Ney and Desaix, are considerably less known than him. Why? Smart people surround themselves with smarter people and achieve success. Remember these words.*

But soon the customers started complaining again. The problem was that they couldn't see, feel, or touch the furniture, and it's natural they complained. Kamprad had two options – either to leave IKEA to die or make the customers trust his company and, by doing so, make the furniture sales profitable. Every day he walked together with Hansen, mulling over ways to handle the situation. IKEA was in a state of decline. There had to be a way out. Finally, on a rainy day Hansen offered the following idea:

"First of all, we should organize something for the customers to touch and see. They should learn about the low prices themselves and make a final decision whether to buy the furniture or not. This can be achieved only through exhibition. We'll inform our customers about the exhibition by means of our magazines. We'll have these words on the front page 'Welcome to Elmhult, and you'll see …' First, we'll arouse curiosity as to what they are going to see, and second, no one has organized such an exhibition yet; many will be interested to see what will be exhibited."

Excited, Kamprad accelerated his steps: Hansen's idea could secure a huge growth in sales for the company. Kamprad's joy was explained by the fact that this idea had not been applied by anyone yet; they would be pioneers in it. He rented a vast area, as there was still no opportunity to buy a store, and the furniture was transported there. As a result, the customers had the chance to see the furniture, pick up the catalogue, and make their choices at home. After selecting, they could call the company, and the order would be filled. Hansen's idea was an excellent one. Only five years later did Kamprad open his first IKEA store. *Ingvar Kamprad opened his first store… five years later. And I will add that patience is rewarded – here's an example.*

On Hansen's suggestion, they decided to sell food and coffee on the second floor, which would cover a part of the costs and give people an opportunity to eat. As a result, people would not leave the exhibition for food, otherwise they might not come back. This idea later transformed into IKEA restaurants, which are located inside the stores and generate an annual revenue of 2 billion kronor. Remember, business fails if the customer's stomach is empty.

On the first day of the exhibition, about 1,000 people were waiting in a queue in front of the building. In the morning people visited the exhibition, and in the evening their orders were sent to them. Kamprad's team saved on everything: They would even tie two different furniture parts together to spare the rope, and, say, if the paper was printed on one side, it wouldn't be thrown away so the other side could also be used.

At 18.00 they would close the doors and have something to eat, and at 19.00 they would switch the phones on and start accepting orders. They worked days and nights and slept only 4 hours a day. Kamprad recalls his wife waking him up while he slept on her shoulder once and reminding him that they had things to do. It was no time to sleep. On Sundays Kamprad went mushroom hunting or fishing with his team. No employee addressed him by his last name, but simply Ingvar; he believed that addressing the boss by the first name strengthened the bonds.

For Kamprad, one of the most important issues facing IKEA was the lack of production. That is, IKEA would buy its furniture from other manufacturers. Kamprad was against production, because selling was dearer to his heart. He kept thinking about how to improve this or that process and make more efficient use of the products. To be able to sell at prices 20% lower than the competitors offered, he measured the chairs and tables to decide how much material - even a few inches - he might eliminate. The focus was mainly on wall furniture, as Kamprad used to repeat that people have more walls than floors.

Everything was going well before the competitors woke up. Inexpensive furniture was a real problem for them. In 1955, IKEA's slogan in one of the catalogs was "Your dream house at a fantastic price." One of the competitors had placed an advertisement in a magazine, "If the house of your dreams at fantastic prices turns into a magpie nest, filled with flashy furniture, please contact us and receive high-quality furniture." It made Kamprad angry: He needed to stop the competitors' blows, as they required that he stop selling cheap furniture.

By bribing furniture manufacturers, the competitors forced them not to cooperate with IKEA. They told the suppliers that if they sold furniture to IKEA, they would stop doing business together. And the suppliers were interested in the sales of the product, not the prospects of a young company whose future was unclear. Many refused to work with IKEA. And the others supplied IKEA in the evenings so that no one saw them cooperating with it. The situation was difficult, and Kamprad spent numerous nights literally crying. He had to find a way out of the situation and not give up.

I should note that these very night sufferings led Kamprad to create the business philosophy of IKEA: Look at every problem as at a new opportunity. He had only one way to surmount this blockade – to find a new supplier outside Sweden's borders. Ingvar managed to find new suppliers in Poland, opening up new opportunities before him – to conquer Europe. In 2009 already 40% of the supply was provided by Poland and China.

IKEA's success started at the point when its competitors, the state, and complaining customers cooled towards Kamprad. When all the suppliers in Sweden turned their backs on IKEA, the whole world opened up in front of it. Today to work with IKEA means to observe many rules. Breaking them can result in the breakup of the partnership. Ingvar always states that no one has made as many mistakes as he has and that only those who are asleep make no mistakes. Let's continue:

Kamprad's first failure had to do with selling pens. He had seen an Austrian businessman's advertisement and contacted him. During the meeting he showed Kamprad ballpoint pens, which cost 2.5 kronor each. Such a price was unheard of, as it was sold for 15 kronor in the region. Kamprad ordered 1,000 pens and placed an announcement in one of the magazines that he sold the pens for 3.95 kronor. When he received an order of 500 pens, he took the money and went to the Austrian.

However, he apologized to Kamprad, saying that he had made a big mistake and couldn't sell the pens for 2.5 kronor, as the real price was 4 kronor. Kamprad was disappointed. They had an agreement, and he was getting such a response. But it was a matter of honor, so he took the pens and returned. By selling them at a higher price, he had losses and was disappointed. But life was going on. *Avoid such mistakes.*

The next gross mistake had to do with advertising a company's chemicals in advance. Kamprad never received the promised goods, for the company had deceived him and sent nothing. He fell into despair again, while his father kept repeating that no one should be trusted – do not undertake any steps unless you have the product at hand. Today Kamprad's employees know that agreements should never be reached by handshake since no lawyers can help them in this case. In 1990, Kamprad failed again in Russia, but this time it was about a significant amount of money. Namely, their team, headed by Jan Aulin, confirmed that they could lease a huge forest area in Siberia.

They had taken out a hundred-year lease of 100 hectares of land. They had also taken the responsibility to plant new trees for each cut down tree and develop their business in Siberia. But everything went wrong because of the Russian Mafia, and Kamprad decided to give up the idea, though he had already invested $7.5 million. *If you sense the ship is sinking, leave.* With a local businessman in Thailand they built a factory to produce chairs, but this individual caused considerable damages as well.

The list is long. I mentioned just a few examples to make it clear to you, dear reader, that nothing comes easily. You have to struggle. Everything is temporary: It is not possible to always win or to lose.

After solving supply and quality issues, Ingvar set about the growth of his business. Discussion with the employees was one of Ingvar's favorite activities, from which wonderful ideas were born. Those were the busiest days of furniture sales through catalogs, and they needed a designer. In one of Malmö's advertising companies Ingvar got acquainted with a young designer named Gillis Lundgren. After negotiating a whole night, the latter agreed to work on the IKEA catalogue and became one of the company's strongest representatives.

Lundgren is credited with creating IKEA's flat-pack, self-assembly furniture. People bought furniture parts and assembled them at home. As the former IKEA CEO Anders Dahlvig used to say, the customers have more time than money. The more of the work they do themselves, the less they will have to pay. The customers chose the furniture themselves and were responsible for its transportation and assembly, a great solution for people who don't have big resources. This concept allowed the company to reduce costs by spending less on packaging and freed it from insurance issues. This approach allowed the company to avoid damage, as many delicate models broke during the transportation of ready-made furniture, and the insurance agencies were not quite willing to compensate for such losses. Another important factor was the distinctiveness. Gillis depicted drawings on the furniture the competitors could not imitate. Thanks to his efforts, IKEA began to dictate its style to the suppliers.

All the employees would pay a visit to Ingvar at home and discuss certain problems they might have; it created a wonderful work and friendly atmosphere. He was the first not to force his employees to wear special uniforms or ties, an unprecedented phenomenon in a corporate country like Sweden. Ingvar didn't invite professionals to join his team but only people who had the potential and will to become professional. And today, IKEA's top management is represented by people who were by Ingvar's side from the first day and had no profession. In the beginning many employees were paid low wages, which increased over time, though. For instance, once Kamprad invited one of the employees to the country and told him:

"Take this sum of $4,000. Go and divide it among the employees. A while ago I concluded a successful deal in Norway."

Kamprad loved to go shopping with his co-workers. Once, in 1991, Kamprad visited China with one of his staff members and encountered an amazing phenomenon. The umbrellas cost little when it rained and a lot in sunny weather. Why were the umbrellas inexpensive? The intention was the following: People would enter the stores to buy an umbrella and, seeing that it was inexpensive, stroll around and do more shopping. Ingvar also decided to apply the technique in IKEA. So in rainy weather the umbrellas were cheaper in IKEA than in sunny weather. *Travel. Travelling allows you to see new, effective approaches and apply them to your business.*

IKEA's most significant achievement with the suppliers was long-term cooperation. Usually, Kamprad signs long-term contracts and wins time to plan things calmly. Low prices are the most important condition of long-term contracts. If the German and English sellers bought furniture at expensive prices in return for quick supply, IKEA was doing the opposite. Here the supply lasted long, but it signed long-term and low-cost contracts.

Ingvar Kamprad always treats all his suppliers respectfully. Yet, to reduce the dependence on the suppliers, Kamprad determined to deviate from the golden rule. IKEA was going to produce furniture too. In 1990,

IKEA's sales amounted to 2.7 billion euros with a total 2,500 suppliers. In 2009, the offered products were the same and the sales had increased to 21.5 billion euros, whereas the number of suppliers was 1220. Great efficiency, the suppliers are half what they were, and the sales are about 10 times more.

IKEA's top priority was the trust of its customers, and the company was responding to all the complaints and criticisms quickly. For instance, in 1993, it was announced in Germany that there was a certain toxic substance in the bookshelves produced by IKEA. The company immediately recalled the bookshelves and refunded all the customers, and the toxic substance was phased out of its furniture production. There is an employee in IKEA who visits the stores and records the work environment, the complaints, and the deadlines of settling them. Due to this employee, the number of complaints has significantly declined: *If you want to have success in business, listen to the complaining customers. Sometimes they give important information about the "gaps" in your business.*

In 1965, the largest IKEA store opened in Kungens Kurva. The number of visitors was shocking – 18,000 people on the first day. It was so crowded that the checkout staff could hardly work, and some were going out of the store without paying. The choice of Kungens Kurva was one of Kamprad's excellent initiatives, as this area was on the outskirts of town. The area was affordable, and a new district was being built here. As the employees would get caught in traffic jams in the mornings and evenings, the working hours were shifted to 11:00-19:00, as a solution to the problem. Besides, they worked in shifts. In other words, a working week followed by a rest week. 75 percent of IKEA's employees work in the stores, because on average 2 million people visit the stores every year.

There is an interesting anecdote connected with the store sign. Two of IKEA's employees were quarreling over the store sign. One of the employees said it should be MobellIKEA; the other one insisted it should simply be left IKEA. The IKEA supporter explained his stance by claiming that the store didn't solely sell furniture. The dispute was settled by attaching IKEA to the southern roof and MobellIKEA to the northern roof of the store.

Nevertheless, in 1970, the MobellIKEA side of the building was damaged in a fire IKEA, after which Kamprad decided to only use the name IKEA.

After the fire the company made a decision to increase the flow of people once again and immediately announced sales of 50%-90%. And the number of visitors exceeded 8,000. Some slept in tents in front of IKEA. Imagine a queue in front of the store that stretched 5 km.

After the fire, self-service started to be practiced in IKEA. IKEA created special playrooms for kids in its stores, so the parents could leave them there and do the shopping freely. Amazingly, the children liked the playrooms so much they would ask their parents to take them to IKEA to play. The parents would then have to stroll around the store out of boredom and would do shopping.

It turns out women are in charge of 70% of household purchases, meaning that in most cases it's the women who choose furniture, crockery, chairs, lamps and similar items. For the majority of men it was a real torment to walk behind their wives in IKEA. But they were well aware in IKEA that the absence of even one family member was not good for sales, so they needed to bring the whole family to IKEA.

IKEA found a way to address this situation. In the Australian branches rooms appeared for men with free hot dogs and pizza, a shooting gallery, table football, big TVs with sport events, entertaining games and stuff that would interest men. These rooms came to be called Manland. Men felt good here while their wives did the shopping. So that men were not carried away by the games, the rooms had special big timers that warned of the time every half an hour. IKEA management could easily observe how a child played with other children, a father talked or did something interesting, and a mother did the shopping. According to Tom Peters, a good entrepreneur is one who knows how to attract female buyers.

The playroom for kids was a requirement for all IKEA stores. In order not to build one in a newly-opened store, special permission had to be obtained, and it was still open to question. In addition, a new department, Acceten, was opened. It sold crockery and gifts. The originator of the idea was one of the store managers. Another employee offered to sell Småland food. If the furniture was produced in Småland, he reasoned, the food should also have the spirit of Småland and be sold in IKEA. So Småland dishes appeared in IKEA and became one of company's branded products. On leaving the store, the customers could buy Swedish dishes. *Likewise, listen to the advice of your staff.* If we look back at IKEA's story, we'll see that the majority of the innovations started with the unfortunate (or perhaps not so unfortunate) fire.

Since 1995 IKEA has sold hot dogs at the entrance for 5 kronor. These hot dogs cost between 10-15 kronor in general. The restaurant and hot dog sales departments provide around 2 billion kronor annual profit. It already became clear that IKEA places emphasis on low prices, so hot dogs also had to fit within this strategy. At first, the staff opposed the idea of selling hot dogs in a furniture store, but Kamprad said that business could not develop if the customer's stomach was empty, and the issue was closed.

Kamprad did some research and found out that 2 sales people could sell 300 hot dogs in an hour. In every country the hot dog is priced accordingly - an amount equal to 5 kronor. The price was determined as follows: 3+1+1, that is, 3 for the production, 1 for taxes, and 1 for profit. Ingvar would visit his competitors and examine their collections, prices, placement of items, and cleanliness. Once, he accidentally noticed that one of his competitors sold cups for 18 kronor. He told the head of the procurement department, Björn, he wanted those cups, but they had to cost 1 krona. Björn answered that they could have them if they ordered 5 million items.

Björn managed to find a supplier who provided cups on these terms. Some time later, the cups also became a bestseller. The first IKEA store outside Sweden's borders opened in Norway, in 1963. Worldwide expansion followed. Initially, IKEA would enter medium sized towns, open a store in the center, and study the consumer behavior. And now, as the company is more confident, it opens its stores in the suburbs of large cities from the start.

IKEA stores tend to create an environment around them. New bank branches, cafes, etc. pop up next to them like mushrooms. After signing a franchise contract, all the new employees undergo a probationary period, learn to serve, and get familiar with the company's corporate culture. One of the most important factors of IKEA's business model is its independence, meaning that the majority of its land is not leased and belongs to the company. Ingvar always stresses:

"The most dangerous enemy of business is dependence. We have to neutralize it."

IKEA managers must have business experience at all levels and spend quite a lot of time in the store and with the suppliers. The reason is that before becoming a manager, the specialist must be personally aware of all business processes. Therefore, IKEA sometimes holds anti-bureaucratic days when everyone works in the stores to better understand the reality and the customers' needs.

When Anders Dahlvig became CEO, he appointed two women to senior management positions. This ruffled feathers inside the company, as the majority of the company's leaders were middle-aged, Swedish men. But Dahlvig wanted to keep the focus on the customers. How? If the company wants to understand its customers, most of whom are women, then females will have a better understanding of the new opportunities and approaches than males. So women began to be trusted by executives in IKEA because a woman better understands a female customer's psychology.

If the company supports only like-minded people, it does not yield big results. It is therefore important for every leader to approach the tasks and problems from a different standpoint. There's this comparison Dahlvig makes that's quite to the point, "I don't know of any such statistics yet that say that middle-aged Swedish men better understand household items than women."

By 1983, IKEA already had 41 stores, mainly in Sweden and Germany, with sales equal to 600 million euros. At first, Sweden accounted for the 80 percent of total sales, and now Germany leads the list with 45 percent.

Having conquered Europe, now it was time to turn to North America, and the first store was opened in 1976 in Vancouver. The first store in the USA was opened in 1985 in Philadelphia. Following it, 5 stores opened in the eastern part, and 3 stores opened in the western part of the country, but the business only suffered losses. The reason was that the competition in the retail business in the United States is really fierce, and no matter where the store was, before reaching IKEA, people would enter several large trade centers. If they needed any marketing research, then it was much more expensive in the US than in Europe. The prices of land and construction were also more expensive; the same was true for the staff costs. Staff turnover was higher than in Europe. IKEA encountered similar problems in the United

States. For example, in the United States larger sizes are preferred – it's the only country for which IKEA revised the sizes of its products. Each environment has its own complexity. So you just need to find a solution and everything will fall into place over time.

When in 1998 an IKEA outlet opened in Chicago, one of the customers asked in surprise if the prices were only for the first day and when the furniture would be sold at its real price. Other Americans were also surprised by the low prices.

The prices were so low in Russia that people thought they were written in dollars. The manager had to underline the word *ruble* so the buyers would see it. There's this well-known case when during the opening of the company's first store in Moscow, Ingvar Kamprad had to stand behind the cash register himself – the visitors had, in fact, taken everything from the shelves and there were not enough salespeople. The top management of the company's Russian branch had to do the packing.

The IKEA business model is:

Thrift in everything - IKEA managers must drive inexpensive cars, travel economy class, stay in three-star hotels, and so on. Ingvar's co-workers should do as Kamprad does, meaning no senseless waste of money. For example, IKEA Norden tables are made from the top part of the tree. For the majority of other furniture companies, this part of the tree is considered useless. Annually, the company produces more than 280,000 tons of waste. About 81 percent of it is fully recycled.

Being distinctive – In the 50s and 60's, the furniture business was conservative, and the players in this field put the emphasis on older families. IKEA put the emphasis on families with children. The other players built not big but specialized stores, and IKEA built big stores where every necessary item for the house can be found. The other players only advertised; IKEA distributed free catalogs. The other players added additional services and created a self-service approach, and IKEA was self-service. To the other players, the high-priced segment mattered most of all. In contrast, IKEA focused on the low-priced products. The other players offered ready-made furniture, and IKEA offered parts of furniture that was possible to assemble at home. The other players were supplied by the local manufacturers only, and IKEA has long been supplied from Poland, China, etc. The other players sold furniture of different manufacturers, and IKEA founded its own production as well. And it was by being distinctive in everything that IKEA created its unique brand.

Low prices for all the products – Selling at a low price is IKEA's strategy, a strategy on which the whole business has been based for already half a century. The low prices are stated in all ads and posted throughout the stores every 50 meters. IKEA cuts costs in an interesting way. It calculates whether it is more profitable to move the furniture to the store or the warehouse right after producing it. For instance, if it is moved to the store, the cost could be cut by 20%.

First the price, then the manufacturing – Few know that before the manufacturing starts, IKEA sets the price. Until the crisis of 2008, IKEA maintained the catalogue prices throughout a year after it was released. In other words, whenever you ordered a catalogue during the year, there would be no change in price, and now it is changing every 6 months, which is done for protection only.

No megastores in the center of the city – Kamprad's character is already clear to you. He'd save on everything, and the plot of land is no exception: The stores were chosen to be located on the outskirts of the city where the land prices were less costly. As Anders Dahlvig points out, Kamprad never regretted building a large store, but he regretted having a small store, because when the store was too large for IKEA, it could rent out the area. More than 8.5 thousand types of products are displayed in each store; the large area is not intended to increase the variety, but rather to secure a large flow of customers.

The stores are given maximum freedom. Each store has to analyze its competitive environment and make its own marketing plan. And the store manager is allowed to actively participate in the affairs of the store and sometimes act as an owner.

Comfort – In IKEA stores there are playrooms for kids 3-6 years old. This model is a must for all the stores. In addition, there is a special room for mothers where they can feed their children, or, say, change a diaper. It is clear that every mother appreciates such care.

Pencil and paper – Another interesting tactic of IKEA is about providing the customers with a pencil and paper so they make notes about where to collect their purchases, and in the end the employees simply bring the selected products to the customer. By this step the IKEA employees rid people of the discomfort of constantly holding something in the hands, further simplifying the shopping process. After this model was applied, the sales grew by nearly 7%.

Complementary products – If you buy a bed from IKEA, you are more likely to buy the mattress from IKEA as well, because the dimensions of their products are made to match one another only.

Long, but comfortable – The interior of IKEA stores is designed in a way that the customer will have to walk along the entire store, but not everyone is patient enough. So there exist secret passages through which it's possible to shorten the way. The regular customers are well-informed of the passages, and the layout of the store is clearly visible to customers.

Discounted holidays – All IKEA stores worldwide offer discounts on the national holidays of Sweden.

Terms of cooperation – The company works only with suppliers that can meet IKEA quality standards down to the smallest detail. In one of the cities in the Vologda region, a company purchased equipment for a few hundred thousand rubles and signed a contract with IKEA for the supply of simple wooden furniture parts. Right after this, the company had to invest several million more in acquiring equipment to create eco-friendly and standard IKEA packaging under the threat of contract termination.

Customer service standards – According to IKEA customer service standards, the buyer can lie on the sofa, take a nap and even sleep on it. Inside the store various household items are placed throughout the different departments. Interestingly, the same type of cup can be seen 5 times in the store, constantly reminding the customer of it.

Tips from Ingvar Kamprad:

- If you work and do not feel genuine enthusiasm, consider that at least a third of your life has gone down the drain.

- In leadership the most important thing is love. If people don't love you, they will not sell anything with love.

- Only those who are asleep make no mistakes.

- IKEA is not completely perfect. We have to still develop the IKEA group.

- Simplicity and common sense should characterize planning and strategic direction.

- To design a desk that may cost $1,000 is easy for a furniture designer but to design a functional and good desk that costs only $50 can only be done by the best.

- We ought to have more women in various management positions, because women decide almost everything in the home.

- The word "impossible" has been and must remain deleted from our dictionary.

- IKEA managers freely check the co-workers personal email addresses. The company's motto is to be tender towards the customer and strict towards the supplier.

Secret 25. In order to sell at a low price, eliminate the middlemen and distributors.

* Enjoy the next 25-50 interesting secrets and ideas in Book 2 of

100 Business Secrets

References

Ariely, D. 2010. *Predictably Irrational, Revised and Expanded Edition: The Hidden Forces That Shape Our Decisions.*

Barden, Ph. 2013. *Decoded: The Science Behind Why We Buy.*

Beckwith, H. 2012. *Selling the Invisible: A Field Guide to Modern Marketing.*

Bock, L. 2015. *Work Rules! Insights from Inside Google That Will Transform How You Live and Lead.*

Charmasson, H. 1998. *The Name's the Thing: Creating the Perfect Name for Your Company or Product* (AMERICAN MANAGEMENT ASSOCIA-TION).

Cialdini, R. 2001. *Influence: The Psychology of Persuasion.* 4th Edition.

Corey, L. 1930. *The House of Morgan: A Social Biography of the Masters of Money.*

Cram, T. 2006. *Smarter Pricing: How to Capture More Value In Your Market* (Financial Times).

Cunningham A. 2001. *The Essays of Warren Buffett Lessons for Corporate America.* First Revised Edition.

Dahlvig, A. 2011. *The IKEA Edge: Building Global Growth and Social Good at the World's Most Iconic Home Store.*

Ferrazzi, K. 2014. *Never Eat Alone, Expanded and Updated: And Other Secrets to Success, One Relationship at a Time.*

Ford, H. 2013. *My Life & Work.* An Autobiography of Henry Ford.

Hermann, S. 2015. *Confessions of the Pricing Man: How Price Affects Everything*

Kravtsov, A. 2016. *The Next Level. A Book for Those Who've Reached Their Ceiling*

Landram, G. 1994. *Profiles of Female Genius.*

Landram, G. 1993. *Profiles of Genius*

Larionov, V. 2002. *Business Legends, or How to Become Rich.*

Lewis, D. 2013. *The Brain Sell: When Science Meets Shopping.*

Lindstrom, M. 2010. *Buyology: Truth and Lies About Why We Buy.*

Lindstrom, M. 2011. *Brandwashed: Tricks Companies Use to Manipulate Our Minds and Persuade Us to Buy.*

Livingston, J. 2008. *Founders at Work: Stories of Startups Early Days.*

Lowe, J. 2009. *Google Speaks: Secrets of the World's Greatest Billionaire Entrepreneurs, Sergey Brin and Larry Page.*

Manoukyan, H. 2012. *Change your life.*

Mesnyanko, A. 2015. *Oil: People Who Changed the World.*

Mitchell, J. 2008. *Hug Your People: The Proven Way to Hire, Inspire, and Recognize Your Employees and Achieve Remarkable Results.*

O'Shea, C. 2012. *The Man from Zara: The Story of the Genius Behind the Inditex Group.*

Poundstone, W. 2012. *Are You Smart Enough to Work at Google?: Trick Questions, Zen-like Riddles, Insanely Difficult Puzzles, and Other Devious Interviewing Techniques You ... Know to Get a Job Anywhere in the New Economy.*

Ries, L. 2015. *Visual Hammer: Nail your brand into the mind with the emotional power of a visual.*

Seller, B. 2010. *Forbes Best Business Mistakes: How Today's Top Business Leaders Turned Missteps into Success.*

Sewell, C. 2002. *Customers for Life: How to Turn That One-Time Buyer Into a Lifetime Customer.*

Sir Branson, R. 2006. *Screw It, Let's Do It: Lessons In Life.*

Sir Branson, R. 2011. *Losing My Virginity.*

Soros, G. 1995. *Soros on Soros.*

Tinkov, O. 2010. *How to Become a Businessman*

Tinkov, O. 2010. *I'm Just Like Everyone Else.*

Torekull, B., Kamprad, I. 1999. *Leading By Design: The Ikea Story.*

Tracy, B. 2002. *The 100 Absolutely Unbreakable Laws of Business Success.*

Traut, J., Ries, A. 1994. *The 22 Immutable Laws of Marketing: Violate Them at Your Own Risk!*

Traut, J., Ries, A. 2000. *Positioning: The Battle for Your Mind.*

Traut, J., Ries , A. - Marketing Warfare, 1997

Traut J., Ries, A. 2008. *Differentiate or Die: Survival in Our Era of Killer Competition.*

Traut J., Ries, A. 1990. *Horse Sense: The Key to Success Is Finding a Horse to Ride.*

Traut J., Rivkin, S. 2001. *The Power Of Simplicity: A Management Guide to Cutting Through the Nonsense and Doing Things Right.*

Tzu Sun. 2012. *The Art of War.*

Underhill, P. 2000. *Why We Buy: The Science Of Shopping.*

Underhill, P. 2004. *Call of the Mall: The Author of Why We Buy on the Geography of Shopping.*

Walton, S. 1993. *Made In America.*

Weiss, S. 2010. *The Billion Dollar Mistake LEARNING THE ART OF INVESTING THROUGH*

THE MISSTEPS OF LEGENDARY INVESTORS.

Wise, D. 2008. *The Google Story: For Google's 10th Birthday.*

http://www.forbes.ru

http://www.kommersant.ru

http://www.forbes.com

http://www.podfm.ru

http://www.slon.ru

http://www.fresher.ru

http://www.adme.ru

http://www.dailycomm.ru

http://hi-news.ru/

http://shard-copywriting.ru/

http://rbcdaily.ru/

http://ubiznes.ru/

http://vatel.rmat.ru/

http://www.e-xecutive.ru/

http://www.nytimes.com/

http://otherreferats.allbest.ru

http://sales-support.com.ua/

http://www.businessinsider.com/

http://www.nngroup.com/

http://listverse.com/

http://myautoworld.com/

Made in the USA
San Bernardino, CA
14 October 2018